The Christian Left

The Christian Left
An Introduction to Radical and Socialist Christian Thought

Anthony A.J. Williams

polity

First published in 2022 by Polity Press

Polity Press
65 Bridge Street
Cambridge CB2 1UR, UK

Polity Press
101 Station Landing
Suite 300
Medford, MA 02155, USA

ISBN-13: 978-1-5095-4281-9 (hardback)
ISBN-13: 978-1-5095-4282-6 (paperback)

A catalogue record for this book is available from the British Library.
Library of Congress Control Number: 2021947044

Typeset in 11 on 13 pt Sabon LT Pro
by Cheshire Typesetting Ltd, Cuddington, Cheshire
Printed and bound in Great Britain by TJ Books Ltd, Padstow, Cornwall

For further information on Polity, visit our website: politybooks.com

Contents

Introduction

In June 2020 then-US President Donald Trump staged a photo-op outside Washington DC's St John's Episcopal Church. Amid the Black Lives Matter protests, which had engulfed Washington and other inner cities since the racist murder of George Floyd a week previously, Trump walked from the White House to the church building, held aloft a Bible for the assembled press, and then walked back again.[1] Trump's aim in this 'religious performance' was to signal his faith commitment and Christian credentials to a voter base of white evangelicals.[2] Predictably, many of these – three-quarters of whom would cast their vote for Trump that November – were delighted with the president's performance.[3] One such, a Republican candidate for the Florida Senate, described scenes of joy as his family watched Trump on TV: 'My mother just shouted out, "God give him strength! He's doing a Jericho walk!" ... My mother started crying [...] she started speaking in tongues [...] I thought, look at my president! He's establishing the Lord's kingdom in the world.'[4] Encapsulated in this one example is all we know – or think we know – about the relationship between Christianity and politics.

Yet, not everybody was impressed with Donald Trump's religious signalling. Mariann Edgar Budde, the Episcopal Bishop of Washington DC, led the denunciations.

> I just want the world to know, that we in the diocese of Washington, following Jesus and his way of love [...] distance ourselves from the incendiary language of this President. We follow someone who lived a life of nonviolence and sacrificial love. We align ourselves with those seeking justice for the death of George Floyd and countless others [...] Let me be clear: the President just used a Bible, the most sacred text of the Judeo-Christian tradition, and one of the churches of my diocese, without permission, as a backdrop for a message antithetical to the teachings of Jesus.[5]

A statement by the Episcopal bishops of New England also criticised Trump's 'disgraceful and morally repugnant' actions, reaffirming the church's mission to 'serve our Lord Jesus Christ's higher purpose: to extend love and mercy and justice for all, and especially for those whose life, liberty, and very humanity is threatened by the persistent sin of systemic racism and the contagion of white supremacy'.[6] This is an entirely different interaction between Christianity and politics than the one many of us have come to expect.

The critical responses to Trump's photo-op and the positioning of the church as an ally to the poor, the oppressed, and the mistreated are not an aberration or an anomaly. The Episcopalian bishops of Washington DC and New England, and others who spoke out, represent a long tradition of socialist and radical religion. The link between the (white) evangelical church of the United States and the economically neo-liberal, socially conservative agenda of the Republican Party should not be assumed to be the default setting for Christian political thought and action. The bishops' intervention reminds us that many Christians have taken socially liberal or progressive positions. Many others have adopted left-wing, socialist critiques of capitalism and have sought a world in which *laissez-faire* individualism is replaced with a commitment to co-operation, collectivism and economic equality. In the pages that follow we examine this tradition, the Christian Left.

Biblical theology of the Christian Left

Despite theological variety – there are Christians of the Left from all denominations and theological traditions – all the movements and individuals considered in these pages share the characteristic that, at least in theory, they have drawn their radical or socialist views from the Bible, church teaching, and Christian history. The Christian Left does not see a commitment to co-operative, equality, social justice and liberty as an optional extra to the Gospel or as principles which Christians should only apply if, at some stage, they turn their attention to politics, but rather as the core of the Christian message itself. That God created the world and gave it to humanity – whether the Genesis account is understood literally or figuratively – proves that it is not for a few to own and exploit the natural resources of the world or oppress others with their privilege and dominant perspective. The prelapsarian world of the Garden of Eden was a place of co-operation and equality – 'When Adam delved and Eve span, who was then the Gentleman?' – as well as a situation in which everything was done justly and God's children enjoyed perfect liberty.

The Exodus account – so crucial for theologies of liberation – was God breaking into history, bringing liberty to the captives, freedom to the oppressed. The Egyptian rulers and slave-owners are made to represent the capitalist class, the global centre, the one per cent, the white supremacists, the patriarchy. God chooses to identify rather with the exploited. The rest of the Old Testament bears witness to the freedom with which God sets his people free – the land laws of Israel, such as the year of jubilee, are designed to prevent those who have recognised the Fatherhood of God and the brotherhood of man from slipping back into unequal, oppressive relationships with one another:

> When you reap the harvest of your land, you shall not reap your field right up to its edge, neither shall you gather the gleanings after your harvest. And you shall not strip your vineyard bare, neither shall you gather the fallen grapes of your vineyard. You shall leave them for the poor and for the sojourner: I am the LORD your God.

> You shall not oppress your neighbour or rob him. The wages of a hired servant shall not remain with you all night until the morning. You shall not curse the deaf or put a stumbling block before the blind, but you shall fear your God: I am the LORD.

> You shall do no injustice in court. You shall not be partial to the poor or defer to the great, but in righteousness shall you judge your neighbour.

> (Leviticus 19:10–11, 13–15)

The prophets who followed – 'fiery publicists of the description we should now call Socialists or Anarchists', according to UK Labour Party founder James Keir Hardie – were fierce in their denunciation of Israel's failure to measure up to this standard.[7] 'Woe to those who devise wickedness […] They covet fields and seize them, and houses, and take them away; they oppress a man and his house, a man and his inheritance' (Micah 2:1a, 2). 'But let justice roll down like waters, and righteousness like an ever-flowing stream' (Amos 5:24).

This 'prophetic-liberating tradition', as feminist theologian Rosemary Radford Ruether referred to it, reaches its culmination in the life and ministry of Jesus Christ.[8] In the Christian Left understanding of the Gospel, Christ comes to proclaim and to inaugurate a new order in which economically and socially oppressive relationships are abolished, the first become last, and the world is turned upside down. 'My soul magnifies the Lord', sings Mary upon hearing the news of the miraculous conception. 'He has shown strength with his arm; he has scattered the proud in the thoughts of their hearts; he has brought down the mighty from their thrones and exalted those of humble estate; he has filled the hungry with good things, and the rich he has sent away empty' (Luke 1:46, 51–3). The British Anglo-Catholic Stewart Headlam regarded this *Magnificat* as 'the hymn of the universal revolution', 'the Marseillaise of humanity', the heralding of God's Kingdom of righteousness and justice upon the earth.[9] This Kingdom, those on the Christian Left argue, is not a distant eschatological promise – 'pie in the sky when we die, by and by' – but, as exemplified in Christ, something to be fought for and won in the here and now.

Christ – the lowly carpenter, Jesus of Nazareth – befriended the poor and the outcast, acknowledging the worth and dignity of those crushed and oppressed by the selfish and individualistic world. He warned his followers not to seek material gain – 'You cannot serve God and money' (Matthew 6:24) or, in the more familiar King James translation, 'Ye cannot serve God and mammon' – but rather to love and to serve others as themselves (Matthew 22:39). The followers of Christ were not to lord it over their companions, nor to place burdens on each other, for they were to regard one another as brothers and sisters (Matthew 23:4–12). The Sermon on the Mount, in which Christ raises up the poor and the meek and the peaceable, is, according to Keir Hardie, 'full of the spirit of pure Communism'.[10] Christ's radical, revolutionary mission is summed up, it is argued, in the synagogue sermon in which the liberative nature of the Old Testament year of jubilee is explained and applied: 'The Spirit of the Lord is upon me, because he has anointed me to proclaim good news to the poor. He has sent me to proclaim liberty to the captives and recovering of sight to the blind, to set at liberty those who are oppressed, to proclaim the year of the Lord's favour' (Luke 4:18–19). 'In the Bible,' maintains Peruvian liberation theologian Gustavo Gutiérrez, 'Christ is presented as the one who brings us liberation [...] Christ makes man truly free, that is to say, he enables man to live in communion with him; and this is the basis for all human brotherhood.'[11]

Christ's death, in this understanding, was a result of his radical mission, which was opposed by the religious and political authorities of his day. Labour Party leader George Lansbury declared Christ to be 'the greatest revolutionary force of His times', 'the lonely Galilean – Communist, agitator, martyr – crucified as one who stirred up the people and set class against class'.[12] Theologian Robyn J. Whitaker, responding to Donald Trump, links the death of Christ to systemic racial injustice, describing Jesus as 'a brown-skinned Jew killed by the Roman State'.[13] The folk singer Woody Guthrie summed up this perspective in his 1940 song 'Jesus Christ':

Jesus Christ was a man who travelled through the land
A hard-working man and brave
He said to the rich, 'Give your money to the poor',
But they laid Jesus Christ in His grave.

When Jesus come to town, all the working folks around
Believed what He did say
But the bankers and the preachers, they nailed Him on the cross,
And they laid Jesus Christ in his grave.

This song was written in New York City
Of rich man, preacher, and slave
If Jesus was to preach what He preached in Galilee,
They would lay poor Jesus in His grave.[14]

There are certainly questions arising from this summary of a Christian Left biblical theology, particularly from a theologically (but not necessarily politically) conservative perspective. An understanding of God's absolute holiness and the sinfulness of people is absent, as consequently is an understanding of how the sinner can be reconciled to God. The substitutionary theory of the atonement, supported by two millennia of church history and a plain reading of the Bible – 'that Christ died for our sins in accordance with the Scriptures' (1 Corinthians 15:4b) – has been replaced. In a justifiable attempt to broaden the scope of the Gospel beyond individual piety, the Gospel itself has arguably been pushed aside in favour of economic collectivism and social liberation.

Radicalism and socialism in the church

It would be an anachronism to attribute the term 'socialist' or 'communist' to movements active long before modern political ideologies began to develop throughout the long nineteenth century. The term 'radical', being less precise, can be employed more freely. In any case, those on the Christian Left can point to a long church tradition of collectivism and social conscience – we might use the term proto-socialism – to show that their position is no postmodern novelty. The collectivism recorded in Acts of the Apostles (Acts 2:44–5; 4:32, 34–5) is seen as the first fruits of a new order of society, the application of Christ's denunciations of selfishness and materialism, the immediate consequence of the ministry of the Holy Spirit which began at Pentecost; it was the realisation of brotherhood and justice. The church community represented not a disparate conglomeration of individuals but, as the Apostle Paul described it, a body of many members all working towards the same goal (1 Corinthians 12:12–27). In this community '[t]here is neither Jew nor Greek, there is neither slave nor free, there is no male and female, for you are all one in Christ Jesus' (Galatians 3:28). These truths are reflected in the sacraments of the church, especially communion, which speaks of collective unity and togetherness.

Radical and socialist Christians often accuse the institutional church of not living up to this grand creed, at the same time as noting the individuals and the movements that have. Samuel E. Keeble, the British Wesleyan Methodist, quotes freely from the early church fathers, first pointing to the words of Tertullian: 'We who mingle in mind and soul have no hesitation as to fellowship in property.' Cyprian is then quoted, commanding that Christians should 'imitate the equality of God in the common gifts of nature, which the whole human race should equally enjoy'. 'The unequal division of wealth,' writes Ambrose of Milan, 'is the result of egoism and violence.'[15] Ambrose is also quoted by the American Catholic John C. Cort: 'God has ordered all things to be produced so that there should be food in common for all, and that the earth should be the common possession of all. Nature, therefore, has produced a common right for all, but greed has made it a right for a few.'[16] Keeble refers to the warnings of Augustine of Hippo Regius about private property: 'Let us, therefore, my brethren, abstain from the possession of private property, or from the love of it if we cannot abstain from the possession of it.'[17] Augustine's condemnation of economic injustice is, says Cort, 'the cornerstone of Christian socialism'.[18]

Radical movements of the late medieval and early modern periods are also co-opted into this account of a radical tradition. The peasants' uprisings of fourteenth-century England and sixteenth-century Germany, including figures such as John Wycliffe, John Ball and Thomas Muntzer, are held up as examples of prophetic opposition to the corruption of state and church, as is the Diggers movement of the seventeenth century, which declared the earth a 'Common Treasury' for all mankind.[19] Denominational differences account for whether the precapitalist guild economy and the monasteries of Roman Catholic Europe, or the modernising zeal of the magisterial reformers – Martin Luther, John Calvin, Ulrich Zwingli – are held up as part of the back-story of religious socialism but, in either case, the social conscience and opposition to economic exploitation of Catholics such as Thomas Moore and Protestants such as Hugh Latimer are cited by way of proof that Christianity has not always gone hand-in-hand with the spirit of capitalism.

These movements are just some of those making up a thread of radicalism, which underpinned the American and French revolutions and informed the liberal and socialist ideologies that developed throughout the long nineteenth century. Radical movements were often secular in nature, such as the attempt of the French Revolution to depose Christianity and install in its place a state religion devoted to the worship of Reason, possibly in an attempt to fulfil the ideas of Jean-Jacques Rousseau in *The Social Contract*.[20] Yet there was always a religious component, calling attention to a message of brotherhood, collectivism, equality, justice and liberty, which had seemingly been forgotten by both secular radicals and the conservative-minded established churches. These movements constitute both the prehistory and philosophical foundation of the Christian Left. The term Christian Left should not be taken to signify a mirror image of the US religious Right. Rather, the phrase is here used to encompass broad and disparate political-theological trends which may be summed with the terms radical and socialist. This, as we shall see, encompasses many different movements and ideological positions.

This book considers the Christian Socialism of the UK; the religious socialism of continental Europe; the Social Gospel, civil rights and black liberation movements, and 'red-letter' evangelicalism of the United States; the liberation theology of Latin America, as well as of Africa and the Middle East; feminist, womanist and LGBT+ theologies of liberation. Some of these focused more on economic socialism or social democracy; others on progressive, intersectional or identarian politics. Each movement is itself diverse, and there are many others outside the scope of these pages, which have made their own significant contributions. One of the things the author has discovered in studying radical and socialist Christianity is that there are always movements and individuals that are accidentally overlooked or not given the consideration they perhaps deserve. Some readers may be disappointed to find that movements or persons with which they are familiar have been omitted or neglected. As John Cort commented upon beginning his own account of Christian Socialism, '[i]n a book of this ambitious, arrogant scope, it is inevitable that much will be missed or neglected'.[21] Nonetheless, this book provides a concise and accessible introduction to the key traditions of the radical and socialist Christian Left.

1

The Spirit of Brotherhood: Foundations of British Christian Socialism

The first socialist organisation in Britain was not a trade union or a political party. Rather, it was a society founded to promote Eucharistic observance at St Matthew's Church in Bethnal Green. The Guild of St Matthew (GSM), founded in 1877, was the child of Stewart Headlam (1847–1924), an eccentric Anglican priest with a dual commitment to Anglo-Catholic sacramentalism and socialism. The GSM had among its aims both the promotion of 'frequent and reverent worship in the Holy Communion' and the promotion of 'the study of social and political questions in the light of the Incarnation'. Headlam's view of politics was stark: he declared as the leader of the GSM that the 'contrast between the great body of workers who produce much and consume little, and those classes which produce little and consume much, is contrary to the Christian doctrines of brotherhood and justice', and that all Christians should seek to 'bring about a better distribution of the wealth created by labour'.[1] The connection between a high-church sacramentalism and socialism may not be immediately obvious, but for Headlam and others like him the two were intrinsically linked.

British Christian Socialism arguably has its origins in 1848 when Frederick Denison Maurice (1805–72), Charles Kingsley (1819–75) and John Malcolm Forbes Ludlow (1821–1911) joined forces to offer a Christian view of social questions as a response to the Chartist campaign for voting rights and parliamentary reform in the UK and the radical forces at work across the continent of Europe. Question marks remain, however, over whether these men, Maurice in particular, were fully committed to socialism. Nevertheless, they did bequeath a theology of God's Fatherhood and human brotherhood, which was to become the keystone of the socialism espoused so clearly by Headlam. Headlam was followed by other Anglican clergy who took up the message of Christian Socialism, among them Henry Scott Holland, Charles Gore, Conrad Noel and William Temple, as well as Nonconformists such as the Wesleyan Methodist Samuel E. Keeble and the Baptist John Clifford. These men established a vibrant tradition of church socialism, which has lasted until the present day.

Christian Socialism did not remain purely the concern of the church. Unlike continental Europe, where mutual distrust characterised the relationship between the church and the political Left, the ethics of Christianity became part of the very DNA of the nascent Labour movement. James Keir Hardie was the key figure in the founding of the Scottish and the Independent Labour parties before he helped to form the Labour Representation Committee – later the Labour Party – in 1900. Hardie did not disavow the theories of Karl Marx – whether the orthodox doctrine enshrined by Friedrich Engels and Karl Kautsky, or the revisionist version offered by Eduard Bernstein – but, nevertheless, declared unambiguously that 'the impetus which drove me first of all into the Labour movement, and the inspiration which has carried me on in it, has been derived more from the teachings of Jesus of Nazareth, than from all other sources combined'.[2] In this Hardie was followed by George Lansbury, Arthur Henderson, Margaret Bondfield, John Wheatley, R.H. Tawney, and many others. The Christian Socialist principles first declared by Headlam on behalf of the GSM fundamentally shaped the Labour Party and had their ultimate triumph in the social democratic agenda enacted by the post-war Labour government.

Origins

It was the social and political turmoil of 1848 which proved to be the catalyst for Maurice, Kingsley and Ludlow to join forces. The three men met at Maurice's house after the mass Chartist demonstration at Kennington Common in London, spending much of the night discussing how Christianity might respond to socialism. The immediate response was a leaflet, most probably written by Kingsley, seeking to dissuade the Chartist protestors from turning to violence and highlighting for them the necessity of seeking morality and virtue.[3] Consider, the 'Workmen of England' were urged, the 'men who are drudging and sacrificing themselves to get you your rights, men who know what your rights are better than you know yourselves'. '[T]urn back from the precipice of riot [for] there will be no true freedom without virtue.'[4] This unblushingly paternalistic, moral-force argument hardly represents a thoroughgoing radicalism. Kingsley, according to historian of Christian Socialism Chris Bryant, had the instincts of a 'Tory paternalist' who was concerned less with economic or political reform than with the moral standing of the working class.[5] Nevertheless, Kingsley would go on to draw attention to the ways in which the capitalist system exploited workers in novels such as *Yeast* and *Cheap Clothes and Nasty*, which stirred the consciences of his readers and garnered support for the co-operative ventures of himself, Maurice and Ludlow.[6] Kingsley also condemned a hypocritical Christianity that sought to quash complaints about such an exploitative system, arguing: 'We have used the Bible as if it were a special constable's handbook – an opium-dose for keeping beasts of burden patient while they were being overloaded – a mere book to keep the poor in order.'[7] The Bible, Kingsley pointed out, speaks far more of the rights of workers and the duties of those who own property than contemporary preaching reflected.

After the initial leaflet the three men set up a journal, *Politics for the People*, 'a rag-bag fusion of radical politics, liberal churchmanship and social conservatism', which tended to lack concrete proposals and attracted criticism from the Chartists and other radical movements as much as it did from the conservative elements within the Church of England.[8] This was followed by a series of *Tracts on Christian Socialism*, a name approved by Maurice, who had quickly emerged as the dominant figure within the group: 'Christian Socialism [is] the only title which will define our object, and will commit us at once to the conflict we must engage in sooner or later with the unsocial Christians and the unchristian Socialists.'[9] The fact that Maurice predicted such a conflict indicates that he saw himself or his colleagues as having to battle with secular socialists no less than with Christians who opposed socialism; by contrast, Christian Socialists in Britain, from the late nineteenth century onwards, would often work within, or at least alongside, the main current of left-wing and labour politics, even while they emphasised the unique religious reasoning for their socialism.

Maurice contributed the first Tract, in which his commitment to socialism was as ambiguous as that of Kingsley. In the opening paragraphs he declared that 'I seriously believe that Christianity is the only foundation of Socialism, and that a true Socialism is the necessary result of a sound Christianity'; yet, in what followed, he remained vague on what that socialism actually entailed.[10] Robert Owen and Charles Fourier were advanced as examples of social-ism, yet Maurice argued that the co-operative schemes of these men failed because they erred in trying to build a new form of society. This, according to Maurice, was a mistaken endeavour, for a co-operative society already existed – all that was required was for the co-operative nature of society to be recognised.[11] This somewhat bewildering argument perhaps goes some way towards explaining Maurice's cautious approach, for radical action was unnecessary and potentially harmful, insofar as attempts to build new co-operative structures risked damaging the already-existing co-operative nature of society, which needed only to be brought into view. Instinctively conservative, Maurice remained a sup-porter of monarchy and social order, opposed to trade unions and attempts to undertake significant structural changes to politics or the economy.[12]

Maurice's view of society as co-operative was derived from his ecclesiology – his theology of the church. For historian and theologian Jeremy Morris, the politics of Maurice 'was never anything other than a direct application of his ecclesiological convictions [...] his Christian Socialism was simply another pres-entation of his thinking on the church'.[13] The church, argued Maurice, declared the 'unity of God', which was the basis for 'all unity among men'. It was the church, he wrote, which represented 'Universal fellowship' and unity 'for all kindreds and races', as well as being 'the divine means of declaring to all men their relationship to God; and of transmitting its blessings to succeeding genera-tions'.[14] It was this emphasis that explains Maurice's reluctance to support reform movements, trade unions, political parties, or even the co-operative ventures to which he did, at length, give his approval: the church was already, as Morris terms it, 'a universal, spiritual society for all human beings', and none other was needed.[15] The task at hand, thought Maurice, was to draw attention to the church as the basis for a co-operative society, not to create a new basis. In Maurice's view, society was made up of three spheres: church, nation and family. Unlike other theories of this type – for example, the sphere sovereignty of Abraham Kuyper – which posited autonomous, non-overlapping spheres, Maurice's spheres were in hierarchical relationship to one another: church at the top, then nation, and then family. Furthermore, Maurice at times seems to suggest that the church encompassed all – a complete overlap between universal church and universal society.[16] As such, the church was the basis for all societal co-operation.

Though significant, Maurice's ecclesiological arguments were not as durable as his theology of the incarnation, which would be a key emphasis in the work of the next generation of, especially high-church Anglican, Christian Socialists.[17] Maurice 'sees the union between Godhead and humanity as the central message of Christian Scripture', for it 'reveals the unity of God with humanity'.[18] This is not an exclusive unity, but underlines the presence of Christ in all human lives – hence, the universality of the church and its message of unity and co-operation. It demonstrates that all human beings are linked together in a common brotherhood, as a common family, and therefore that a society based on economic competition and rivalry is unnatural and inhumane.[19] In place of such a competitive society, Maurice called for a co-operative society based on 'fellowship' or 'communion'.[20] Nowhere are these ideas represented more clearly than in the Eucharist, which represented for Maurice the incarnate Christ as well as the communion – the fellowship – of all people, both with each other and with God.[21] Thus incarnational theology was linked to the core Christian Socialist concept of brotherhood, as well as to co-operation.

Maurician co-operation, though based on the fraternal fellowship of all people, was not egalitarian. Indeed, it is noticeable that Maurice employed the phrase 'Liberty, Fraternity, Unity' in place of the more familiar conceptual trio, with unity replacing equality.[22] Nevertheless, Maurice wanted all to take their place in a society based on the fraternal, co-operative values of God's kingdom. For

Maurice – and for Kingsley – socialism was the expression of a kingdom of God, which already existed if men would but realise it. This, however, meant that socialism must be kept from party politics, unions, strikes and revolutions, all of which mitigated against this reality.[23] 'Every successful strike tends to give the workmen a very undue and dangerous sense of their own power, and a very alarming contempt for their employer,' Maurice declared, while unsuccessful strikes led, he claimed, to even more radicalism.[24] 'Organizations, political parties, trade unions, strikes – these implied a denial of "the Divine Order",' explains John Cort. 'It was all rather pathetic. The message, in effect, was: "Politics are not for the people – at least not yet".'[25]

Cort gives rather a more charitable assessment of Ludlow, whom he regards as the true founder of British Christian Socialism. Ludlow had spent time in France, was influenced by ethical socialists such as Henri Saint-Simon (see Chapter 3) and Charles Fourier, and was supportive of the co-operative initiatives he observed in Paris. He went far further than Maurice or Kingsley in arguing for state ownership and worker management of key industries.[26] Maurice certainly emphasised the significance of co-operation. In his Christian Socialist Tract he declared that the 'principle of co-operation' is the core principle of socialism and that all who prefer it to competition are socialists; co-operation would allow the working class to assert their share of ownership in society, a share denied to them by the capitalist system.[27] Maurice, however, needed his arm twisting before he would commit to putting his principle into practice – perhaps he feared attempts to create rather than simply recognise co-operation – and it was Ludlow who was the driving force behind the associations for tailors, shoemakers, builders, bakers, needlewomen, and other professions, all of which were affiliated to a new Society for the Promotion of Workingmen's Associations, which was responsible for providing guidance and raising funds where necessary.[28] Yet Maurice's unwillingness to countenance union activity and strikes prevented this developing co-operative movement from forming links with the trade unions; the movement faltered and finally failed in 1855, the progress of Christian Socialism itself coming to a simultaneous halt. Its supporters reflected that things might have been different had Ludlow rather than Maurice been the leading figure.[29]

Maurice's achievements should not be denigrated – he founded the Working Men's College, also known as The Camden College, which still exists today, and was a champion of adult education in a similar manner to R.H. Tawney in the early twentieth century – but these were the achievements of a Christian reformer rather than a Christian Socialist. Maurice protested that his view of co-operation as a present reality, embodied by the church, which needed to be recognised in society rather than of co-operation as a future objective which needed to be created did not mean he was less of a socialist than Owen or Fourier – yet insofar as it kept him from actually trying to establish co-operation, this is exactly what it did mean.[30] Ludlow was regretful that he deferred to Maurice's cautious approach and continued political activism for many years, serving as a member of the executive committee of the London Christian Social Union from 1891–1903. Henry Scott Holland described how Ludlow 'retained to the last his democratic faith in the people, his passionate pity for the poor and downtrodden, his fiery cry for righteousness'.[31] Maurice, however – always more a theologian than a political or economic theorist – did provide for the next generation of Christian Socialists a theology of God as universal Father and the consequent brotherhood of all people, which would be the lasting foundation of Christian Left thought.

Church socialism

It was Stewart Headlam more than anybody else in the next generation of Christian Socialists who acknowledged his debt to Maurice. In his estimation Maurice and the others revealed 'the theological basis of Socialism, by showing how essentially Christian it was [...] They brought into the world of thought all the suggestion which is contained in that most pregnant phrase, "Christian Socialism".'[32] It was not, argued Headlam, that Maurice was responsible for a new form of socialism, but rather that he demonstrated that socialism was inherently Christian regardless of whether socialists recognised the fact. Given Maurice's intention to battle against the 'unchristian Socialists', Headlam may here be overstating his case; he certainly overstates it in the assertion that Maurice wanted to go further than any 'mere co-operative store or association of workmen'.[33] Nevertheless Headlam viewed his own Guild of St Matthew (GSM) as continuing the work of Christian Socialism. As noted above, the basis of the GSM was more thoroughly socialist than Maurice, or indeed than any organisation that came before in British politics. It was not therefore when it came to practical politics or socialist theory that Headlam was indebted to Maurice, but rather in theology. Headlam's socialism was based on the foundation laid by Maurice – as Headlam phrased it, 'the fact of the Fatherhood of God, implying as it does the Brotherhood of men [...] as children of one God we are all united in one common Brotherhood'.[34]

Headlam was an eclectic mix of opinions and preferences – yet somehow he shaped them into a coherent perspective. He was an aesthete who founded the Anti-Puritan League as a protest against the drabness of Victorian Christianity, lauding instead art and music, dancing and theatre. Keir Hardie later recalled, '[a]s a Scotsman and a Nonconformist, I well remember the shock it gave me that the leading member of the Guild divided his attention fairly evenly between socialism and the ballet'.[35] It may have been this taste for theatrical show that inclined him towards Anglo-Catholic liturgy rather than what he regarded as the severity of low-church and Nonconformist worship. For Headlam the sacraments were the indispensable foundation of socialism; he described baptism as 'the Sacrament of Equality' and Holy Communion as 'the Sacrament of Brotherhood', adding that 'these two are fundamental, the one abolishing all class distinctions, and admitting all into the Christian Church, simply on the ground of humanity; the other pledging and enabling all to live the life of brotherhood'.[36] Such a perspective was simply not possible, Headlam averred, on the basis of a Christian theology that drew distinctions between saved and unsaved, redeemed and lost, elect and reprobate, and which offered the sacraments only to those accounted part of the first set of categories. Headlam's theology was the basis for socialism because it was universal – God was the Father of all, all people were brothers and sisters – and the indiscriminate administration of the sacraments was a picture of that fact.[37]

In his idiosyncratic Anglo-Catholic way Headlam viewed the Eucharist as being central to worship, not the reading and preaching of the Word. Nevertheless he was not shy about turning to the Bible to offer arguments in favour of socialism. The parable of the sheep and the goats, argued Headlam, in which Christ judges the world in righteousness, commending those who provided for the poor and needy and condemning those who failed to do so, 'seems to compel every Christian to be a socialist'.[38] Headlam saw that Christ often warned against the love of money, the pursuit of wealth and the selfish misuse of property, all while urging his followers to behave as brothers and sisters by sacrificially providing for one another: 'All those ideas which we now express vaguely under the terms solidarity, brotherhood, co-operation, socialism, seem to have been vividly present in Jesus Christ's teaching.' For Headlam then, Christ was 'a radical reformer', 'a Socialistic carpenter', the 'revolutionary Socialist from Galilee'.[39] Headlam discovered the same socialist ideals throughout scripture, New Testament and Old, a key example being the common ownership of the earliest Christians recorded in Acts of the Apostles. These first-century believers were, according to Headlam, 'in the simplest sense of the word communists' – and the same should apply today.[40]

The GSM was soon followed by a similarly minded organisation, the Christian Social Union (CSU), founded in 1889 by Henry Scott Holland (1847–1918) and Charles Gore (1853–1932). The CSU was more vague in its commitment to socialism than the GSM – according to Gary Dorrien 'purposively vague – Christian socialism in the broad sense of Maurician Christian idealism, not a political programme' – but did have a definite purpose, Scott Holland explaining that policies must be found to prevent Christians flitting between the amoral principles of political economy and conscience-driven attempts at providing charity.[41] It was also alleged that the CSU was founded in order for Anglicans to commit to Christian Socialism and social reform without having to work alongside Headlam.[42] The CSU was less sectarian than the GSM – it was exclusively Anglican but membership was not restricted to Anglo-Catholics.[43] It was also more devoted to research than activism, with Scott Holland describing the process:

We form Reading Circles. We gather round the study of this or that qualified and adequate book. We meet to talk it round, and through, and over [...] At the end we, perhaps, can manage to formulate certain conclusions, certain definite issues, which have resulted from the talks. Those can be reduced to print, and circulated. Our experiences are recorded; and we can go on to the next book.[44]

The scathing response from those who remained members of the GSM: 'Here's a glaring social evil; let's read a paper about it.'[45] Holland in turn mocked Headlam and his GSM colleague Henry Cary Shuttleworth (1850–1900) as 'Headlong and Shuttlecock'.[46]

It is probably fair to say that Scott Holland and Gore were rather more radical than their pedestrian method of social analysis suggests. Scott Holland rejected Marxism and lauded Christian reformers such as Lord Shaftesbury, but he nevertheless viewed socialism as being an extension of Christianity; socialism, he insisted, gives voice 'to pleas and claims to which Jesus Christ alone could give value and solidarity [...] It tells of the Fatherhood of God, bringing Peace and Goodwill: of the universal brother-hood of men'.[47] This socialist Christianity had been lost because of the fear of those who benefited from *laissez-faire* capitalism that religious morals and ethics would place limits on their ability to make a profit.[48] Yet such limits were the necessary consequence of an economic system that enshrined the Christian principle of love for neighbour; love of neighbour, Scott Holland asserted, was not merely an act of charity but the requirement of justice, for your neighbour 'might be some stranger lying by the road-side, unknown and unnamed, who had been nothing to you, and whom you might never see again. Nevertheless, if he was there, and you happened to be going that way, and could do anything for him, that was enough. He held you fast by a moral claim.'[49] Furthermore, in an increasingly globalised economy there was no person upon the face of the earth who was not your neighbour.

Holland did not shy away from the conclusion that the state must be involved in this process. He begins by focusing on the municipality, arguing that local government is one of the things that bind the members of a locality together as neighbours as well as the means by which they may govern lovingly and responsi-bly, thereby demonstrating their neighbourly commitment to one another. 'The Municipality is sacred to us. It is our only instrument by which to fulfil the commandment of our Lord – "You shall love your neighbour as yourself".'[50] Yet, Holland adds, there is another instrument that can achieve even more – the state itself. Given Holland's view of the interconnectedness of the national and international economy, it is the state by which Christian love may be demonstrated to all the inhabitants of a nation and to those in other nations. 'We invoke the State, then. We call upon it to relieve our individual conscience by doing for us what we are powerless to do for ourselves.'[51] This, argues Holland, is not an abdication of responsibility but the recognition of a practical reality – economic relations have grown into such a complex system that the structures of local and national government must be brought into play in order to establish the social ethics of Christianity. It might not be necessary for the state to do all the things that socialists desire, but some regulation of the economy is necessary in order to enshrine love for neighbour. 'Law is liberty', declares Holland. 'Why do we fail to see this?'[52]

To twenty-first-century readers Scott Holland's invocation of the state sounds troublingly authoritarian, the slogan 'Law is liberty' alarmingly Orwellian. Holland, though, has nothing so sinister in mind. His view here is, for example, of factory legislation, which frees workers from the exploitative demands of their employers, or welfare reforms, which set individuals at liberty from the fear and the threat of destitution.[53] This is a positive conception of liberty, which to be sure may lend itself to an authoritarian agenda – but such was not Holland's agenda. Individuals had inalienable rights. Local government kept a check on national government, and vice-versa. Democracy ensured that the state served the people rather than the people serving the state.[54] There was no reason that legislating Christian ethics would lead to authoritarianism; rather, it would lead to 'a Kingdom of earthly righteousness and social happiness [...] The Holy Jerusalem descends from heaven to Earth: the City of God.'[55]

Scott Holland's friend and colleague Charles Gore took a similar view of *laissez-faire* capitalism. It was a 'profound revolt against the central law of Christian morality, "Thou shalt love thy neighbour as thyself"', he said, adding: 'There are few things in history more astonishing than the silent acquiescence of the Christian world in the radical betrayal of its ethical foundation.'[56] Gore emphasised that human beings were made equally in the image of God; the exploitation which characterised the capitalist system served therefore to damage and corrupt this image in whom it should be reverenced.[57] He argued that society must provide for every person the 'equal right to realise himself', which might be taken as an argument in favour of equality of opportunity.[58] If Scott Holland took aim at the inviolability of *laissez-faire* economics then Gore gave the same treatment to property rights.

A society in which a wealthy few could amass more property than they needed, while others were excluded from the right to own property, was not functioning as it should – an argument which might appeal to conservative critics of neo-liberalism more so than socialists.[59] Gore's solution, however – a 'redistribution of property' – brings us back to socialism; such a redistribution was possible because, in Gore's estimation, there is frankly no absolute right to property, only a qualified right to property based on whether property ownership benefits or serves any useful function for the community, an argument which would be echoed by R.H. Tawney a few years later.[60] 'Much,' argued Gore, 'that we are accustomed to hear called the legitimate rights of property, the Old Testament would call the robbery of God, and the grinding of the faces of the poor'; it was a violation of 'the Christian idea of brotherhood'.[61]

Gore was ambivalent on whether he regarded himself as a socialist, suggesting that society would do well to take a few steps towards socialism without going the whole way.[62] This argument, taken alongside Gore's denial of absolute rights to property and Holland's view that the state could and should bound the economy with regulations, suggests that their vision was one that today we would label as social democratic – not the abolition but the management of capitalism. The CSU was 'definitely anticapitalist and indefinitely socialist'.[63] The CSU however, though it did support important reforms, did not declare any firm programme for economic or political change, retaining a 'non-committal attitude' which, despite Gore and Holland's awareness that this was an issue, 'began to make the more radical Christian Socialists somewhat disillusioned'.[64]

Among those who left the CSU was Conrad Noel (1869–1942), who declared in frustration that the organisation was 'forever learning but never coming to a knowledge of the truth'.[65] Noel was an Anglican priest who combined a high-church focus on the sacraments with a radical socialism in a manner similar to Headlam. He repudiated the Maurician idea that seemed to have taken hold in the CSU that Christian Socialism should be moderate and non-committal: 'Christian Socialism [...] is not, as some appear to think, a particular variety of Socialism, milder than the secular brand, but economic Socialism come to by the road of the Christian faith and inspired by the ideas of the Gospel.'[66] Noel was one of the founders of the Church Socialist League (CSL), a third Anglican Christian Socialist organisation, which was far more radical and committed to socialism than the CSU, as well as being more working-class than both the GSM and CSU.[67] He became best known as the infamous 'red vicar' of Thaxted, where he turned the parish into a centre of sacramental socialism, causing local and national scandal by hanging both the Red Flag and the flag of Sinn Fein inside the church building.[68] In sermons, Noel raged against the system of 'Christo-capitalism', which exploited workers and co-opted the Gospel for its own ends; like Vida Scudder (see Chapter 4) he pointed to the Trinity as an example of the love and co-operation that should be practised on earth and, like Headlam, he lauded the *Magnificat* of Mary as a hymn 'more revolutionary than the *Marseillaise*'.[69]

Noel and Headlam both held that a sacramental Christianity was the only legitimate basis for socialism; they looked down on low-church and evangelical Anglicans, reserving particular scorn for Nonconformists. Yet church socialism was not an exclusively Anglo-Catholic phenomenon, nor was it reserved for the established church. A key figure was John Clifford (1836–1923), President of the Baptist Union of England and Wales, who also served as president of the predominantly Nonconformist Christian Socialist League, as well as being active in the Free Church Socialist League. The declaration of this latter organisation expressed its commitment to socialism in a manner that, excepting the lack of sacramental emphasis, would have satisfied Noel or Headlam:

> Believing that the principle of Brotherhood as taught by Jesus Christ cannot adequately be wrought out under existing industrial and commercial conditions, and that the faithful and commonplace application of this principle must result in the Socialization of all natural resources, as well as the instruments of production, distribution and exchange, the League exists to assist in the work of eliminating the former by building the latter Social Order.[70]

For Clifford, the ethical principles of Christianity required a collectivist rather than competitive order of society. There were, he noted, some advantages to competitive capitalism – men were motivated to work hard and innovate – but the system also encouraged 'the crushing of competitors and thrusting aside of rivals' rather than the 'brotherly helpfulness' summed up in the teaching of Christ.[71] Collectivism was no guarantee against sin and vice, but it encouraged co-operation and mutual support rather than self-centred individualism; such a system, Clifford declared, 'will abolish poverty, reduce the hungry to an imperceptible quantity, and systematically care for the aged poor and for the sick'.[72]

Another notable representative of Nonconformist socialism was Samuel E. Keeble (1853–1946), a Wesleyan Methodist minister and founder of the Wesleyan Methodist Union for Social Service along similar lines to the CSU. As well as being committed to social service, Keeble was a gifted student of economics and a prolific writer, producing many books and pamphlets on social and economic – as well as theological – issues. Chief among these was *Industrial Day-Dreams* (1896) in which he declared straightforwardly:

> No system of industry which proceeds upon the principle of unscrupulous competition, of treating human labour as a mere commodity, and human beings as mere 'pawns' in the game of making money, as mere means to a selfish end; of taking advantage of one man's poverty and necessity, and of another man's ignorance; which sanctions the law of might, and not of right, and the principle of survival of the fittest for success in the scramble for material wealth – no such system [...] can by any stretch of generosity be called Christian.[73]

While no slavish adherent of Marx – Keeble doubted the labour theory of value, for example – he nevertheless valued the insight of Marx and Engels on the systematic ways in which capitalism exploits the working class.[74] Keeble did not believe that state ownership of industry should be the universal rule but, like Scott Holland, favoured a system in which both local and national government would regulate the economy to prevent such exploitation.[75] This, he held, was required by 'the great Christian principles of the Fatherhood of God and the Brotherhood of Man'.[76] The Christian Gospel, Keeble explained, had two elements, individual and social, and '[t]he social gospel is as sacred and as indispensable as the individual gospel'.[77]

The men noted above are just a few examples of the many from various denominations and sects who embraced socialism – or something very close to it – and condemned capitalism as incompatible with the teaching of Christianity. The impact this had on the church – the Church of England in particular – is evident in the appointment of William Temple to the see of York in 1929 and then Canterbury in 1942. Temple (1881–1944) was a throughgoing socialist, who in his younger years made some strikingly radical statements, declaring, for example, that the capitalist system 'is simply organized selfishness' while socialism 'is the economic realisation of the Christian Gospel [...] The alternative stands before us – Socialism or Heresy.'[78] Temple mellowed as he grew older – especially after his appointment as Bishop of Manchester – but he lost nothing of his determination to pursue economic and social justice. In 1924 Temple organised the Conference on Christian Politics, Economics and Citizenship (COPEC), which included Christians from several different denominations and produced papers on a wide variety of economic and social questions. The conclusions of COPEC were perhaps overly cautious and conservative, but the conference nevertheless symbolised that Christian Socialism was growing and that the church was asserting its right to speak into social issues.[79]

Temple continued to assert that right, nowhere more so than in *Christianity and the Social Order* (1942), an exploration of the Christian principles that should underpin the post-war reconstruction of society. Temple declared that the capitalist system was not condemned merely on the selfish say-so of those who did not benefit from it, but precisely because, in favouring a small class of wealthy people and exploiting the rest, such a system outraged the principles of justice.[80] No individual should be subject to exploitation because – contrary to what appearances would suggest – all people are equal, for 'all are children of one Father [...] all are equal heirs of a status in comparison with which the apparent differences of quality and capacity are unimportant'.[81] Temple echoed Gore – and, indeed, his friend Tawney – in asserting that property rights were not absolute, as well as Scott Holland in his argument that '[l]aw exists to preserve and extend real freedom'. Here, Temple also asserts a positive conception of liberty: freedom, he argued, 'must be freedom for something as well as freedom from something'.[82] A system that produces material benefits, even where those benefits are not absolutely restricted to the wealthiest class, is nevertheless condemned insofar as it does not conform to the principles of justice, equality and freedom.

These arguments are at the level of principle rather than practical policy. While Temple was relentless in his view that the church must speak into social issues, he denied that it was the proper role of the church to advance specific policies. Nevertheless, he was persuaded to include in his work a section on what sort of policies might be derived from the principles he was advocating, a section which gained the support of both Tawney and William Beveridge, who was at that time preparing his own contribution to post-war planning.[83] The government, according to Temple, might do well to acquire land for the building of houses; it might increase the support given to families, perhaps in the form of food or coupons for the purchase of clothes; schools should supply food and milk to all pupils; public works funded by the state would benefit all of society as well as providing jobs for the unemployed.[84] These suggestions were intended by Temple as illustrations, sometimes called middle-axioms because they bridge the gap between the levels of principle and of practical policy. What is striking, however, is the extent to which Temple's proposals actually were put into practice by the 1945–51 Labour government, thereby demonstrating the significance of the church socialism, which began with Stewart Headlam and the Guild of St Matthew, for the shape of our politics to this day. Temple, sadly, did not live to see it; he died in 1944. His death, notes Dorrien, may be viewed as 'the symbol of a passing age'.[85]

Christianity and Labour

The Labour successes of 1945 demonstrate for us that Christian Socialism was not solely restricted to the church. James Keir Hardie (1856–1915) is regarded as the founder of both the Scottish Labour Party and the Independent Labour Party (ILP), and latterly the Labour Party itself. Hardie's poverty-stricken upbringing left him with a hatred of both capitalist exploitation and hypocritical Christianity, yet he himself had a religious commitment that was expressed in his membership of the Evangelical Union. 'The only way you can serve God,' asserted Hardie, 'is by serving mankind. There is no other way. It is taught in the Old Testament; it is taught in the New Testament.'[86] The same themes are evident in Hardie's thought that can be observed in the varieties of church socialism considered above. The Gospel, in Hardie's estimation, declared that all people were children of God and consequently brothers and sisters to each other; capitalism stood condemned because it prompted competition and strife rather than the familial co-operation which should be the outworking of this spiritual reality.[87] For Hardie, socialism was 'the application to industry of the teachings contained in the Sermon on the Mount'. While Hardie allowed that the Sermon did not specify state socialism with its aims of owning and managing industry, it nevertheless provided the principles for this form of collectivism by denouncing property and the selfish pursuit of individual wealth. Striking something of a Marxist note, Hardie argued that it would be 'an easy task to show that Communism, the final goal of Socialism, is a form of Social Economy very closely akin to the principles set forth in the Sermon on the Mount'.[88] This, for Hardie, is exemplified in the common ownership practised in the Acts of the Apostles; the earliest Christians could not bear to have differences in wealth and the ownership of property cause divisions in a community characterised by brotherhood and consequently by equality and co-operation.[89]

Hardie's Marxism, though, was inconsistent. He appealed to Marx to support his own political activism, arguing that the policy and methods of the ILP and the Labour Party were in keeping with those laid down by Marx and Engels, and was happy to refer to Marxist analysis in order to denounce capitalism.[90] Yet he was no systematic Marxist, his biographer Bob Holman suggesting that 'Hardie read some Marx and selected bits which fitted with his own views of an ethical and peaceful socialism'.[91] Hardie's assertion that the teaching and arguments of Jesus Christ were the basis of his socialism must be taken seriously; anything else, even the theories of Marx and Engels, was an optional extra. In this Hardie stands as representative for the labour movement and the mainstream British Left, which holds to a non-Marxist ethical socialism of which Christianity was a key component. This differs from the social democratic parties of Europe – the German SPD being the chief example (see Chapter 3) – which, whether orthodox or revisionist, absorbed an anticlericalism and, indeed, an atheism that remained a minority position in the early days of the Labour Party.

As such, Hardie was joined by other Christian Socialists. Hardie did not live long enough to see it, but the first Labour cabinet of 1924, headed by James Ramsay MacDonald, included Christian Socialists such as Philip Snowden (1864–1937), Arthur

Henderson (1863–1935) and John Wheatley (1869–1930). Snowden and Henderson returned in MacDonald's second Labour government of 1929–31, and were joined by Margaret Bondfield (1873–1953) and George Lansbury (1859–1940). Snowden was a strict Methodist, who came to politics via the ILP and the Free Church Socialist League, of which John Clifford had been a keen member. As Chancellor of the Exchequer, Snowden was committed to maintaining free trade, balancing the budget and remaining on the gold standard, enduring criticism that he did not allow for a truly socialist budget; in his defence, however, both of these Labour governments were minority administrations that relied upon the support of Liberal MPs.[92] Henderson was brought up as a Congregationalist but later committed himself to Wesleyan Methodism along with trade unionism; he was a key figure in the creation of Labour's 1918 constitution, including the Clause IV, which would generate so much heated discussion in the decades which followed; he went on to serve as leader of the Labour Party from 1931 to 1932, after MacDonald had formed the National Government coalition.[93]

Wheatley, a devout Roman Catholic, was excluded from the second Labour government because – along with his fellow Red Clydesider James Maxton – he had been critical of MacDonald and Snowden for not pursing a more radical agenda.[94] Indeed Wheatley was responsible for one of the few successes of the first, short-lived Labour administration, the Housing (Financial Provisions) Act (1924), which extended more central funding to municipal governments or the building of homes. Wheatley held that it is socialism 'which emanates from that spirit of brotherhood which is ever present in the heart of man but is so often suppressed by the struggle for existence', arguing that the competitive environment engendered by capitalism did not allow for people to live as children of God.[95] Wheatley struggled to reconcile his political views with the opposition – both official and unofficial – of his church. The official opposition came in the 1891 papal encyclical *Rerum novarum*, when Pope Leo XIII, while attacking the abuses and injustice of capitalism, condemned socialism.[96] The unofficial came when Wheatley's own parish priest incited a mob to protest outside his house; Wheatley responded to this with what, especially under the circumstance, was a highly eloquent speech attacking the capitalist class for stealing the universal God-given right to share in the beauty of creation and enjoy a flourishing life.[97] 'The Catholic Church,' Wheatley maintained, 'has always leaned more to socialism or collectivism and equality, than to individualism and inequality. It has always been the church of the poor and all historical attacks on it have emanated from the rich.'[98]

Bondfield, a Congregationalist and trade-union activist, became the first female cabinet minister in 1929. Although she spent a part of her life away from the church after a deacon admonished her to choose between church and union – taking him at his word she chose the latter – it was her Nonconformist upbringing that provided the basis for her socialism and the campaigns against the exploitation of female shop workers such as she had been.[99] Bondfield's aim was to see the Golden Rule – 'Thou shalt love thy neighbour as thyself' – applied to economy and society, suggesting that this would involve state ownership of key industries and the financial sector.[100] Crucially for Bondfield it was not sufficient merely for industries to be nationalised, but that their priority should be service to the public rather than the pursuit of profit.[101] Neither would state ownership go far enough if workers and consumers were not involved in the management of industry; while such a situation would be an improvement upon private ownership, it would not allow fully the spirit of co-operation to develop. Socialism, Bondfield argued, must involve 'the reorganisation of society on the basis of both political and industrial democracy'.[102] Another noteworthy figure is Ellen Wilkinson (1891–1947), distinguished by her role as co-author of the 1945 Labour Party manifesto, who declared the need to combat 'injustice' wherever it afflicted 'human beings, the children of God'.[103]

Lansbury remains among the best known of the British Christian Socialists. A committed Anglican, he was one of the most forceful and consistent exponents of Christian Socialism's core concept of, as he phrased it, God's 'Fatherhood and the consequent Brotherhood of man'.[104] For Lansbury all the injustices and exploitation of capitalist society come as a result of humanity's failure to live according to these universal principles; yet he never lost hope that people could unlearn the selfishness of capitalistic Mammon worship and live together as children of one Father.[105] Sadly Lansbury's reputation has been tarnished by his unwillingness as Labour Party leader in the mid 1930s to countenance war against the Axis powers; he was 'efficiently and brutally removed from the leadership in 1935'.[106] Lansbury committed himself to a peace crusade in the years leading up to the war, meeting with Adolf Hitler in 1937 in an ill-fated attempt to avert the inevitable and, as late as 1939, imploring Hitler by telegram: 'All mankind is looking to you and Signor Mussolini for such a response as will lead all nations away from war and along the road to peace through cooperation and sharing territories, markets and resources for the service of each other.'[107]

It is easy from our historical vantage point to hold in contempt those such as Lansbury – a sincere and unyielding pacifist in any and all circumstances – who, even faced with such evil, sought peace at all costs. We need to remember that the Great War – the first total war, unprecedented in its bloodshed and carnage – was still fresh in the minds of those who hoped they could prevent another cataclysm. Lansbury in particular has been painted as naive, too saintly minded for the dirty world of real-life politics. This view is mistaken: it overlooks Lansbury's hard-headed leadership of the Poplar Rates Rebellion in which many concessions were won for the residents of that impoverished borough; it cannot account for Lansbury's achievements as the First Commissioner for Works in the 1929–31 government; nor does it give Lansbury enough credit for sustaining the Labour Party after the electoral disaster of 1931, ensuring, with Clement Attlee as his deputy, that there remained a genuine opposition to MacDonald's Conservative-dominated National Government and an alternative vision for the country which could be put to the electorate in 1945.

We have already noted William Temple as one of the proximate architects of that vision. Another was Temple's close friend and fellow Anglican Richard H. Tawney (1880–1962). Tawney, an economic historian and Labour Party activist, set out his view on the events of 1931 in a famous essay, 'The Choice Before the Labour Party', published in *Political Quarterly* in 1932. Tawney argued, while naming no names, that the Labour Party had been overly cautious, failing to commit itself to restructuring the social order and allowing itself to be satisfied with a few efforts to make capitalism more bearable.[108] Is it surprising, asked Tawney, given Labour's lack of vision, if the electorate 'concluded that, since capitalism was the order of the day, it had better continue to be administered by capitalists, who, at any rate – so, poor innocents, they supposed – knew how to make the thing work?'[109] In place of this noncommittal attitude Tawney called for 'a serious effort [...] to create organs through which the nation can control, in coop- eration with other nations, its own economic destinies; plan its business as it deems most conducive to the general well-being; override, for the sake of economic efficiency, the obstruction of vested interests; and distribute the product of its labours in accord- ance with some generally recognised principles of justice'.[110] Tawney was well placed to make such criticisms. He had drafted the 1929 manifesto *Labour and the Nation*, committing the party – at least on paper – to a socialism that he framed as a moral imperative.[111] If MacDonald's actions in forming the National Government are a betrayal of socialism, then they are a betrayal of Tawney's socialism.

Tawney's socialism was clearly and unapologetically Christian. For Tawney, the 'essence of all morality' is 'to believe that every human being is of infinite importance, and that no consideration of expediency can justify the oppression of one by another'. But, he added, 'to believe this it is necessary to believe in God'.[112] This remark, though, was made in Tawney's private diary and only published posthumously. Some have suggested, on the basis of Tawney's public writing, that he is rather more secular-minded than is often interpreted; some of Tawney's key works – for example, most of *The Acquisitive Society*, published 1920 – keep rather quiet about any religious basis for socialism.[113] This argument, though, is hard to square with the final chapter of *The Acquisitive Society*, which sets out unmistakably the Christian ethic driving Tawney's argument. Tawney describes the anti-materialistic teaching of scrip- ture, as exemplified in the *Magnificat* and in the life and teaching of Christ, as a 'revolutionary' creed with which the church can and should seek to remodel society. If taken seriously, the Christian message 'destroys alike the arbitrary power of the few and the slavery of many'.[114] Political historians Matt Beech and Kevin Hickson conclude that, 'for Tawney democratic socialism is only possible because it flows from his Christian faith'.[115]

Tawney's socialism is based on an ideal of service. At its most basic this is a call for a spirit of co-operation rather than compe- tition, based on the concept of brotherhood. 'A well-conducted family,' argued Tawney, 'does not, when in low water, encourage some of its members to grab all they can, while leaving others to go short. On the contrary, it endeavours to ensure that its diminished resources shall be used to the best advantage in the interests of all.'[116] Here, Alan Wilkinson suggests, Tawney is drawing upon the Pauline image of the body (1 Corinthians 12:12–26; Romans 12:4–5) to say that all members of society are members of one body – each has its own function, but all must co-operate. More deeply, Tawney's ideal of service is a call for the economy to be based on function rather than functionless property rights. He excoriates those who defend the rights of landowners who provide no service or function to merely receive payments for the use of their land – for example, the owners of coal mines who profited from the activity on their land through the payment of royalties, but play no part in the mining or distribution of coal, nor even the planning and management of the work. 'Such rights,' he says, 'are, strictly speaking, privileges. For the definition of a privilege is a right to which no corresponding function is attached.'[117] In place of an acquisitive society, which allowed such profiteering shorn of any contribution to the common good, Tawney advocated a 'Functional Society', which would aim at 'making the acquisition of wealth contingent upon the discharge of social obligations' and in which 'the main subject of social emphasis would be the performance of functions'.[118]

Tawney was not opposed to state ownership if it allowed industry to be conducted in a spirit of service and with an eye to function rather than an eye to profit, particularly as state ownership need not necessarily involve direct state management.[119] The key thing for Tawney was to cultivate a sense of professionalism, in which all workers – whether manual labourers or managers – would make service rather than profit their aim. Such a sense could be cultivated by professional associations or guilds: Tawney cites the creation of guilds in the building trade which were organised, he said, 'for the discharge of professional duties'.[120] A society in which workers co-operatively maintained 'the standards of their profession' was, for him, 'the alternative to the discipline which Capitalism exercised in the past'.[121] Tawney's hope to replace amoral profiteering with a professional commitment to service for the common good has similarities with the 'civil economy' advocated by Adrian Pabst (see Chapter 2). Tawney also shares with radical orthodoxy and Blue Labour that his critique of capitalism is effectively a critique of liberalism, for having replaced an ideal of community-minded service with self-centred individualism; as such, it shares some points in common with a conservative critique of liberal capitalism. In modern society, Tawney argues, 'men recognize no law superior to their desires', having instead adopted an individualism which 'appeals to the self-assertive instincts, to which it promises opportunities of unlimited expansion'.[122] Tawney's view – set out famously in *Religion and the Rise of Capitalism*, published in 1922 and dedicated to Charles Gore – was that capitalism was a product of modernity, of an individualism linked to the Protestant Reformation.[123] The solution then was not to look ahead and discard the past as progressivism is apt to do, but rather to recover and restore the ideals of a former age characterised by service and community-mindedness.

Tawney, despite this overlap with conservatism, was most certainly a socialist. In another of his key works, *Equality*, published in 1931, he urged a socialist vision committed to tackling the inequalities caused by capitalism. Tawney did not suggest that all individuals are naturally equal to one another, as though 'all men are equally intelligent or equally virtuous, any more than they are equally tall or equally fat', but that 'it is the mark of a civilized society to aim at eliminating such inequalities as have their source, not in individual differences, but in its own organization'.[124] Equality of opportunity, argued Tawney, was an illusion in a society that systematically excluded whole classes of people from educational opportunities, the highest-paying jobs, and all positions of power and influence; it was necessary to seek equality of outcome, or at least to minimise inequality of outcome. Without this 'the phrase equality of opportunity is obviously a jest, to be described as amusing or heartless according to taste'.[125] It was not in Tawney's view necessary to observe a strict equalisation of incomes, even if such a thing were possible; rather, the aim was 'the pooling of [the nation's] surplus resources by means of taxation, and the use of the funds thus obtained to make accessible to all, irrespective of their income, occupation, or social position the conditions of civilization, which, in the absence of such measures, can only be enjoyed by the rich'.[126] It is this vision that Tawney commended to the Labour Party, and which the party set about putting into practice at the end of the Second World War.

Conclusion

It was F.D. Maurice, Charles Kingsley and John Ludlow who provided the theological grounding for the Christian Socialist vision, expounding the universal Fatherhood of God and the consequent brotherhood of all people, as well as asserting co-operation to be the natural outworking of these spiritual truths. The next generation of church socialists expanded this political theology into a recognisably socialist or social democratic vision of a whole society characterised by equality, co-operation and democracy.[127] Unlike European socialism, which, following Marx and Engels, remained largely opposed to religion as a reactionary force and a form of false consciousness, this Christian Socialist vision also had adherents in the Labour Party: James Keir Hardie, George Lansbury, John Wheatley and others. After two unsuccessful terms in office the Labour Party, guided by figures such as William Temple and R.H. Tawney, finally succeeded in translating this vision into a programme of real social and economic change.

2

Identity Crisis: Christian Socialism in Post-War Britain

In January 1960 R.H. Tawney made one of his final public appearances to attend a meeting of left-wing Christians at Kingsway Hall in Holborn, London. At this meeting – chaired by Donald Soper – two organisations, the Society of Socialist Clergy and Ministers and the Socialist Christian League, came together to form the Christian Socialist Movement (CSM).[1] The CSM – now known as Christians on the Left – has represented Christian Socialism in Britain ever since, with several dozen members among the parliamentary Labour Party and around 2,000 members overall.[2] Tawney's attendance provides a historical link between Christians on the Left and the Christian Socialism of those formative pre-war years. That Tawney was a member of the Christian Social Union, as was John Ludlow, gives an even greater sense of apostolic succession, linking Christians on the Left with the work of F.D. Maurice and the ethical socialism of France, which Ludlow combined.

The CSM emerged at a time when the Labour Party was divided between those who wanted to press on towards a more socialist agenda, those who wished to maintain the existing social democratic consensus, and those who felt that the party needed to move away from ideas of state ownership and control. These issues, which have dogged the party and the wider British Left since the 1951 election defeat, have never been resolved. At first the CSM, though not officially affiliated until 1988, was firmly to the left of the party, opposing any attempt to rewrite Labour's Clause IV commitment to collectivism and with leading figures such as Soper and Tom Driberg linked to the Bevanite wing of the parliamentary party. In a similar way Christian Socialism, as represented by Church of England criticism of Margaret Thatcher's Conservative government, was thoroughly opposed to the neo-liberalism of the new Right.

Yet, in the years following Thatcher's resignation, Christian Socialism came to be represented by John Smith and Tony Blair – figures who wanted to move the Labour Party away from the hard-left policies of the 1980s, as symbolised by Blair's successful redefinition of Clause IV in 1995. Blair's communitarian values were certainly in keeping with an ethical social democracy (or, as he preferred to call it, democratic socialism), yet the Third Way politics, which drifted away from a communitarian vision in extending privatisation and placing faith in market competition, could be characterised as symptomatic of a new post-1979 neo-liberal consensus. Groups such as Jubilee and Ekklesia represent the more radical face of Christian Socialism, as well as rejection of this New Labour economic liberalism. The more moderate, even conservative, face of Christian Socialism is represented by the 'faith, family and flag' approach of figures such as Frank Field, associated with the Blue Labour movement. Blue Labour, however, while opposing social liberalism and progressivism, nevertheless departs from New Labour in seeking, in the terminology of Adrian Pabst, a new 'civil economy' which would replace an economy based on individualistic profiteering with an ethical, community-minded commitment to the common good, and is in that sense rather more radical than a progressive Left that has often accepted liberal individualism.

A party divided

Despite what can be characterised as the triumph of Christian Socialism and the Labour movement in general in the accomplishments of the 1945–51 government, the Labour Party of the 1950s was divided in spirit and thoroughly unsure of what it was or what it should be doing. In part this was due to the success of 1945: with 'the welfare state in place, the worst deficiencies of labour law corrected, the nationalisation of significant parts of the economy and the eradication of the worst excesses of poverty', the party did not know how to proceed.[3] Following the loss of the 1951 general election the party can be seen as split into three factions: the left (associated with Nye Bevan), who wanted to continue down the path towards socialism, the centre (Herbert Morrison), who focused more on what had been achieved than what had yet to be done, and the right (Hugh Gaitskell), which urged that Labour must revise or moderate its aims in the new post-war economic and social context.[4] It was the party's right which appeared to have the ascendancy, at least among the parliamentary party: Gaitskell overcame Bevan and Morrison in the leadership election of 1955 following Labour's second successive general election defeat. The driving force behind this modernising impulse was Anthony Crosland, who held that the growing affluence of society allied to the disintegration of the working class necessitated a change of strategy: 'the Labour Party [...] would be ill-advised to continue making a largely proletarian class appeal when a majority of the population is gradually attaining a middle-class standard of life, and distinct symptoms even of a middle-class psychology'.[5]

It was into this ideological milieu that the CSM emerged. Among the key figures in its foundation was Tom Driberg (1905–76), a Labour MP who served as party chairman from 1957 to 1958. Driberg was a larger-than-life figure, a high-church Anglo-Catholic in the mould of Stewart Headlam or Conrad Noel. His obituary in *The Times* would describe him as 'a journalist, an intellectual, a drinking man, a gossip, a high churchman, a liturgist, a homosexual [...] a politician of the left [...] a stylist, an unreliable man of undoubted distinction'.[6] Driberg held a series of meetings in the late 1950s with prominent Christians of the Left – among them Donald Soper – at The Lamb pub in Soho. These discussions led to the publication of a Christian Socialist manifesto, *Papers from the Lamb*, in 1959.[7] This took the form of essays on various topics, authored by Driberg but with the aim of being as representative as possible, which urged the importance of 'the divine purpose of so reordering society that the lives of countless human beings, made in the image of God, do not end in degradation and despair'.[8] *Papers* called for 'distributive communism' after the pattern of the early church, and 'common ownership' tempered by 'a concern with abundant living for individual human persons within society'.[9] This, though, did not necessarily mean state ownership, but any way in which industry and economy could be reorganised so as to promote co-operation and fair distribution rather than competition and individualism.[10]

The main figure in the formation and subsequent life of the CSM was Donald Soper (1903–98). Soper was a Methodist minister who served as president of the Methodist Conference in 1953–4 and was a founder member of the Campaign for Nuclear Disarmament (CND) in 1957. He had a devotion to the eucharist, which is perhaps not typical of British Nonconformism – like Anglo-Catholic socialists he emphasised the sacrament as a symbol of 'peace and justice and love' – but was otherwise quite unlike Driberg and other high-church Anglicans in his more austere and socially conservative lifestyle.[11] Soper was opposed to an exclusively spiritual, other-worldly interpretation of the Gospel, which denied that there was a role for Christians in helping the poor and destitute and building a better form of society here on earth. He argued that Christianity was incompatible with the individualism of free-market capitalism, which he saw being embraced by the Conservatives in the 1950s.[12] 'The foundation of my Socialist belief,' he declared, 'is that I regard Socialism as the economic and political expression, in time, of what I believe to be the Kingdom of God.'[13] Soper became the first chairman of the CSM at the Kingsway Hall meeting in 1960, an office he held until 1975; he then served as CSM president until the end of his life.

The CSM – although not formally affiliated to the Labour Party – was deeply involved in party politics. Despite prevailing views that Christian forms of socialism are necessarily more moderate, the CSM was a consistent left-wing critic of Hugh Gaitskell's plans of reforming the party. Driberg, associated with the Bevanites in the party and a member of the Keep Left group, was an active opponent of Gaitskell's revisionist agenda.[14] Soper was a member of the Victory for Socialism group, which advocated 'common ownership of the means of production'.[15] His advocacy of unilateral nuclear disarmament and common ownership placed him firmly to the Left of the party at a time when even Bevan began to move away from unilateralism. This positioning is crystallised in Soper's support for Clause IV, which he argued 'expresses, within the framework of a contemporary economic situation, what I believe to be the ultimate principle that emerges from our Lord's teaching'.[16] Soper became 'increasingly antagonistic' towards Gaitskell for his attempt to drop Clause IV from Labour's constitution.[17] Tawney too, in the final years of his life, was deeply disappointed at Gaitskell's desire to abolish Clause IV, but did not speak out publicly.[18] The CSM in the 1960s and 1970s remained committed to common ownership, most of its members taking this as a commitment to the state ownership and management that Gaitskell and Crosland had urged was no longer a realistic aspiration.[19]

The response to Thatcherism

The 1945–51 Labour government represented, says Gary Dorrien, the coming-of-age of British social democracy.[20] This is especially so when we consider that the economic and welfare policies introduced by that government would remain largely unchallenged for years to come, the 'basis of a new political consensus', which would last into the 1970s. 'Labour's values were effectively incorporated into a cross-party consensus, sometimes described as social democratic.'[21] It was the 1979–90 Conservative government headed by Margaret Thatcher that finally smashed the social democratic post-war consensus, replacing it with a neo-liberal view of economic *laissez-faire*, small government, and a shrinking welfare state.[22] To Christian Socialists as much as others on the Left this was an unacceptable turn of events, the very set of social and economic policies that Donald Soper had decried as antithetical to the Christian Gospel some two decades previously.

The divisions within the Labour Party and the wider Left became at this stage even more marked, reaching their culmination in 1981 when Labour MPs Roy Jenkins, David Owen, Bill Rodgers and Shirley Williams split from the party to form the Social Democratic Party (SDP). The SDP claimed to represent the tradition of ethical socialism that was being abandoned by an, allegedly, increasingly far-left Labour Party under Michael Foot. For this reason the SDP named its new thinktank, which lasted until the merger with the Liberal Party in 1988, after R.H. Tawney. Foot responded by claiming Tawney as part of Labour's socialist history and tradition.[23] Shirley Williams (1930–2021),

herself a Roman Catholic, argued that Christian Socialism in the
Labour Party had been replaced by scientific socialism, and that a
faith-based commitment to social democracy had been squeezed
out by the party's hard left.[24] Interestingly, the present itera-
tion of the SDP, in advocating socially conservative policies and
traditional values allied to centre-Left views of a 'social market
economy', along with promises to protect the welfare state from
neo-liberal incursion, represents something analogous to continental Christian Democracy (see Chapter 3).[25]

Not everybody, however, agreed with the assessment of Williams
and others that Christian Socialism was no longer welcome
within the Labour Party. Tony Benn, personally an agnostic but
one who valued the tradition of Christian ethics that shaped
British radicalism, remained a key figure on the left of the party.
Benn seemed to embody the creed of Clement Attlee: 'Believe in
the ethics of Christianity. Can't believe the mumbo-jumbo.'[26]
Another Christian who kept faith with Labour in this period was
Eric Heffer (1922–91), who served as MP for Liverpool Walton
from 1964 until his death; indeed, Heffer was a supporter of the
Militant group which ran the local council in his adopted city and
had become a by-word for hard-headed leftism, especially as Neil
Kinnock sought to move the party back towards the centre.[27] As
a young man Heffer attended a meeting for the Jarrow hunger
marchers in 1936 when they arrived in his native Hertford on their
way to London. He also heard Conrad Noel preaching. He went
on to join the Communist Party, partly out of disillusionment with
mainstream parties during the National Government coalition,
and remained a Communist until he was expelled from the party
in the post-war period, possibly as a result of his campaigning for
Labour in the 1945 election. Heffer argued that 'Jesus was crucified because he took the side of the poor', and saw co-operative
values embedded in both the Protestant and Roman Catholic communities of highly sectarian Liverpool.[28]

Thatcherism prompted a response outside the party as well. In
1980 a group of nineteen Christian societies came together to form
Christian Organisation for Social, Political and Economic Change
(COSPEC) with the express aim of opposing the government's
neo-liberal policies from a Christian perspective. These societies
included the Quaker Socialist Society, the Alliance of Radical
Methodists, the Student Christian Movement, Christian Action,

Jubilee and the Urban Theology Unit, as well as a Manchester-based group called Christians for Socialism.[29] COSPEC stressed five points: true equality of opportunity; workers' ownership and management; community control of capital; a planned, co-operative economy; and full democratic participation in political and economic decision making.[30] These themes were present in a Christian Manifesto issued at the 1983 general election and the 'Christians for a Change' campaign, which followed at the 1987 general election.[31] COSPEC, however, remained rather too unwieldy and, like the Labour Party, divided to make as much of an impact as it might; plans to develop a 'Christian Institute' for the UK, perhaps in a similar manner to the Christian Institute of South Africa (see Chapter 7), came to nothing. COSPEC did, however, succeed in arranging much-needed practical support for mining communities during the 1984–5 miners' strike, as well as maintaining 'a radical witness' at a time when it seemed little could stop the Thatcherite agenda.[32]

Opposition to the government also came from the established church itself, in the form of bishops such as David Sheppard (1929–2005) of Liverpool and David Jenkins (1925–2016) of Durham. Sheppard's encounter with poverty in London's East End, prior to his appointment to the see of Liverpool, moved his theology away from an evangelical focus on salvation and towards a view, closer to that of liberation theology (see Chapter 6), emphasising freedom from the oppression of poverty.[33] Jenkins, active at the William Temple Foundation in Manchester, criticised individualistic Thatcherism as antithetical to the Gospel in a manner similar to Donald Soper.[34] Thatcher herself disagreed. In a 1981 speech at St Lawrence Jewry in the City of London, she proposed that the Bible is 'preoccupied with the individual', and from this is derived the importance of 'personal moral responsibility'. 'We must always beware,' warned Thatcher, 'of supposing that somehow we can get rid of our own moral duties by handing them over to the community'.[35]

The Anglican opposition to Thatcher's individualistic emphasis and denial that the state bore the responsibility of care for the impoverished was stated most notably in the 1985 report *Faith in the City* published by the Archbishop of Canterbury's Commission on Urban Priority Areas. The report begins by condemning the 'evident and apparently increasing inequality in our society

[which] exceeds the limits that would be thought acceptable by
most of our fellow citizens'. Poverty, inequality and polarisation
of society represent, it is argued, 'a grave and fundamental injustice'.[36] This, it was implied, was a direct result of the faith placed
in the markets by the Conservative government, for 'the market
has intrinsic tendencies towards inequality'.[37] In what may be read
as a direct response to the theology of Thatcher, the report declares
that the biblical injunction to provide for the poor

> can legitimately take the form of social and political action aimed
> at altering the circumstances which appear to cause poverty and
> distress [...] The evidence of the gospels makes it clear that Jesus'
> proclamation of the Kingdom of God had from the start profound
> social and political implications. It was to be embodied in a commu-
> nity in which the normal priorities of wealth, power, position and
> respectability would be overturned.[38]

Many in the church, it was argued, had failed to recognise this,
engaging in the 'ambulance work' of providing charity rather than
fighting for systemic change in the name of justice.[39]

Conservative MP Ian Gow was among those who denounced
Faith in the City and the broader Anglican opposition to government policy as Marxism, perhaps with some justification.[40] The
report stated plainly that it was 'against the background of the
excessive individualism of much Christian thinking in the nineteenth century' – and remember that Thatcher herself embodied a
return to these Victorian values – 'that we must place Marx's perception that evil is to be found, not just in the human heart, but in
the very structures of economic and social relationships'.[41] Other
Marxist concepts were in evidence: references to the alienating
nature of capitalist society; the argument that commodities must
have an intrinsic, not merely an exchange, value; the declaration
that the wealth created by capitalism was not being fairly distributed, certainly not 'trickling down' as some believed it would, and
was by implication being stolen.[42]

Yet, in other ways, Gow's criticism was overly simplistic. The
idea that evil was to be found in the unjust structures of society
was also attributed, *contra* Thatcher, to the Bible itself, especially
the Old Testament ('from which, in fact, Marx may have derived
it').[43] The Old Testament gives 'explicit recognition of the inevitable tendency of the rich to get richer and the poor to get poorer

unless some constraint is imposed to limit the freedom of individuals to profit without restraint from a market economy'.[44] These constraints take the form of such rules and regulations as the year of jubilee, the instructions to maintain a portion of the harvest for the poor and needy, the prohibition of charging usury, and other community-minded provisions. These social ethics came to the fore again in the New Testament, as evidenced by the *Magnificat* of Mary and the Beatitudes of Christ's Sermon on the Mount. These indicated the need to work towards a form of society instilled with the values of the Kingdom as revealed in Christ. In making these arguments *Faith in the City* disavowed a reliance on the theories of Marx and Engels, even if those theories were of some use, and placed itself within the Christian Left tradition of making 'a prophetic call for justice' to keep 'alive the fundamental Christian conviction that even in this fallen world there are possibilities for a better ordering of society'.[45]

Reclaiming the ground

Christian Socialism began to take a more prominent role in the Labour Party after Margaret Thatcher's tenure in office, as seen in the leadership of first John Smith and then Tony Blair, both of whom were members of the CSM and committed themselves to a Christian-based ethical understanding of politics. The emphasis on Christian or more broadly ethical socialism was a move away from the perception of Labour being dominated by its hard, uncompromising left wing during the Thatcher years. This was a shift from trade unions and hard-left shibboleths and towards a democratic socialism drawn from moral values.[46] This period also marked the collapse of communism, the end of the Cold War, and 'the end of History' – the eschaton of liberal democracy and free-market capitalism. Socialism, it seemed, was discredited; capitalism, it was supposed, had proved itself the victor in the twentieth century's clash of ideologies, a situation that 'confirmed the supremacy of the free market and discredited planning'.[47] Parties of the Left had to respond accordingly, reframing their alternative to the individualism and injustice of the free-market system, in a manner that accepted that there was a new political consensus around the superiority of that system.

After the general election defeat of 1992, it fell to John Smith (1938–94) to continue the reforming agenda of Neil Kinnock as party leader. Smith, a committed member of the Church of Scotland, was 'someone whose Christian Socialism permeated both his personal and political life'.[48] He had fought against Labour's moves towards the Left in the 1980s, supporting Denis Healey against Michael Foot in the 1980 leadership election. Demonstrating a traditional Presbyterian morality, Smith was an opponent of abortion and generally 'voted with the anti-abortion lobby' – a position that would be impossible for a politician of the Left or centre-Left today.[49] 'For me,' declared Smith, 'socialism is largely Christian ethical values [...] Politics is a moral activity. Value should shine through at all times.'[50] In the 1993 Tawney Lecture, given at Bloomsbury Baptist Church, he identified himself with the tradition of Tawney who, Smith argued, 'was through-out the whole of his long and productive life an uncompromising ethical socialist. He founded his political outlook on the moral principles of his Christian commitment. From that strong redoubt he assailed the deficiencies of both communism and capitalism and espoused the cause of a democratic socialism.'[51]

In that lecture, subsequently published as part of the Christian Socialist volume *Reclaiming the Ground*, Smith declared himself against the 'nihilistic individualism' espoused by the Conservative Party, which assumed that 'human beings conduct their lives on the basis of self-interested decisions taken in radical isolation from others'.[52] Instead, Smith pointed to 'the interdependence of the individual and society'. Human beings are more than 'homo-economicus'; they are 'people living in families, in communities, in regions, and in nations'.[53] Market systems work well, Smith conceded, but not when they are based on atomistic self-interest; rather, markets should be embedded in the broader community and its social and political institutions. The commandment to love our neighbours as ourselves (Matthew 23:29) cannot be achieved on a solely individual basis but involves a 'care and concern for our fellow citizens which is reflected in the organisa-tion of our society'.[54] A minimal state does not suffice to safe-guard and promote the common good; neither does a negative conception of liberty, which holds non-interference as the highest ideal of freedom. Instead, Smith urged a positive conception of liberty, which would underpin an 'infrastructure of freedom that

would require collective provision of basic needs through an enabling state'. Such a view of freedom, linked to mutual support
rather than non-interference, 'is the moral basis of democratic
socialism'.[55]

Sadly, Smith died a little less than two years after becoming
leader of the opposition. His successor Tony Blair (b.1953) continued both the reforming agenda and the emphasis on ethical
socialism. Indeed, Blair argued, 'since the collapse of Communism,
the ethical basis of socialism is the only one that has stood the
test of time'.[56] Blair drew on an 'ecumenical' understanding of
Christianity – he was first confirmed into the Church of England
before converting formally to Roman Catholicism in 2007 – to
underpin his political vision.[57] Alan Wilkinson argues that Blair's
leadership 'exemplifies and has powerfully promoted the rediscovery and reinterpretation of the ethical and Christian roots
of British socialism'.[58] This was clear in Blair's foreword to
Reclaiming the Ground in which he set out his desire to 'reunite
the ethical code of Christianity with the basic values of democratic
socialism'. Like Smith, Blair pointed to 'the union between individual and community', adding that 'the Christian message is that
self is best realised through communion with others. The act of
Holy Communion is symbolic of this message.'[59] Blair highlighted
the concepts of equality and justice, but – in perhaps a hint of later
accusations that New Labour had abandoned its socialism – these
were not conceptualised in an overtly socialist way. Justice was
linked to international aid and equality of opportunity. Equality
was not equality of outcome, nor even equality of opportunity:
to Blair it meant 'that despite our differences we are entitled to
be treated equally, without regard to our wealth, race, gender or
standing in society', a fairly conventional understanding of formal
equality shared by liberals and modern conservatives.[60]

Blair made his opposition known to the 'narrow self-interest'
represented by the Conservatives, yet he also criticised a Marxist
conception of socialism, which subjugated the needs of the individual to that of the state.[61] Socialism, for Blair, was a 'belief
in society, working together, solidarity, cooperation, partner-
ship [...] Socialism to me was never about nationalisation or
the power of the state; not just economics or politics even. It is
a moral purpose to life; a set of values.'[62] He thus rejected both
the Marxist understanding of community and the neo-liberal

emphasis on the autonomous individual, substituting for both a communitarianism derived from the Christian philosopher John Macmurray (1891–1976). Macmurray argued that individuals could only fully realise their potential and their humanity within community, through relationships with others.[63] Such interdependence does not rely upon a large, powerful or controlling state, but it does disavow the atomistic nature of neo-liberal capitalism in which each individual pursues their self-interest, often divorced from the interests of others. Blair explained that 'individuals are interdependent [and] owe duties to one another as well as themselves', the basis of New Labour's rhetoric of rights and responsibilities. 'It was,' continued Blair, 'only by recognising their interdependence will individuals flourish, because the good of each does depend on the good of all.'[64]

It was the indebtedness to another philosopher, Anthony Giddens, which arguably underpins the argument that Blair's political outlook was not socialist at all. Giddens developed a philosophy of 'Third Way' which, although he presented it as part of the social democratic tradition, was a *via media* between the economics of the Left and the Right.[65] There remains some dispute about whether social democracy should be considered a variant of socialism, or a separate ideological tradition. If there is a difference, then it lies in the fact that socialism – whether through revolutionary or democratic means – seeks to abolish the capitalist system and replace it with a co-operative, collectivist order of society. Social democracy, by contrast, does not seek the abolition but rather the management of capitalism, regulating economic activity to prevent injustice and minimise equality of outcome, as well as using the wealth created by a market economy to fund state-provided services. Social democracy remains sceptical of free markets; markets do not, left to themselves, deliver the goods. The Third Way, however, places much greater faith in the role of the market, with Giddens arguing that the case for free-market capitalism had been made.[66] The Third Way departed from a social democratic 'social security state' to a 'social investment state' in which government is no longer responsible for the provision of social goods, merely for the provision of access to social goods. The emphasis is placed on equalising opportunities rather than outcomes.[67]

Insofar as Blair's New Labour followed this agenda – for example in introducing 'more competition and increased private-sector involvement' into the provision of public services – it might be argued that this was not socialism at all.[68] The National Health Service was subject to internal marketisation, the privatisation of public transport initiated by the governments of Margaret Thatcher and John Major continued, and income tax for the wealthiest remained lower than in many other countries. Indeed, in the words of Peter Mandelson, New Labour was 'intensely relaxed about people getting filthy rich'.[69] The much-trumpeted language of rights and responsibilities came to be used as a reason to penalise the lower strata of society, for example in removing benefits as punishment for anti-social behaviour, but seemed not to apply to the social responsibilities of the wealthy.[70] Successes of the New Labour government, often overlooked by left-wing critics, should be noted: measurable improvements in healthcare and education, the introduction of the minimum wage, the reduction in child poverty, the SureStart programme for disadvantaged preschool children.[71] Yet much of Blair's policy agenda seems to point to the abandonment of the communitarian values expressed in opposition and the continuation of a new neo-liberal consensus around the efficiency of the market and the autonomy of the individual, replacing the earlier social–democratic consensus that had emerged from 1945–51.

Blair's modernising agenda and his opponents' accusations that he had abandoned socialism are symbolised in his successful campaign in 1995 as leader of the opposition to replace the party's Clause IV, successfully implementing the revisionist agenda of Gaitskell and Crosland. John Smith had made plans to replace the clause but had not lived long enough to put them into practice.[72] The new Clause IV replaced a commitment to 'common ownership of the means of production, distribution and exchange' with a declaration that:

> The Labour Party is a democratic socialist party. It believes that by the strength of our common endeavour we achieve more than we achieve alone, so as to create for each of us the means to realise our true potential and for all of us a community in which power, wealth and opportunity are in the hands of the many, not the few, where the rights we enjoy reflect the duties we owe, and where we live together, freely, in a spirit of solidarity, tolerance and respect.[73]

Critics thought it vague, and argued that a party that was no longer committed to collectivism was not a socialist party, democratic or otherwise. Yet, whether or not such criticism is valid, it does have to be noted that the new Clause IV does not reflect the neo-liberalism of which New Labour is often accused. The focus on 'community' and on rights being linked to 'duties' reflects the communitarianism that Blair derived from his faith, while the phrase 'the many, not the few' would become the basis for Jeremy Corbyn's campaign slogan in 2017.

The Christian faith, argued Blair, provides 'principles of living that are timeless' rather than specific policies, allowing us to make a distinction 'between values themselves and their application'.[74] This perspective explains how Blair could disavow a commitment to collective ownership yet still regard himself as a Christian Socialist, and continue to speak of Christian Socialist values: 'One Britain, where your child in distress is my child; your parent ill and in pain is my parent; your friend unemployed or helpless, my friend; your neighbour my neighbour.' Whether those values were actually reflected in New Labour's approach while in office, or whether they were merely rhetorical camouflage for a rebranding exercise that allowed the party to persist in a Thatcherite neo-liberal consensus, will remain a matter of contention.

Two faces of Christian Socialism

Donald Soper, nearing the end of his life, remained opposed to any attempt to remove or replace Clause IV, repeating his argument that a commitment to collective ownership was the teaching of Christ applied to socio-economic matters.[75] Indeed, Soper criticised New Labour and Blair's Giddens-inspired Third Way for, as he phrased it, 'canoodling with capitalism', arguing that a Labour Party not committed to socialism would be 'a waste of time'.[76] The CSM, however, was no longer united on the matter. Having affiliated to the Labour Party in 1988 and voted 'overwhelmingly' for John Smith and Tony Blair in successive leadership elections, roughly three-quarters of CSM members at the 1995 AGM voted for the adoption of Blair's new Clause IV.[77] It seems that the CSM was no longer universally to the left of the party – though neither does it constitute a reliable ally of the New Labour right of the party. In September 2016, the day after his re-election as leader at the party conference in Liverpool, Jeremy Corbyn received a rapturous welcome at the Christians on the Left conference service at St James in the City church as he described the 'fundamental tenets of Christianity' as being 'social justice', 'sharing' and 'compassion'.[78]

These two faces of Christian Socialism, the one more moderate and reformist, the other more radical, are also reflected outside the CSM; indeed, it must be remembered that neither Christians on the Left now nor the CSM previously represented all of the Christian Left. While, for example, in its opening decades the CSM was dominated by Anglicans and Methodists, radical-minded Catholics – many of them University of Cambridge students – came together to form the Slant group, which lasted from 1964 to 1970. Members sought to develop a theology for a New Left Church drawing from Marxism, Catholic social teaching and the first stirrings of liberation theology in Latin America (see Chapters 3 and 6). The writer Terry Eagleton (b.1943), a prominent Slant member, argued that the answer to the alienation endured under the capitalist system, as identified by Marx, was a community which was found in unity with Christ.[79] Another group influenced by liberation theology is the Sheffield-based Urban Theology Unit (UTU) of Methodist minister John Vincent (b.1929). All theology, argues Vincent, 'begins because of the situation of the poor'. The Bible reveals 'a God who is not in favour of the powers, who all the time through scripture is at war either with the kings, or the priests, or the authorities, and who then appears in Jesus Christ, who futilely rides on his donkey down into Jerusalem, representing the Galilean uprising of the peasants'.[80]

The UTU was among the organisations that joined COSPEC in 1980, as was the Jubilee Group, an Anglo-Catholic socialist movement in the mould of Stewart Headlam or Conrad Noel.[81] Jubilee was described by one of its key founding members Kenneth Leech (b.1939) as 'a loose framework through which left-wing Catholics in the Anglican tradition can think through issues, support one another and can help to forward ideas'.[82] Another key member was Rowan Williams (b.1950), later Archbishop of Canterbury, who in 1975 co-authored a Jubilee manifesto – albeit never officially adopted – which condemned 'the institutionalised egotism of all forms of capitalism, including the Soviet collectivised form' and called upon Christians to 'make our stand with the oppressed, with the movement for liberation throughout the world'.[83] A more recent example is Ekklesia, a Christian Left thinktank founded in 2002 by Simon Barrow (b.1971) who had previously served as the convenor of COSPEC from 1987 to 1990, and Jonathan Bartley (b.1971), who was co-leader of the Green Party of England and Wales from 2016 to 2021. Ekklesia is committed to 'favouring the poorest and most vulnerable', 'redressing social and economic injustices and inequalities', as well as promoting a Green New Deal with 'radical measures to decarbonise the economy, with major investments in renewable energy'.[84]

If groups such as this represent the more radical face of Christian Socialism then the more moderate – indeed, conservative – face is probably represented nowhere better than in former Labour MP Frank Field (b.1942). Field has adopted what Chris Bryant calls 'a resolutely right-wing socialist critique' of the Labour Party, arguing that instead of outright opposition to free-market capitalism, 'Labour should embrace the market and spend the whole of its effort expressing its disapproval of the market's unacceptable faces – particularly its inability to tackle unemployment and its power to punish the poor and least strong.'[85] Field is known as a critique of the welfare state for creating dependence rather than encouraging moral improvement, arguing that 'a major consequence of welfare is now the cultivation of idleness, fecklessness and dishonesty', which serves to 'block the very process we should be aiming to achieve – maximising a person's natural instincts to leave the welfare roll'.[86] Never entirely comfortable in the Labour Party, Field resigned the Labour whip in 2018 during Jeremy Corbyn's tenure as party leader and instead formed his own Birkenhead Social Justice Party.[87]

Field is also one of the contributors to *Blue Labour: Forging A New Politics* (2015), co-edited by former executive member of Christians on the Left Ian Geary (b.1976) alongside theologian and political theorist Adrian Pabst (b.1976). Field's contribution to Blue Labour is to call for a new politics of the common good, which neither abandons nor infantilises the impoverished of society.[88] Other contributors include Rowan Williams – demonstrating that the divisions within the Christian Left are not strict – and Jon Cruddas (b.1962), a Labour MP and member of Christians on the Left.[89] The Blue Labour movement seeks to combine centre-Left economic and welfare policies with social conservatism and traditional values, offering 'a critique of metropolitan liberal values' and emphasising 'the importance of the role of family, faith and flag'.[90] Although more conservative in the sense of emphasising tradition and rejecting both the state socialism and social liberalism that characterises much of the Left, Blue Labour is also more radical than much of the Left insofar as it seeks to achieve economic justice by changing the very nature and spirit of society. This can be seen in the 'radical orthodoxy' of Anglican theologian John Milbank (b.1952), another key figure in the Blue Labour movement. Radical orthodoxy is orthodox in the sense of a commitment to the historic, catholic faith, as represented in the ancient creeds and confessions of the church; it is radical most clearly in the use of this 'patristic and medieval' perspective 'systematically to criticise modern society'.[91]

Blue Labour – and the radical orthodoxy to which it is linked – is an anti-Enlightenment position, not in the sense of being anti-intellectual but in the sense of rejecting liberalism, atomistic individualism, and progressivism. Milbank and Pabst describe 'two liberalisms' that have 'dominated the Western politics for the last half century: the social–cultural liberalism of the left since the 1960s and the economic–political liberalism of the right since the 1980s'.[92] These two positions are not antithetical as is often supposed, but draw on the same liberal conception of the isolated, self-regarding individual. In place of this liberal malaise, Milbank and Pabst call for 'a post-liberal politics of virtue that seeks to fuse greater economic justice with social reciprocity'.[93] The Jewish philosopher and historian Maurice Glasman – arguably the founding father of Blue Labour – argues similarly that the excesses and injustices of the free market need to be curtailed, not by the state, but by encouraging a greater role for non-state institutions and reviving an ethical underpinning to social and economic activity.[94] While much of the contemporary Left seeks to jettison tradition, proponents of Blue Labour view tradition as a necessary guide to crafting an ethic of social virtue and economic justice; things, argues Glasman, 'do not always get better, and that is part of the critique of the concept of "progressivism".'[95]

Although not explicitly Christian, the Blue Labour movement does recognise the importance of recovering Christian values as the underpinning for economic activity. 'The Labour tradition,' says Glasman, 'is continuous with Christianity in asserting that the humanity of the person is not exclusively defined by their price.'[96] For Milbank, all disciplines, all human knowledge, 'must be framed by a theological perspective; otherwise these disciplines will define a zone apart from God, grounded in literally nothing'.[97] An example of this is Milbank and Pabst's citing of the Christian concept of the 'person' in opposition to the liberal concept of the individual; a person is not separate or atomised as an individual, but rooted in a network of relationships with other persons and non-state institutions, part of a community with shared aims and values.[98] Pabst calls for 'a renewed resistance against the impersonal forces of liberalism that have disembodied the economy from society', a move away from narrow individualism and towards 'mutual flourishing'.[99]

Despite Blue Labour's 'family, faith and flag' image, Pabst focuses more on critiquing the neo-liberal conception of the free market than the progressivism of the liberal Left. Capitalism, especially since Thatcher and Ronald Reagan resuscitated the ideas of Friedrich von Hayek and Milton Friedman, has become an amoral system with immoral outcomes. Despite hopes that recovery from the 2007–09 recession would lead to a change in how the market works, many remain in underpaid, precarious, low-skilled jobs; living costs continue to rise ahead of wages; these factors continue to result in chronic indebtedness; the 'super rich' are able to engage in risky economic ventures for which the bulk of society must absorb the cost; the programme of privatisation initiated by Thatcher and perpetuated by New Labour has resulted in increased inequality and social polarisation.[100] Britain has joined a global 'race to the bottom' in terms of low wages for the poorest and low taxes for the wealthiest, and now faces 'the paradox of a richer economy with poorer people'. Globally the capitalist system 'combines the nakedly honest pursuit of power and wealth for the few with a legal license for objectively criminal, immoral behaviour that harms the many'.[101]

Pabst's alternative to this is a 'civil economy', which 'ties economic profit to ethical and social purpose'.[102] In such an economy the state passes laws and regulations that link economic activity to the common good; for example, the creation of financial and business legislation that rewards those companies that pursue profits in ways that contribute to the society's wellbeing, or the granting of licences only to those companies that formally incorporate 'social purpose and profit sharing' into their activities. Instead of companies and individuals being rewarded for risky ventures, which bring no benefit to the community, there would be rewards and incentives for ethical behaviour that looks to the common good. The individualistic pursuit of ever-increasing wealth would be replaced with 'the relational pursuit of both private profit and social benefit for the sake of mutual flourishing'.[103] This vision draws upon Catholic social teaching, and ideas of community and common good derived from Anglicanism and British Nonconformity (along with other religions), as well as a Labour tradition grounded in small-'c' conservative concepts of organic society and rootedness in community, which has been devalued by both the party left, latterly represented by Jeremy Corbyn, and – despite the communitarian rhetoric – the New Labour right represented by Tony Blair.[104]

Pabst's civil economy differs in two key respects from a typical social democratic economy. Firstly, the aim of the civil economy is to infuse the market with moral principles, not simply to delimit and regulate a market that continues to operate according to amoral principles. Socio-economics requires 'a new culture of virtue and ethos', which will be achieved 'by linking profit to a wider social and civic purpose'.[105] Secondly, this is not solely the role of the state: Pabst, in a manner similar to Tawney, proposes the formation of professional associations and guilds that would regulate economic activity but, more importantly, set a social-minded ethos.[106] The ethics of professionalism and community-mindedness inculcated by these bodies would be key bulwarks against the free-market tendency to make profits by cutting production costs, lowering wages, and selling at unjustifiably high prices. Critics might argue that this vision of a morally responsible market economy, dependent to such an extent on the self-regulation of its key actors, is unrealistic. Pabst's response is that an economy based on 'honourable behaviour' is 'only utopian in terms of the current capitalist logic and liberal ideology'.[107] Ultimately, 'a more moral market would also be a more genuinely free market'.[108]

Conclusion

Like the broader Labour movement, the Christian Left is divided over what it should stand for. Some of those belonging to

Christians on the Left, along with groups such as Jubilee and Ekklesia, have allied themselves to the more traditionally left-wing policies advocated by Jeremy Corbyn or minor parties such as the Greens. Others, such as the Blue Labour movement, have melded together opposition to progressive social liberalism with a vision of a new, ethicised economy, which serves as an alternative to both the selfish individualism of Thatcherism, perpetuated by New Labour, and the traditional social democratic approach of state ownership and management. Labour's defeat in the May 2021 Hartlepool by-election, on top of the loss of traditional Labour seats in the December 2019 general election, represents a Labour movement in crisis. In the post-Brexit era, Christians are abandoning their support for the Labour Party, with 2019 the first election in history at which Roman Catholics were more likely to vote Conservative than the average voter.[109] The Christian Left has an important role to play in responding to these challenges.

3

A Hostile Environment: Religious Socialism in Europe

The Christian Left in continental Europe was never as significant a movement as its counterpart in the UK. While from the mid nineteenth century, as we have seen, the Church of England gradually came to accept – indeed, to embrace – socialism, and Nonconformists also committed themselves to radical politics, the relationship between the church and the Left in Europe was more often one of mutual antipathy. Individual clergymen and laypeople might embrace the ideas of democracy and collectivism, but the hierarchy of the Roman Catholic Church remained implacably opposed; for example, 33 priests attended a Christian Socialist dinner party in Paris in 1849, toasting 'Jesus of Nazareth, the father of socialism', but all were censured by their bishops.[1] One of the chief critics of socialism was Pope Pius IX, in office from 1846 to 1878, who, three years into his tenure, issued an encyclical, *Nostis et nobiscum*, condemning those within the church who aimed 'to drive people to overthrow the entire order of human affairs and to draw them over to the wicked theories of socialism and communism' in the false belief that 'the property of others can be taken and divided or in some other way turned to the use of everyone'.[2] It would be another half century until Pope Leo XIII's *Rerum novarum* would give anything close to an official sanction of socialism.

The socialists of Europe were in turn opposed to the church. Statements such as those of Pope Pius indicated that the church was on the side of the rich and powerful, and had no interest in the hardships endured by the growing number of workers who were forced to sell their labour to an increasingly opulent capitalist class. The church's alliance with Emperor Napoleon III was evidence enough of this.[3] French socialism became staunchly anti-clerical; indeed, 'France contributed mightily to the idea that socialism got rid of God.'[4] This anti-clericalism had its antecedent in the French Revolution and the Terror that followed: as many as 5,000 clergy were executed from late 1793 and 'an active programme of "de-Christianization"' accompanied the revolutionary cults of Reason and the Supreme Being, which sought to supplant Christianity.[5] In a similar way the church's support for the nationalist movement of Francisco Franco in Spain led to virulent anti-clericalism and, during the Civil War, the killing of some 7,000 Roman Catholic priests and nuns, for the revolutionary Left regarded the priests as being representatives of the capitalist system.[6] Anti-clericalism became a hallmark of the anarchist and syndicalist movements – 'No Gods; No Masters' – as much as it did the theories of Karl Marx and Friedrich Engels, which came to dominate socialism in German-speaking Europe, Italy and France (though, crucially, not the UK), and in the form of Marxism–Leninism was the driving force behind the Bolshevik Revolution; persecution of the Russian Orthodox Church was a persistent feature of Stalin's USSR.[7] Socialists and radicals vehemently opposed the 'established churches, allied as they were with the ruling monarchies and oligarchies against which revolutionary fervour was directed'.[8]

Europe therefore represented a hostile environment for Christian Socialism, which was neither fully accepted by the church nor fully part of the socialist movement. Yet despite this a Christian Left tradition did emerge from continental Europe. Before Marx ever put pen to paper, an ethical socialism had developed in France, which, in figures such as Henri Saint-Simon, Hugues-Félicitié Robert de Lamennais, and Philippe Buchez, linked the ethical imperatives of socialism with the teaching of Christianity. In the German-speaking world, Christoph Blumhardt, Herman Kutter and Leonhard Ragaz were key figures in the development of a Protestant socialism, which came to fruition in the theology of Paul Tillich and provided the impetus for the ecumenical International League of Religious Socialists. At the same time, the German bishop Wilhelm Emmanuel von Ketteler developed a left-leaning critique of free-market capitalism, which was the major influence behind Pope Leo's *Rerum novarum* and the tradition of Catholic social teaching, which allowed Roman Catholics – whether they identified as democratic socialists, social democrats or Christian Democrats – to oppose capitalism in the name of co-operation, as well as preparing the ground for the emergence of liberation theology.

Christian Socialism against Marx

Marxist theory went beyond a dislike of the church for its role in maintaining the capitalist status quo. Religion, according to Marx and Engels, is the main example of a false consciousness generated by the material – that is to say, economic – conditions of society. 'All religion,' writes Engels, 'is nothing but the fantastic reflection in men's minds of those external forces which control their daily life, a reflection in which terrestrial forces assume the form of supernatural forces.' For Engels, 'God' was no more than 'the alien domination of the capitalist mode of production'.[9] On this basis Marx writes:

> Man makes religion, religion does not make man. In other words, religion is the self-consciousness and self-feeling of man who has either not yet found himself or has already lost himself again [...] Religion is the sigh of the oppressed creature, the heart of a heartless world, just as it is the spirit of a spiritless situation. It is the opium of the people. The abolition of religion as the illusory happiness of the people is required for their real happiness.[10]

On this basis no thoroughgoing Marxist could accept the claim of Christian Socialists such as James Keir Hardie (see Chapter 1) that it was the spirit and teaching of Jesus Christ that more than anything else compelled him to fight for socialism. What Christians held to be the spirit and teaching of Christ could only be a false consciousness generated by the present mode of production; it could not serve those who fought to realise a new mode of production, but must be abolished.

In *The Communist Manifesto* Marx and Engels lump Christian Socialism in with what they term 'Feudal Socialism', that

indictment of the property-owning bourgeoisie and its capitalist
mode of production by the aristocratic rulers of the now-perished
feudal system. The old feudal lords developed a social conscience
regarding the struggles of the proletariat, argued Marx and Engels,
a symptom of their mourning for the old way of doing things and
in forgetfulness that they themselves had once exploited the poor
to the fullest possible extent. The so-called socialism of the church
was only a reactionary creed, which seeks to salve the collective
conscience of the old ruling class: 'Christian Socialism is but the
holy water with which the priest consecrates the heart-burnings
of the aristocrat.'[11] The ethical socialism of France came in for
similar treatment: this was mere 'Petty-Bourgeois Socialism' or
'Utopian Socialism', which, while capable of recognising and
drawing attention to all the misery caused by the capitalist
system, failed to understand how this system might be defeated
and replaced with a new socialist order of society.[12] There is no
reason, however, for the non-Marxist observer of the political Left
to accept the diagnosis of Marx and Engels. Socialism as an ideology emerged in the 1820s and 1830s, some two or three decades
before the *Manifesto* and half a century before Marx's *Critique of
the Gotha Programme* sought to protect the integrity of his doctrine from contamination by non-Marxist variants of socialism.[13]
In short, Marx and Engels were not the first word on socialism;
neither need they be the last.

Christian Socialism might be regarded as a form of ethical
socialism, but not all ethical socialists based their thinking on a
recognisably Christian ethics. The early French socialist Charlies
Fourier, for example, based his co-operative ideas on his own
understanding of human nature as being shaped by the twelve
components: the five physical senses as well as parental affection,
ambition, group identity, variety, commitment to an activity, and
romantic or physical love.[14] This led him to encourage the practice
of 'free love, bisexuality, lesbianism and polygamy'.[15] Among the
several phalanxes – co-operative communities that followed more
or less Fourierist ideas – later founded in the United States there
remained a division of opinion over the acceptability of 'Fourier's
sexual radicalism'.[16]

Henri Saint-Simon (1760–1825) held to something more closely
akin to a Christian-based socialism, identifying the establishment
of a co-operative rather than competitive form of society as the

true aim of Christianity. 'God has said, "Men should treat one another as brothers"', he declared. 'Now, according to this principle, which God has given us as a rule for our conduct, we should organize society in a way that will be the most advantageous for the greatest number.'[17] Saint-Simon, though, was no orthodox Christian; he held rather that Christianity must be stripped 'of all its superstitious or useless beliefs and practices', an uncompromising position given that for him these useless beliefs and practices included both Roman Catholic liturgy and Protestant doctrine.[18] Saint-Simon's final work, *The New Christianity* (1825), in which these ideas were expounded was taken by his followers as a 'quasi-religious doctrine' in and of itself.[19] Another key figure of early French socialism was Hugues-Félicitié Robert de Lamennais (1782–1854), a Roman Catholic priest whose scepticism about the developing capitalist system prefigures that of Catholic social teaching. 'We must,' argued Lamennais, 'assure to labour that fair share of the products of labour that belongs to it.'[20] Lamennais was much more orthodox in his religion than Saint-Simon, and, though he remains not nearly so well known, John Cort regards him as 'one of the first and most persuasive apostles of Christian socialism in the modern era'.[21] Others of this type included Auguste Boulland (1799–1859), who argued in *Doctrine politique du christianisme* (1845) that the democratic values of the French Revolution were one with those of sacramental Roman Catholicism, Anthime Corbon (1808–91) who criticised the church for not supporting the oppressed classes, and Désiré Laverdant (1809–84) whose *Socialisme Catholique* (1851) equated the vision of a socialist society with the Kingdom of God on earth.[22]

Boulland, Corbon and Laverdant were comrades and supporters of Philippe Buchez (1796–1865), an atheist from a Catholic background for whom the ethical socialism of Saint-Simon proved to be a pathway back to religious faith; he rejected both the Church of Rome and the teaching of Protestantism but held to a Christianity which he regarded as separate from both.[23] Buchez, however, went further than Saint-Simon in his interpretation of the capitalist system, prefiguring some of the key aspects of Marx's economic and social analysis. 'Today,' he wrote, 'European society is, with regard to material interests, split into two classes [...]. Of these two classes, one is in possession of all the instruments of labour:

land, factories, houses, capital. The other has nothing. It works for the former.'[24] This latter class, Buchez argued, generates value for their property-owning employers but cannot share in the creation of wealth, given that it is systematically excluded from the ownership of both capital and the means of production – a reasonable enough summary of what Marx would later theorise regarding value, exploitation and surplus profit. In place of such an exploitative system Buchez foresaw 'the land covered with agricultural and manufacturing communities where all the members would be associated and cooperating in a common effort and using for this end the capital of the community'.[25] This voluntarist co-operation of workers and producers – also expressed by John Ludlow in the UK (see Chapter 1) – was in the view of Cort the 'mainstream of early socialism' before Marx and Engels established instead state ownership and management as the ineliminable core of left-wing thought.[26]

If Marx and Engels succeeded in writing off the ethical socialists of France as hopeless utopians, then the Christian Socialists of German-speaking Europe fared even worse, for they had the unenviable task of competing directly with the doctrine of Marx. An example is that of Wilhelm Weitling (1808–71) who, influenced in part by Saint-Simon, Lamennais, and others in the French tradition, set out in *The Poor Sinner's Gospel* (1845) a socialism based on Christian ethics and a portrayal of Jesus Christ as a socialist revolutionary. 'Poverty,' he argued, 'must be overcome, not by almsgiving but the abolition of private property.'[27] Weitling, though, came off second best in a debate with Marx about how this might be carried out in practice; his ethical precepts did not stack up against Marx's 'scientific' methodology. Weitling, it should be noted, was not an upstanding example of a Christian Socialist – the first section of his work is 'devoted to an effort to prove that the Bible is full of errors and contradictions and that Jesus Christ was merely another sinner like the rest of us' – but the point here is that socialism based, albeit in this case vaguely, on Christian ethics was excluded from the mainstream of German thought.[28]

This came to be reflected in the attitude of Germany's Marxist Social Democratic Party (SPD). August Bebel, who served as SPD chairman from 1892 until his death in 1913, held that the party should be committed to socialism in economics, republicanism in constitutional theory, and atheism in religion.[29] Wilhelm Liebknecht, another key party figure among the organisers of the Second International, made his position abundantly clear: 'It is our duty as socialists to root out the faith in God with all our zeal, nor is anyone worthy of the name who does not consecrate himself to the spread of atheism.'[30] The revisionist socialism of Eduard Bernstein was less diametrically opposed to Christianity, but Bernstein was still a critic of religion, who found himself shocked at the extent of Christian involvement in left-wing politics when he discovered Reformed Protestants, including pastors, active in the Democratic Party of Zurich and the Swiss Workers League.[31] The SPD's antipathy to Christianity diminished over time – both Bebel and Bernstein acknowledged that the teaching of Jesus appeared compatible with their socialism – but the suspicion did not entirely disappear.[32] Some Christians of the Left, it has to be said, gave mainstream socialists every reason to be suspicious. Lutheran theologian Adolf von Harnack (1851–1930) was a proponent of economic justice and staunch critic of *laissez-faire* capitalism; however, Harnack's focus was more on persuading the church to do more for the relief of poverty, and insofar as he prescribed a new economic system it came in the form of reforms to rather than the abolition of capitalism.[33] Another example is that of Lutheran pastor Adolf Stöcker, who attacked German socialism for its rejection of Christianity and founded the Christian Social Labour Party in 1878; the left-wing credentials of Stöcker's party are rather brought into question by the fact that it entered into electoral coalition with the German Conservative Party the following year.[34]

Others, though, had more convincing credentials. Wilhelm Emmanuel von Ketteler (1811–77), the Bishop of Mainz, is one such example. Ketteler always had a concern for the poor, but this – influenced by the ideas of the non-Marxist socialist Ferdinand Lassalle – morphed into a throughgoing socialist commitment.[35] Denouncing the self-centredness of capitalist society, Ketteler declared that 'it is my deepest conviction that we could even bring about common ownership of the goods of this world as well as eternal peace along with maximum freedom in our social and political institutions'.[36] Ketteler did not deny the right to private property – so long as it was remembered that all property ultimately belonged to God – nor did he wish the state to enforce common ownership. Yet he was critical of the wealthy, who sought to enrich themselves at the expense of others, declaring that refusing to share wealth and resources amounted to theft: 'stealing means not only to take what belongs to others, but also to hold back what rightfully ought to belong to others'.[37] If Ketteler was the foremost example of Roman Catholic Socialism, then Christoph Blumhardt (1842–1919), a Lutheran pastor, represented the Protestant side, linking together economic and social justice with the teaching of Christianity:

> If then today socialism has its eye on the goal that specifies an equal right to bread for everyone, which necessitates that property relationships assume such a form that the life of man rather than money and possessions, has the highest value – why is that an objectionable desire? I am certain that it is based on the spirit of Christ [...] and that there will be uprisings until it is reached.[38]

Blumhardt shared an emphasis which is near-universal in left-wing Christian thought, that the Kingdom of God was something to be realised here on earth through socialist values of collectivism and co-operation. He held that God was bringing about this Kingdom through the socialist movement, whether or not the atheistic members of that movement were willing to believe it, and therefore bridged the chasm between the conservative-minded religious establishment and the anti-clerical Left by joining the SPD, the first Lutheran clergyman to do so; for this he was forced to resign from his pastorate.[39] Both Ketteler and Blumhardt were to have a significant impact on the Christian Left, Ketteler on Catholic social teaching – to which we shall return – and Blumhardt on the German-speaking Protestant Left that followed.

Protestant Socialist theology

Leonhard Ragaz (1869–1945) and Herman Kutter (1863–1931) were both theologians from the Swiss Reformed tradition, who came under the influence of Blumhardt's view that the Kingdom of God was to be recognised in a reformed and renewed society on earth, a new society in which, said Ragaz, 'people work together for a common goal, no longer against each other but for each other'.[40] This was the case, argued Ragaz, because 'Socialism is not just an economic or political system [...] Socialism is a moral ideal, and the political or economic system is simply the means by which it gets realized [...] Socialism is a form of community that is based on the principle of solidarity rather than on the principle of mutual combat.'[41] This, added Kutter, would be the work of God, 'the greatest of all revolutionists', who would destroy the Mammon worship of capitalist society by – as Blumhardt had argued – working through the social democratic movement.[42] Both men were disappointed at the lack of a Christian Socialist movement such as that which had appeared in the UK, and that across Europe socialists and Christians remained opposed to one another – Kutter noted sadly that the term 'Evangelical' meant effectively 'anti-Socialist', while Ragaz criticised those on the Left who proclaimed that socialism required the exaltation of 'adultery', 'birth control and abortion'.[43] They therefore established a 'Religious Social' movement which, in Kutter's words, aimed to combine 'the radicalism of the Social Democratic belief with a warm and enthusiastic religious devotion'.[44] There were differences between the two men. Ragaz believed that Christians should join political parties and trade unions – he himself joined the Swiss Social Democratic Party (SP) – while Kutter believed the focus should remain on developing the church into a vehicle for socialism; strangely, though, it was Kutter who held to a more orthodox version of Marxism, while Ragaz favoured the revisionist socialism of Bernstein.[45] Despite this, Ragaz and Kutter together articulated the vision of a co-operation and egalitarian society that would be the visible realisation of the Kingdom of God.

Blumhardt, Kutter and Ragaz crafted a foundation that would be built upon by two of the best-known Protestant theologians of the past century, Karl Barth (1886–1968) and Paul Tillich (1886–1965). In his earlier years Barth, a theologian from the Reformed tradition, was a committed socialist, declaring: 'Real socialism is real Christianity in our time.'[46] He was reluctant, however, to use terms such as 'Christian Socialist' or 'religious socialist', refusing to discuss politics in his theology seminars, on the grounds that 'politics was not a subject for theology'.[47] In this attitude we might perceive the roots of Barth's later disavowal of socialism, as illustrated by his argument that – despite the understanding of Christian Socialists in various contexts – there was a clear and decisive division between the Kingdom of God and

merely human political progress.[48] Tillich, a theologian from the
Lutheran tradition, became less outspoken about socialism in his
later years, but this was because, having been given the opportunity to move to the United States and escape Nazi persecution, he
'never entirely overcame the feeling that it was unseemly for him
to stump for socialism in the colossal bastion of capitalism that
saved his life'.[49] Tillich nevertheless became a member of Reinhold
Niebuhr's Fellowship of Socialist Christians – before Niebuhr
rejected his own religious socialism and became instead the
founder of the realism school of international relations theory.[50]

Tillich was critical of Protestantism for not espousing socialism, arguing that because it focused on an individual relationship to God it had not properly developed the social ethics that
it therefore needed to learn from the socialist movement.[51] He
credited Blumhardt with the recognition that God may speak
more clearly and powerfully through a secular organisation such
as the SPD than through the church, and Kutter and Ragaz for
breaking down the distinction between sacred and secular, which
prevented Christians from speaking prophetically, into politics or
into culture more generally.[52] For Tillich:

> The decisive idea of religious socialism is that religion does not have
> to do with a specific religious sphere but with God's dealing with
> the world, and that therefore it is possible that God's activity may
> be more clearly seen in a profane, even anti-Christian, phenomenon
> like socialism than in the explicitly religious sphere of the church.[53]

With this understanding Tillich went on to join the SPD in order
to participate fully in the socialist movement, notwithstanding
that he favoured socialist revolution and opposed what he viewed
as the party's reformist policies.[54] Taking these themes, Tillich
went further in developing a theology of religious socialism: 'It
was Tillich's special contribution to place the whole discussion of
socialism within a theological perspective.'[55]

Tillich's socialist theology consisted of three key elements: theonomy, *kairos*, and the demonic. The view of theonomy expressed
by Tillich was not, as the term sometimes suggests, the wholesale
adoption of the civil law given to Old Testament Israel, but simply
a society where all aspects of culture – politics included – were
linked to the divine.[56] The concept of *kairos* meant for Tillich 'the

right time' or 'the fullness of time', the dialectical point at which human society would be unalterably changed:

> Kairos in its unique and universal sense is, for Christian faith, the appearing of Jesus as the Christ. Kairos in its general and special sense for the philosopher of history is every turning-point in history in which the eternal judges and transforms the temporal. Kairos in its special sense, as decisive for the present situation, is the coming of a new theonomy on the soil of a secularized and emptied autonomous culture.[57]

The 'emptied' culture that Tillich believed was ready to produce a 'new theonomy' was the imperialistic and capitalist Germany – and wider Western world – of the long nineteenth century. It was for this reason that Tillich and his colleagues in publishing the *Journal of Christian Socialism* became known as the Kairos circle.[58]

The third key element was the demonic. For Tillich the demonic was evident when society moved in directions that oppose the norms of the Kingdom of God and used creative processes to serve destructive ends, nationalism and capitalism being two key examples.[59] Capitalism, he argued, is demonic because of its 'union of creative and destructive powers', and this demonic spirit in a sense possesses all individuals who operate within the capitalist system.[60] The solution then was theonomy – restructuring society in accordance with the norms and values of God's Kingdom. Here – as in other places – Tillich departed from Barth, asserting that there was no clear and decisive separation between the Kingdom and human progress. This progress towards the values of the Kingdom was the particular responsibility of religious socialism: 'The point of religious socialism was to imagine and inspire a new social order, born of a fusion of Christianity and socialism that broke the power of nationalism and capitalism and recovered a premodern sense of the sacred.'[61]

Yet Tillich did not simplistically link the realisation of a theonomised society with the Kingdom, arguing that the Kingdom itself could only be realised outside of human history; society, nevertheless, bore the responsibility of shaping in accordance with and imitation of that Kingdom.[62] 'The Kingdom of God will always remain transcendent,' he explained, 'but it appears as a judgement on a given form of society and as a norm for a coming one.'[63] Again, Tillich argued: 'In the struggle *against* a demonised society and *for* a meaningful society religious socialism discerns a necessary expression for the expectation of the kingdom of God. But it repudiates the identification of socialism with the kingdom of God.'[64] This perspective is perhaps linked to Tillich's disavowal of utopianism. Christians of the Left, who directly associated a socialist society with the appearing of the Kingdom, were apt to view such a society in strikingly utopian terms (Tillich's assertion that 'religious socialism rejects every utopian ethic' holds true only if one discounts a large chunk of the Christian Socialist tradition).[65] This rejection of utopianism may also account for Tillich's move away from a Marxist-influenced commitment to revolutionary socialism towards an acceptance of the social democratic attempt to reform capitalism by means of a mixed economy and a welfare state.[66]

Roman Catholicism and Catholic social teaching

If Blumhardt was the key figure behind the Protestant socialism that gradually rose to prominence through Tillich and, to a lesser extent, Barth, then his Roman Catholic contemporary Bishop Ketteler made a similarly sized contribution on his side of the Tiber. Most of the church hierarchy, ever conservative in instinct, had been implacably opposed to socialism; this, as already noted, included Pope Pius IX in the mid nineteenth century. Yet the successor to Pius, Pope Leo XIII, demonstrated a much softer attitude towards socialism – or, at least, a more critical attitude towards capitalism. Leo reflected a Catholic perspective which 'often regarded capitalism as another illustration of the excesses of the enlightenment. Economic liberalism allowed the individual or entrepreneur to do whatever he or she wanted in the pursuit of profit, with no concern for others involved in the enterprise'.[67] In this he credited Ketteler, regarding the German bishop rather than Pius as 'my great predecessor', and describing him as among 'the first openly to declare that employers and government had a responsibility and a duty to the workers of our time'.[68] Ketteler, then, might be regarded as the formative influence in what came to be known as Catholic social teaching.

The founding document of Catholic social teaching is Pope Leo's 1891 encyclical *Rerum novarum*. Here Leo set out his critique of the capitalist system in terms that, at least in theory, might be agreeable to many socialist – even Marxist – opponents of that system, for example:

> The present age [has] handed over to the workers, each alone and defenceless, to the inhumanity of employers and the unbridled greed of competitors [...] In addition the whole process of production as well as trade in every kind of goods has been brought almost entirely under the power of a few, so that a very few rich and exceedingly rich men have laid a yoke almost of slavery itself on the unnumbered masses of non-owning workers.[69]

'It is incontestable,' maintained Leo, 'that the wealth of nations originates from no other source than from the labour of workers.'[70] Capitalism, in short, was oppressive, and Leo was quite willing to see the state intervene in the economy in order to protect the oppressed and provide for those who are materially disadvantaged by their position in its hierarchy of owners and workers.[71] Yet, despite these radical statements about the exploitative nature of capitalism, Leo did not give his blessing to the socialist alternative. The Pope continued to oppose socialism for its rejection of private property, arguing that 'the main tenet of socialism, the community of goods, must be utterly rejected'.[72] Leo, despite his willingness to see state management of welfare and the economy, still feared giving too much power to the state; he also maintained that the socialist goal of an egalitarian society was unobtainable: 'in capability, in diligence, in health, and in strength; an unequal fortune is a necessary result of inequality in condition'.[73] Leo certainly imbued Catholic social teaching with an understanding of the oppression resulting from the exploitation of labour, as well as a concern for the restoration of justice, but this, it seems, led more to the Christian Democratic position of rejecting economic liberalism without advocating socialist collectivism.

The ideology of Christian Democracy came to the fore in many parts of Europe, though the UK remains a notable exception. One of the main examples is Germany's Christian Democratic Union (CDU) founded in 1945 and, before this, the Roman Catholic German Centre Party (*Zentrumpartei* or *Zentrum*). One key figure in *Zentrum* was Heinrich Pesch (1854–1926), a Catholic priest and economist who developed the concept of 'solidarism' as a middle way between the atomistic individualism of economic liberalism and the class-contingent solidarity preached by both orthodox and revisionist Marxists. Solidarism remains one of the key concepts of Christian Democracy as a political ideology.[74] Like Pope Leo, Pesch was a trenchant critic of capitalism – he viewed as the goal of economics not private profit but 'the sufficient provision of the people [...] with fair-priced food, clothing, shelter, with all the material goods which they require for the satisfaction of their wants' – without counting himself a socialist.[75] Pesch, however, wrote a *Zentrum* pamphlet in 1918 to which he gave the title, *Not Communistic but Christian Socialism*. Here he described what he termed 'a workable system of Christian socialism':

> We agree with Marxian socialism that the future no longer belongs to the economic license of individualistic capitalism. However, neither will it belong to the compulsory economic system of communism, but to a truly socialized national economy, i.e. regulated in accordance with its end [...] which is the satisfaction of the entire national community in accordance with the prevailing level of civilization.[76]

Pesch's solidarist vision looks very much like the kind of economic system advocated by social democrats, including those who might term themselves democratic socialists. 'Public welfare,' argued Pesch, 'is the direct purpose of the state', and this fits exactly with the social democratic position that the proper role of the state is to provide or maintain social goods such as welfare, healthcare, education and the natural environment.[77] Here we can see both that there is a significant overlap between the economic programmes of social democracy and Christian Democracy, and that there is not a clear ideological boundary between Christian Democracy and Christian Socialism. Indeed, this overlap was the basis for much of the co-operation between *Zentrum* and the SPD during the time of the Weimar Republic, and Maurice Glasman regards the German economy as the result of 'an alliance between Christian and social democracy'.[78]

Pesch's contribution was to the dual currents of Christian Democracy and Catholic social teaching; his concept of solidarism became 'the conceptual core' of the 1931 encyclical of Pope Pius XI, *Quadragesimo anno* (or 'On the fortieth year', as it was published on the fortieth anniversary of *Rerum novarum*) in which Pius expanded Catholic social teaching by focusing on the ethical aspects of social and economic questions.[79] *Quadragesimo* was in keeping with *Rerum novarum* insofar as Pius criticised capitalism and allowed for solutions that may be described from our perspective as social democratic, but all the while maintaining a hostility towards socialism itself. The encyclical taught that the purpose of production and economic activity should be to supply needs rather than primarily to make profit, and suggested that workers should have a share in decision making via industrial councils or guilds; the wages system, however, was not viewed as inherently unjust or exploitative.[80] Furthermore, lest any Christian Socialists should draw too much encouragement from the Pope's disavowal of capitalist profiteering, Pius was careful to note:

> Whether socialism be considered as a doctrine, or as a historical fact, or as a 'movement', if it really remains socialism, it cannot be brought into harmony with the dogmas of the Catholic Church [...] 'Religious socialism', 'Christian socialism' are expressions implying a contradiction in terms. No one can be at the same time a sincere Catholic and a true socialist.[81]

The extent to which Catholic social teaching then can be used to support socialism is debatable. One contemporary scholar of Catholic social teaching argues that 'socialism is intrinsically evil because it contravenes basic Christian teachings on private property and class relations, whereas capitalism is not intrinsically evil but often leads to abuses. Thus, the condemnations are not symmetrical. Socialism alone is intrinsically evil'.[82] That some could conclude that Catholic social teaching permitted, even encouraged socialism, while others derived the view that socialism was 'intrinsically evil', demonstrates the ambiguity of the encyclicals. This ambiguity created theological headaches for Roman Catholic socialists. For a Protestant, armed with his or her own understanding of scripture, it mattered little whether a pastor, a vicar, or even an archbishop opposed socialism – even these men could be wrong. It was a different matter for Catholics when the Pope declared *ex-cathedra* that socialism and Christianity were incompatible. John Wheatley – the Labour MP and founder of the UK's Catholic Socialist Society (see Chapter 1) – was able to use the teaching of Pope Leo to support his own socialist position – yet was reduced to questioning the *ex-cathedra* status of *Rerum novarum* when a Catholic priest pointed out the condemnations of socialism contained within.[83]

Yet this demonstrates that, however difficult it was, Catholics such as Wheatley did not abandon their socialist views. This was the case even in Italy itself where, despite reunification and Italian nationalism, the Catholic Church remained influential. Francesco Nitti (1868–1953) was an economist, a leading figure in the centre-Left Italian Radical Party, and – briefly, from summer 1919 to summer 1920 – Prime Minister of Italy. Nitti 'argued that Christians should hold everything in common, and, if need be, this could be done through the moral agency of a collectivist state', and was an influential figure for Wheatley.[84] Nitti was an opponent of 'Communism', yet – writing after Leo XIII but before Pius XI – he acknowledged that 'the Christian ideal is in no way opposed to the socialistic ideal'.[85] Like Pope Leo, Nitti acknowledged Ketteler as one of 'the great Catholic economists' to have recognised the incompatibility of Christianity and economic liberalism.[86] Given this incompatibility, he expressed frustration that the 'democratic socialists' of Europe persisted in their hostility to religion and wedded themselves instead to 'scientific positivism' – for Nitti, the Darwinist emphasis on struggle and competition was perfectly well suited to the capitalist system, while socialism shared with Christianity the rejection of this competitive spirit – yet a portion of the blame for this situation must rest with the religious estab- lishment that had allowed itself to be 'employed by the bourgeois class to arrest the progress of Socialism among the masses'.[87] Nitti remained confident that Catholicism did not require the complete rejection of socialism: 'what the Catholic Church combats in modern social democracy is not the democratic spirit of fraternity and equality, but the anti-religious tendencies by which it seems to be dominated'.[88] A spirit of fraternity and equality was a precisely Christian spirit.

Another Italian Catholic socialist – indeed, one more radical than Nitti – was Ignazio Silone (1900–78, real name Secondino Tranquilli), who was, with Antonio Gramsci, one of the co- founders of the Communist Party of Italy in 1921. Silone, however, broke with the communists as the horrors of Stalin's USSR became apparent, arguing that the political programme being enacted behind the Iron Curtain was certainly not the crea- tion of a new moral order of society.[89] Silone's contribution to the 1949 anti-communist volume *The God That Failed* is a deeply personal account from his own dealings as an Italian Communist with Stalin and other leading figures from the USSR of how the Russian Revolution morphed into a totalitarian nightmare. Here, Silone made the argument that the world being designed under communism – the totalitarian 'fiction' as Hannah Arendt referred to it – was 'but a new version of the inhuman reality against which, in declaring ourselves Socialists, we had rebelled'.[90] Yet, Silone declared, 'my faith in Socialism' – as distinct from the state-sponsored terror being enacted by Stalin and supported by the Communist International – 'has remained more alive than ever in me'. This, he argued, was a socialism which was 'older than Marxism', 'faith' rather than 'theory', a permanent set of values.[91]

Silone therefore became a key proponent of an ethical social-ism based not on Marxist–Leninist theory but rather derived from acts of love, kindness and co-operation, as Vaneesa Cook explains:

> Socialism, he deduced, presupposes democracy; democracy depends on community; and community grows from the simplest human actions, such as caring for the sick, breaking bread, and sharing wine. These gestures of love and compassion, Silone contended, also defined Christianity – not supernatural, institutional, or doctrinal Christianity, but a kind of sacred experience inherent in the practice of social solidarity.[92]

It was through his contribution to *The God That Failed* as well as his earlier novel *Bread and Wine* that Silone became influential in the United States. The view of socialism as the system founded on day-to-day expressions of care and compassion, built from the bottom up rather than imposed from above, flowed into the thinking of the tradition of 'spiritual socialism' which Cook identi-fies with figures such as A.J. Muste, Sherwood Eddy and Martin Luther King, Jr (see Chapter 4). Silone was a particular influence for Dorothy Day, whose now-global Catholic Worker Movement is based on his ethical understanding of socialism.[93]

Catholic social teaching has continued to be sympathetic towards socialism – albeit, as we have seen, not unambiguously so. Pope John XXIII in the 1961 encyclical *Mater et magistra* argued that workers having a role in management was a 'demand of justice'.[94] Pope John-Paul II in his 1981 encyclical *Laborem exercens* offered his own criticism of capitalism for disregarding biblical principles insofar as 'man is treated as an instrument of production, whereas he – he alone – independently of the work he does – ought to be treated as the effective subject of work and its true maker'.[95] In place of the de-humanising economic relations of capitalism the Pope suggested the 'socialization' of 'certain means of production', including workers having a share in the ownership and management of industry – the kind of co-operative economy advocated by Philippe Buchez more than a century before.[96] Pope Francis, a theological thinker shaped by the Argentine tradition of *la teología del pueblo* ('theology of the people') and with sympathies towards liberation theology, has continued this tradition of papal antipathy towards capitalism. The 'theology of the people', in a similar manner to Catholic social teaching and the various papal encyclicals, is critical of economic liberalism while still cautioning against socialist collectivism; it differs then from liberation theology which is quite open to Marxism as a tool of analysis (see Chapter 6).[97] In encyclicals such as *Evangelii Gaudium* (2013) and *Laudato si'* (2015), 'Francis presents a rich socio-political heritage that can be drawn upon to heal the many wounds of the contemporary world, including new global forms of slavery, hostility to refugees, environmental degradation, and extreme poverty'.[98]

Pope Francis, particularly in *Laudato si'*, places a renewed emphasis on the need to protect and preserve the environment. For Francis, combating climate change is a requirement of justice, particularly as the global South appears to bear the brunt of environmental damage. In order to achieve justice change is needed, not just to government policy and industrial practice but to the global culture of consumerism and perpetual economic growth.[99] The Pope also denies that unregulated market forces can supply the solutions needed to the environmental crisis; rather, strengthened international institutions must have more power to protect the 'global commons' from exploitation.[100] The ultimate aim must be, says Francis, to preserve 'our common home' and to bring about 'sustainable and integral development'.[101] In this encyclical Francis makes ecologism a key concern of Catholic social teaching, adding the official voice of Roman Catholicism to the still-developing Christian response to Lynn White Jr's 1967 thesis that Christianity had contributed to destruction of the environment (see Chapter 5), and drawing links between ecologism and the theories of liberation theology regarding development and exploitation (see Chapter 7).

Liberation theology is now exerting an influence on Catholic social teaching, but at first it was Catholic social teaching which helped prepare the ground for liberation theology. It was Pope Leo XIII in *Rerum novarum* who declared: 'Still when there is a question of protecting the rights of individuals, the poor and helpless have a claim to special consideration'.[102] Here written into the founding document of Catholic social teaching is the 'preferential option for the poor' which forms the core concept within the liberation theology of Gustavo Gutiérrez (see Chapter 6). In this we can see the significance of Catholic social teaching. That significance can also be seen in the way in which, for all their ambiguities, the papal encyclicals allowed Catholics to hold to a non-Marxist form of socialism (whether that was an ethical or spiritual socialism, a revisionist social democracy or democratic socialism, or a particularly left-leaning Christian Democracy). Cort argues that the 1951 Frankfurt Declaration (formally known as *Aims and Tasks of Democratic Socialism*) of the Socialist International is entirely in keeping with *Rerum novarum* and *Quadragesimo anno*, notwithstanding the popes' stated opposition to socialism; the Declaration sets out a de-centralised, democratic vision of socialism, one which accepts state ownership and planning but is not wedded to the state, preferring instead workers' ownership and control.[103] The same argument could be applied to the Bad Godesberg Resolution adopted by the SPD in 1959, which moved the party away from Marxism and committed it instead to social democracy. Furthermore, the Resolution disavowed the SPD's historic anticlericalism, and acknowledged 'Christian ethics' as one of the sources of democratic socialism.[104] With on the one hand Frankfurt and Bad Godesberg and on the other Catholic social teaching, there is, argued Cort, 'no essential difference' between socialism and Christianity.[105]

International League of Religious Socialists

In 1926 German Christian Socialists, including followers of Herman Kutter and Leonhard Ragaz, formed a new Association of Religious Socialists led by Lutheran pastor Erwin Eckert (1893–1972). Eckert followed in the steps of Blumhardt in joining the SPD, a move which by this time was permitted by the

Lutheran church. Eckert however found the SPD too moderate, joining instead the Communist Party of Germany (KPD); for this he was expelled from the pastorate.[106] The Association was disbanded by the Nazi Party after 1933, with many of the leading figures going on to play a role in the anti-Nazi Confessing Church, and reformed after 1945.[107] Also in 1926 came the first international conference for religious socialists, held in the Netherlands and organised by Ragaz, Willem Banning (1888–1971) and Carl Mennicke (1887–1958). Banning was a Dutch Reformed pastor who was a key figure in the Dutch Social Democratic Workers' Party (SDWP) and in 1945 was one of the founders of a new Labour Party (*Partij van de Arbeid*). Banning was also the chairman of the Woodbrookers co-operative community, founded by Quakers who had spent time at the Woodbrooke Quaker Study Centre in Birmingham, UK. It was through joining this group that the German-born Mennicke, a Reformed theologian, came to discover religious socialism.[108] It was out of this and subsequent conferences that the International League of Religious Socialists (ILRS) was founded, to which the German Association of Religious Socialists became affiliated.

As well as these Dutch, German and Swiss origins the ILRS has drawn much of its strength from the Scandinavian countries. Christian Socialists had been active in the Swedish Democratic Party since the nineteenth century, forming in 1929 the Swedish Christian Social Democrats' Association (SKSF, also known as the Brotherhood Movement), which also affiliated to the ILRS. By the 1980s there were Christian Socialist groupings active in each of the Nordic social democratic parties.[109] This illustrates that the ILRS, like so much of European religious socialism, holds 'to a social democratic ideology that regards participation in parliamentary politics as necessary, supports strong state capacity in areas of education, health, and social welfare, and maintains that free-market capitalism requires moral limits'.[110] Günter Ewald (1939–2015), spokesman for the German Association and a member of the Evangelical Church Congress, described a vison of:

> a new order of society, where people will no longer be treated as objects, a society different from both Western capitalism and Eastern communism. Methods and goals of production should be built on democratic structures of economic life and on a concept

of the person not simply as the consumer of a maximum quantity of material goods but as a total human person. For this reason we favour the cooperative form of production.[111]

Evert Svensson (b.1925), a Swedish Social Democratic Workers' Party (SAP) MP, Chairman of the Brotherhood Movement from 1968 to 1986 and President of the ILRS from 1983 to 2003, went even further in acknowledging the necessity of working with rather than against the market: 'we regard the market system as an instrument for achieving equality, freedom, and philanthropic aims. At the same time, we realize that the market must serve the well-being of mankind.'[112]

It was the social democrats of Sweden who provided the impetus for the ILRS, for most of its first sixty years a predominantly central and northern European movement, to become a truly global organisation. A conference held in Bommersvik in 1983 featured speakers from across the world, including Japan, Italy, Tanzania, Brazil and Nicaragua. This conference focused on the need for nuclear disarmament and for addressing the economic disparities between the global North and South. It also voiced support for movements of liberation in Africa such as the South West African People's Organization in Namibia, and argued that churches around the world had a moral obligation to boycott the apartheid regime in South Africa (see Chapter 7), for, the conference concluded, 'we believe that God is present in those liberation movements that are helping oppressed people to achieve freedom and human dignity'.[113] This was followed three years later by a conference in Nicaragua, the first ILRS conference held outside Europe. Throughout the 1980s and 1990s, '[i]mportant links were made between religious socialists in Eastern and Western Europe, Europe and Latin America, and Europe and the Middle East. The ILRS offered these activists a platform for their ideas and helped build bonds of solidarity and support across borders.'[114]

In 1991, after a conference on 'A New Europe: Challenges for Christians and Social Democrats', the ILRS declared that the fall of the USSR need not be a victory for neo-liberalism and free-market fundamentalism, but rather provided the opportunity for democratic socialism to reassert itself as a viable alternative to the capitalist system.[115] This did not prove to be the case; in the 1990s and into the new century even social democracy itself was dominated by the 'Third Way' of Tony Blair's Labour Party (see Chapter 2) or the 'New Centre' (*Die Neue Mitte*) of Gerhard Schroeder's SPD, a conception of social democracy that arguably owed more to the free-market ideas dominating Western politics in the decades prior to the fall of the Berlin Wall.[116] In this context the ILRS has focused on trying to reinvigorate the Left. This includes, for example in Finland and Sweden, religious socialists bringing Europe's growing Islamic community into social democratic politics as a means of strengthening the Left and opposing Islamist fundamentalism.[117] It also includes trying to combat the ingrained secularism of the Left, which never fully dissipated. In Spain, for example, where the political Left remains implacably secular, the ILRS is in a new alliance with CHRISPSOE, the Christian Socialist grouping within the Socialist Party of Spain (PSOE).[118] In some countries such as Germany, where the Association of Religious Socialists is not formally aligned to the SPD, religious socialists have sought to foster co-operation between the parties of the Left by bringing together Christian members of the SPD, The Left (*Die Linke*) and The Greens (*Die Grünen*).[119] Ultimately, as the ILRS delegates to the 2012 conference of the Socialist International explained, the aim is to prevent Christian Socialism from being squeezed out by the religious Right and the secular Left.[120]

Conclusion

The Christian Left faced a hostile environment in continental Europe, created by the antipathy of both the church hierarchy and the secular socialist movement. In the latter part of the nineteenth century the Roman Catholic Church declared that socialism and Christianity were incompatible; simultaneously Karl Marx and Friedrich Engels declared that Christianity was merely a false consciousness derived from the dead-and-buried feudal system and its inevitably doomed capitalist replacement, a false consciousness that must be shaken off if socialism were to be realised. The ethical socialism, however, which pre-dated Marx, had already drawn the link between the values of Christianity and the aims of socialism, and a religious socialism – notwithstanding the initial disdain of the SPD – gradually emerged in the German-speaking world. The result of this was the socialist theology of Paul Tillich, the International League of Religious Socialists, Catholic social teaching and Christian Democracy and, ultimately, liberation theology.

4

What Would Jesus Do? Social Gospel and Socialism in the United States

Charles M. Sheldon (1857–1946), a Congregationalist minister, was among the first in the United States to advocate what would come to be known as the Social Gospel. Sheldon was in 1889 the founding pastor of the Central Congregational Church of Topeka, Kansas. The church was planted by a congregation founded by abolitionists, and Sheldon felt able as pastor to preach 'a Christ for the common people [...] a Christ who bids us all recognize the Brotherhood of the race'.[1] Sheldon, however, was no radical prior to taking up the pastorate; it was the desperate condition of his congregants and the wider community during the winter of 1889/90 that moved him to think more about the social requirements of the Christian Gospel. His best-known contribution to this topic was a novel, *In His Steps* (1896). In this semi-autobiographical work, an unemployed man asks a minister what it means to follow Jesus when the church is not willing to speak on social and economic injustice. The minister is moved to bring Christians together to formulate a response, posing the question: 'What would Jesus do?'

Sheldon stood in a venerable line of Christian radicals and socialists, which can be traced back throughout American history. Among these were figures such as William Lloyd Garrison (1805–79), a prominent abolitionist, whose philosophy of non-violence influenced Henry Thoreau, Leo Tolstoy, Gandhi and Martin Luther King.[2] Abby Kelley (1811–87) was another abolitionist, once powerfully comparing the slaves with the beggar Lazarus, reminding her audience that the rich man was condemned for not using his wealth to alleviate Lazarus' condition.[3] Frederick Douglass (1818–95) is among the best known of the abolitionists, denouncing a hypocritical Christianity he termed the 'slaveholding religion', which had nothing to do with 'the pure, peaceable, and impartial Christianity of Christ'.[4] Sojourner Truth (1797–1883) – like Douglass a freed slave – was 'a potent symbol of the way racial and sexual oppression intersected in the lives of black women', thus pre-empting much of the intersectional theory of thinkers such as bell hooks and Kimberlé Crenshaw.[5]

This radical Christian tradition goes further still than abolitionism, including questions of labour and economic justice. Congregationalist pastor Jesse H. Jones (1836–1904) and Roman Catholic priest T. Wharton Collens (1812–79) joined forces to found the Christian Labor Union in 1879, declaring that 'the resources of life' should become 'the common property of the whole people through the government'.[6] The ideas of George Lippard (1822–54), a novelist and labour organiser, were influential both for Social Gospellers such as Sheldon and socialist leaders such as Eugene V. Debs.[7] These are just a small selection of the radical Christians who campaigned for equality and justice. Throughout the nineteenth century 'labor radicals insisted that the most important religious leader of all was on their side. Had not Jesus himself been a working-class carpenter and a consistent champion of the poor?'[8]

It is difficult – even impossible – to draw firm and decisive boundaries between the different movements of radical and socialist Christians. There are always connections and crossovers however the theorist or historian tries to organise the subject matter. With that caveat in place, however, we will focus in this chapter on three movements. First is the Social Gospel of Sheldon and others, a movement largely consisting of clergymen who aimed to broaden the Gospel from a focus on individual salvation to incorporate social and economic matters. Second is the Christian Socialism of figures such as Debs – activists who sought political power to implement their vision of a new society. Third are the spiritual socialists, of which Dorothy Day is a key example – those who had a more radical vision than that of the Social Gospel, yet focused on developing small-scale co-operative communities rather than fighting elections or stirring up revolution.

The Social Gospel

Sheldon's novels – *In His Steps*, followed by, among others, *The Heart of the World: A Story of Christian Socialism* in 1905 – were highly successful in cultivating the spirit of the Social Gospel. This spirit was still evident when, a century after Sheldon first posed the question, 'What Would Jesus Do?' became a popular slogan and 'WWJD?' wristbands first made their appearance. Yet these works of fiction were largely devoid of practical proposals. The climax of *In His Steps* is a sermon in which the preacher Henry Maxwell exhorts his congregation with such statements as: 'What would be the result if all the church members of this city tried to do as Jesus would do? It is not possible to say in detail what the effect would be. But it is easy to say and it is true that, instantly, the human problem would begin to find an adequate answer.'[9] The congregants are so moved by Maxwell's eloquence that at the close of the service they surge forward to recommit themselves to doing as Jesus would do. Sheldon did have practical ideas on how the federal government might alleviate poverty and provide employment, but the 'senti-mental rhetoric' of his novels could actually serve to obscure the need for systemic economic and political change.[10]

Nevertheless, Sheldon paved the way for the Social Gospel, including perhaps its best-known exponent Walter Rauschenbusch (1861–1918). Rauschenbusch, the son of German immigrants, was born in Rochester, New York, and attended Rochester Seminary before taking up the pastorate of a German Baptist church in the Hell's Kitchen area of Manhattan. Here, like Sheldon in Kansas, the poverty he encountered led him into radical poli-tics.[11] Rauschenbusch's *Christianity and the Social Crisis* (1907) has been called 'the manifesto of a burgeoning Christian social movement', and his influence has been traced on much subsequent radical and socialist Christian thought, including the liberation theology of the mid twentieth century onwards (see Chapters 6 and 7).[12] Like other Social Gospellers, Rauschenbusch empha-sised the social nature of the Gospel, arguing that the evangelical focus on individual salvation was only one part of the message of

Christ. The Kingdom of God, he suggested, was four-dimensional: it referred to a heaven outside of material reality; it referred to the salvation of individuals; it referred to the church; it referred also to the establishment of a reformed society on earth. This latter point had been forgotten – its rediscovery was nothing less than a new Reformation.[13]

Rauschenbusch drew from the 'primitive communism' of the Old Testament – including such provisions as gleaning, the prohibition of usury and the year of jubilee – as well as the 'revolutionary' command of the New Testament 'to institute a brotherly life and to equalise social inequalities', as reflected in the *Magnificat* of Mary, the preaching of John the Baptist, and the Gospel message of Christ himself.[14] While the church since its earliest times has reinterpreted the Kingdom of God as being a purely eschatological reality, in Christ the Kingdom requires the realisation of economic and social justice in the here and now.[15] 'Jesus, like all the prophets and like all his spiritually minded countrymen, lived in the hope of a great transformation of the national, social, and religious life about him.' The Kingdom of God 'is not a matter of getting individuals to heaven, but of transforming the life on earth in to the harmony of heaven'.[16] This view was based on the theme that underpins so much of left-wing Christian thought: 'God is a Father; men are neighbours and brothers; let them act accordingly.'[17] Along with these scriptural exhortations Rauschenbusch was also stronger on practical ideas than Sheldon. He called for approximate equality of outcome as the only way in which the brotherhood revealed in the Gospel could be realised, suggesting that this be achieved by state provision of utilities and the reorganisation of competitive industrialism on co-operative lines.[18] This would serve to overcome the periodic crises of capitalism; with a dash of Marxism, Rauschenbusch asserted that 'industrial crises are not inevitable in nature; they are merely inevitable in capitalism'.[19]

Rauschenbusch followed this work with *Christianizing the Social Order* (1912), an even more hard-headed book written in response to accusations that the Social Gospel lacked practical proposals.[20] Here the critique of capitalism – 'a mammonistic organization with which Christianity can never be content' – is restated: 'If one class is manifestly exploiting another, there is no fraternity between them.'[21] Rauschenbusch argues that public ownership or, at minimum, public oversight is necessary to ensure that justice is done. Yet ownership of property must also be expanded: the workers themselves must have a share in the ownership of their industry, whereas under capitalism their tools and equipment are unjustly owned by others. Industry, suggests Rauschenbusch, must be conducted on a co-operative basis, with all workers taking a share in the profits. State provision of goods and services represents another form of common ownership.[22] The welfare reforms of David Lloyd George's Liberals in the UK and Otto von Bismarck in Germany are cited as real-life examples of what might be accomplished using the power of the state for the good of the community.[23] 'The doctrine that the best State governs least has been drilled into us as civic orthodoxy. In fact, it is a dangerous heresy [...] Against the doctrine that the best State governs least, I set the assertion that the finest public life will exist in a community which has learned to combine its citizens in the largest number of cooperative functions for the common good.'[24]

The views of Rauschenbusch raise the question of whether the Social Gospel was, as Gary Dorrien terms it, the 'Social(ist) Gospel'.[25] Rauschenbusch speaks highly of socialism, calling it 'the most thorough and consistent elaboration of the Christian social ideal' and chiding Christians for their automatic opposition to socialism.[26] His views of collective ownership and co-operation in industry might fairly be regarded as socialist, and – while he never himself joined – Rauschenbusch did regard the Socialist Party as representing both the interests of the working class and a necessary programme, one neglected by the old parties.[27] Rauschenbusch, argues Dorrien, 'advocated socialism' and opposed mere reform and acts of charity.[28] Yet this was not necessarily true of all the Social Gospellers. Shailer Mathews (1863–1941), for example, 'identified the social gospel with moral conversion, reform, and gradual progress. The difference between Christianity and socialism, he argued, was that socialism expected society to make good individuals, but Christianity expected good individuals to make a good society.'[29]

Mathews, like Rauschenbusch a Baptist, was a prolific writer on social issues. He shared the same emphases as Rauschenbusch and others of the Christian Left, describing the Kingdom of God as 'a new social order, established by God, in which the relation of men to God would be like that of sons, and consequently to each other, that of brothers.[30] However, while Rauschenbusch viewed a reformed society in the present age as one of four aspects of this Kingdom, for Mathews the true Kingdom belonged in the future new creation; while our present society should be organised as a reflection of that Kingdom, it could not be the Kingdom itself.[31] It followed from this subtle but important difference that Mathews' focus was not on changing society but on changing individuals within society; the collective ownership and co-operative industry advocated by Rauschenbusch was not his primary concern, and much of his *The Social Gospel* (1910) seems to advocate the changing of attitudes so that men would treat each other as brothers whether they were factory owners or factory workers, without necessarily changing of the economic structure of society. 'There are a number of men calling themselves Christian Socialists who hold that under socialism alone it is possible for the principles of Christianity really to become operative', Mathews asserted. 'But most of us are by no means convinced that this is necessarily true.'[32] Socialism is fundamentally economic, but the Gospel is spiritual. The principles of the Gospel will lead to changes and improvements in conditions, but the restructuring of economic life is not in itself a Gospel aim. This is not to say that Mathews is devoid of helpful insights, but they remain the insights of a reformer rather than those of a socialist.

Washington Gladden (1836–1918) is harder to categorise. For John C. Cort he was, despite his opposition to Marxism, a 'standout representative of the Social Gospel and Christian socialism' who called for society to be reorganised on 'the principle of co-operation'.[33] Gladden's *Christianity and Socialism* (1905), however, shows a thinker rather less certain about his socialism. Gladden draws from F.D. Maurice (see Chapter 1) the principle of God's Fatherhood, making one of the plainest statements ever of the concept that underpins so much of Christian left-wing thought:

> From the fact of the divine Fatherhood is derived the fact of human brotherhood [...] It is not the regenerate alone, but all who are made in God's image, who come under the law of brotherhood. All human relations – domestic, economic, industrial, political – are founded on this fact and must conform to it. Such is the teaching of Jesus Christ. Such is the principle by which, in his conception, society is to be constructed.[34]

In Gladden's view a society based on property, industry and economics rather than the social teaching of Christ will reduce fraternal relationships to mere economic transactions, which do not recognise the essential humanity of other persons. At its worst this leads to slavery but, even without slavery itself, such a system will still be characterised by exploitation and an unwillingness for people to help and support each other.[35] Yet the full socialisation of all property, industry and capital is not practical. It might solve one set of society's problems, but would create another just as harmful. Private enterprise has caused men to be exploited but the solution is for private property to be used rightly, for its abolition would prevent men from being independent, intellectual and moral beings.[36] 'I am very sure,' says Gladden, 'that neither individualism nor Socialism furnishes a safe principle for the organization of society; but that what we need is the coordination of the two principles.'[37] The focus of 'True Socialism' should be to encourage a community-mindedness in each individual, especially at their employment, so that they may serve the community in their day-to-day work. This is more important than socialising industry.[38]

If Gladden's vision falls short of being an endorsement for socialism then William Dwight Porter Bliss (1856–1926) presents one much more avowedly socialist. An Episcopalian priest, Bliss founded the Society of Christian Socialists in 1889, served as leader of the Christian Social Union (modelled on Charles Gore and Henry Scott Holland's organisation of the same name; see Chapter 1), and founded the American Fabian Society in 1897. Bliss held that both the individual and social sides of the Gospel were important, arguing: 'In man's relations to God, Jesus Christ preached an individual gospel; accordingly in their relations to God, Christ's disciples must be individualists. In man's relations to man, Jesus Christ preached a social gospel; accordingly, in these relations, his disciples must be socialists.'[39] In his seminal work *What is Christian Socialism?* (1890) Bliss prefigured many of Rauschenbusch's later ideas. Socialism, for Bliss, was the application of the principles that God is a Father and all people brothers and sisters.[40] Socialism does not involve the confiscation of personal property, but it does involve the collective ownership of all private property and the reorganisation of society into a 'Co-operative Commonwealth'.[41] While the construction of such a commonwealth must be achieved democratically and voluntarily Bliss recognised, in contradiction to Mathews, that this required systemic rather than merely individual change. Further, while the emphasis of F.D. Maurice on the Fatherhood of God was vitally important, Bliss was critical of restricting the Christian Socialist vision to 'co-operative ownership' in industry as he believed Maurice had done: 'Business is conducted to-day on such a gigantic scale that only the State can control it. Small co-operative concerns, competing with each other, will never solve the problem. We need the Co-operative Commonwealth.'[42] The vision of Bliss then is that of a democratic socialist – or at least of a social democrat – rather than merely a social reformer.[43]

Socialist or not, the Social Gospellers tended to stand apart from political parties in general and the Socialist Party in particular. The most notable exception to this was Vida Scudder (1861–1954), who was a Socialist Party member and seemed just as happy in the company of socialists and industrial unionists as she was in that of Social Gospellers such as Bliss and Rauschenbusch.[44] Scudder had, in Cort's words, a 'rare, almost unique combination of appreciation for the spiritual and the material, for "the poets and dreamers" as well as the pragmatic trade unionists and the tough-minded revolutionaries'.[45] She also seems to have had a more radical mindset than her Social Gospel colleagues – consider for example her typical prayer before meals: 'We have food; others have none; God bless the revolution!'[46] Among Scudder's insights is that the doctrine of the Trinity provides a theological basis for fellowship and co-operation in society for the persons of the Godhead fellowship, and co-operate with each other perfectly.[47] In a manner similar to Mathews and contrary to Rauschenbusch, Scudder regards the reformed society on earth as being a reflection of God's ultimate Kingdom rather than the Kingdom itself.[48] She, however, does not follow Mathews in disavowing the need for structural change. Scudder's view – expressed in *Socialism and Character* (1912) – is that society must be changed, the incarnation and sacrificial death of Christ providing the basis for 'the socialist state'.[49] This new society, in keeping with the values of the *Magnificat*, 'should mean the reign of justice and social equality, the exaltation of the poor, while the powerful should be degraded and the rich sent empty away'.[50] Jesus Christ would not have hesitated to regard 'the proletariat as leaders towards social freedom, and welcoming the class struggle, so far as a high idealism suffuses it, as the destined instrument for the abolition of classes'.[51]

Christian Socialists

As well as her own valuable contribution Scudder provides a link between the Social Gospel of Rauschenbusch and the socialism of Eugene Debs and the organised Left. That Left was largely secular, bur not exclusively so; indeed, there was often a religious basis of socialism in the nineteenth and early twentieth centuries. C. Osbourne Ward (1831–1902), building on the work of George Lippard, saw Christianity as the driving force of revolution, a direct contradiction to the Marxist view of religion as representing part of a bourgeois false consciousness. George E. McNeill (1836–1906), a Christian Socialist and prominent ally of the Marxists in the International Labor Union, predicted in 1890 that, '[t]hough the Mammon-worshippers may cry, "Crucify Him Crucify Him!" [...] the new Pentecost will come, when every man shall have according to his needs'.[52] Among the founders of the Socialist Party of America was George Davis Herron (1862–1925), a Congregationalist minister who declared: 'competition is not a law of life, but a contradiction of every principle of Christianity [...] Our economic system is organized social wrong [...] The wage system is economic slavery, a profane traffic in human flesh and blood.'[53] It should, however, be noted that Herron's vision was a pantheistic one, in which a co-operative and collectivist society was linked to the realisation that God and creation were one. Mary G. Harris Jones (1837–1930) – known as 'Mother' Jones – was a founder of the revolutionary Industrial Workers of the World (IWW) who regarded Christ as one who 'agitated' against injustice.[54] Among the other founders of the IWW were Thomas J. Haggerty (1862–1920), a Roman Catholic priest and trade-union activist, who 'sought to meld Christian commitment and radical communism', and James Connolly (1868–1916) who, despite an ingrained anti-clericalism, always professed himself to be a believing Catholic.[55]

Another founder member of the IWW was Eugene V. Debs (1855–1926). Debs was also a founder of the Socialist Party and ran for the presidency five times: for the Social Democratic Party in 1900 and for the Socialist Party in 1904, 1908, 1912 and 1920, the final occasion while he was imprisoned for denouncing American participation in the First World War. Christian Socialists were among those who allegedly 'blunted' the radical edge of the Socialist Party by focusing on brotherhood rather than class conflict; Debs, by contrast, 'campaigned on a program of straight class-struggle socialism'.[56] Socialism, argued Debs, required 'the emancipation of working class from wage slavery', and this was the aim of the 'the class-conscious, revolutionary Socialist Party'.[57] 'The Socialist Party stands for the abolition of the wage system [...] The Socialist Party stands for the collective ownership of the means of wealth production and distribution and the opera-tion of industry in the interest of all.'[58] Yet Debs' socialism was based squarely on his understanding of the Christian Gospel. Herbert. G. Gutman, a professor of labour history, argues that 'Debs bristled with Christian indignation at human suffering and cannot be understood outside of that framework.'[59] Isabel Maclean, a biographer of Debs, views him as seeking to build a 'brotherhood of man' and following Christ as the champion of the poor and oppressed: 'Many believe in Christianity, but Debs is a Christian.'[60]

Debs demonstrated the influence of Marxist thought, for example arguing: 'One class now owns the tools while another class uses them. One class is small and rich and the other large and poor. One wants more profit and the other more wages. One consists of capitalists and the other of workers. These two classes are at war.'[61] The Marxist conception of history is also evident, Debs explaining that men were 'slaves' in the ancient world, 'serfs' in the middle ages, 'wage workers' under capitalism, and will become 'free men in socialism, the next inevitable phase of advancing civilization'.[62] Debs, however, repudiates Marxist–Leninist methodology, asserting that the working class cannot be led out of capitalism by a vanguard or an elite or a single leader, but must free themselves.[63] For Debs a working-class revolutionary union – the IWW – and a working-class political force – the Socialist Party – should work hand-in-hand to bring about socialism.[64] He also repudiated the Marxist view that reli-gious faith must necessarily constitute an anti-revolutionary false consciousness, for:

> Christianity was integral to Debs's socialism, and he indicted the entire prevailing economic system in religious terms [...] These religious allusions were not merely pieces of rhetorical window dressing trotted out to bolster his vision of socialism. Christianity was a basic component of his ideology that was intimately linked to the international and universal values he championed as a socialist.[65]

The clearest statement of Debs' faith came in his 1914 essay 'Jesus the Supreme Leader'. Debs describes the 'proletarian character of Jesus Christ' who lived as a 'master proletarian revolutionist and sower of the social whirlwind'.[66] 'Pure communism was the economic and social gospel preached by Jesus Christ, and every act and utterance that may properly be ascribed to him conclusively affirms it. Private property was to his elevated mind and exalted soul a sacrilege and a horror; an insult to God and a crime against man.'[67]

Debs combined his Christian Socialism with an avowed anti-clericalism. It was, in his view, the Emperor Constantine who succeeded in morphing Christianity into a religion to support the ruling class. Since then the revolutionary message of Jesus has been replaced by the 'superstition' of a Christ who died to wash away sins and save the repentant.[68] Here we get a glimpse of Debs' unorthodoxy. The virgin conception of Christ is merely a 'beautiful myth', which points us to the reality that all human beings are of 'miraculous origin' and have a fundamental value. Furthermore, 'Jesus was not divine because he was less human than his fellowmen but for the opposite reason that he was supremely human, and it is this of which his divinity consists.'[69] Neither Debs' view that Christ's divinity is a result of his humanity, nor the view Debs attributes to his opponents that Christ is divine because he is less human, fall within the bounds of orthodox Christianity. More so we see Debs' impatience with a church that condemned socialism and sided with the oppressors. In a similar way to Keir Hardie in the UK (see Chapter 1) he drew a distinction between on the one hand the teaching and philosophy of Christ and on the other that of the institutional church.[70] Again like Hardie he denounced the religious hypocrisy of those who professed faith, yet exploited and oppressed the working class. The reduction of wages Debs viewed as 'an exhibition of the methods by which Christless capitalists rob labor, and this is done while the brazen pirates prate of religion and the "Spirit of Christ"; who plunder labor that they may build churches, endow universities and found libraries'.[71] Andrew Carnegie came in for particular criticism for his alleged role in the killing of nine striking steelworkers in Homestead, Pennsylvania. Carnegie, blasted Debs, 'out-phariseed all the pharisees who made broad their phylacteries and made long prayers on the streets of Jerusalem that they might be seen of men, while they were "devouring widows' houses" and binding burdens on the backs of men grievous to be borne'.[72]

Following Debs' death, Norman Thomas (1884–1968) became the leading figure in the Socialist Party. Thomas, formerly a Presbyterian minister, ran for the presidency as the Socialist candidate six consecutive times, beginning in 1928. In some ways less radical than Debs, his views were 'an outgrowth of the nineteenth-century Social Gospel movement. Walter Rauschenbusch, who developed a Social Gospel theology most thoroughly, had a profound influence on Thomas.'[73] Thomas, though – like Debs and Rauschenbusch – regarded the capitalist system as incompatible with Christianity, writing in 1919: 'We cannot be Christian so long as we participate or acquiesce in a social structure whose foundation principles are the direct denials of the precepts of the Sermon on the Mount.'[74] He later described how his 'approach to socialism was largely inspired by the so-called "social justice", the "social gospel" of Rauschenbusch and others. My concept then was a Kingdom of God on earth which would have been pretty much an ideal socialist [...] society.'[75] Thomas set out his vision of a non-Marxist, non-Stalinist socialism in *A Socialist's Faith* (1951). Here he argued that true socialism must be democratic in order to reflect the Christian concept of brotherhood and encourage 'rational co-operation' as opposed to the totalitarian system of the Soviet Union which was 'an incredibly dangerous denial of true socialism'.[76] Society should be based on the principle of common ownership rather than mere government oversight, but this should not mean control of everything by the state. 'Sound democratic socialism will seek public ownership of the commanding heights of the modern economic order.' However, 'it is neither necessary nor desirable' to have a 'monolithic type of ownership or control'. These 'commanding heights' include natural resources, the financial sector, and other monopolies which should not remain in private hands, for example public utilities such as water, gas and electricity.[77] Thomas, like R.H. Tawney (see Chapter 1), did not object to ownership of private property where the owner provided a necessary function; he also advocated workers' co-operatives as a form of shared ownership outside of state control.[78]

By this stage, however, Thomas had lost his previous Christian belief, and this is reflected in his scepticism about whether religion can be a useful tool for remaking society. Insofar as religion aids society in seeking brotherhood and co-operation, and in 'transcending the material', it has 'a great role to play'. Religion, though, has often caused people to be less, not more, brotherly – Thomas points to the idea of the Jewish race as a chosen people, the claim of the Roman Catholic Church to be the only way of salvation, the exclusivity of Protestant sects and denominations.[79] While, however, Thomas does not allow that truth belongs to any one religion – or even to religion in general – he also denies that exclusive truth belongs to socialism. Socialism cannot 'present itself as a complete philosophy of the universe, the universal ground of art, science and religion. It must unite the social actions of men of varying beliefs on the common denominator of a conviction that through cooperation men may win plenty, peace, and freedom.'[80] Thomas was never happy or comfortable with his lack of faith. John R. Erickson interviewed Thomas in 1967, commenting: 'Thomas' loss of belief brought him no emotional satisfaction. Instead, he was a man who coveted a faith he could not have, who never believed that a social creed was an adequate substitute for religious faith.'[81]

Henry A. Wallace (1888–1965) was another key figure of the religious Left. He served as vice-president to Franklin D. Roosevelt during the Second World War and ran as a presidential candidate in 1948. Wallace drew inspiration from his Presbyterian upbringing, as well as from the tradition of liberal Catholicism and Native American forms of spirituality.[82] Wallace's view of religion as a transformative force contrasted with Roosevelt's view of civil religion as a means of maintaining stability, Wallace arguing that 'the essence of Christ's teaching is Peace and the bringing of the Kingdom of God on earth'.[83] Like Debs and Thomas of the Socialist Party, as well as Social Gospellers such as Rauschenbusch, Wallace believed that religion should lead to systemic change rather than mere acts of charity: 'It is good religious practice to feed the hungry and give drink to the thirsty and clothes to the naked. It is still better religion when men cooperate together to create an order of life in which nakedness, hunger and thirst become more and more impossible.'[84] As such, Wallace was a supporter of Roosevelt's New Deal programme of social and economic reform, though he also recognised the need for a spiritual change that would under-pin a renewed form of society: 'I know that the social machines set up by the present administration will break down unless they are inspired by men who in their hearts catch a larger vision than the hard driving profit mongers of the past.'[85]

It is unlikely that Debs would have been a supporter of the New Deal, arguing as he had that, '[a]s a rule, large capitalists are Republicans and small capitalists are Democrats, but work-ingmen must remember that they are all capitalists' and that real change must come from 'the class-conscious, revolutionary Socialist Party'.[86] Thomas, perhaps more moderate than Debs, did give tentative support to New Deal reforms such as the creation of social security, but argued that these did not go far enough in alleviating poverty and achieving justice.[87] Thomas acknowledged Wallace's critique of the capitalist system, but did not regard him as a socialist.[88] This was possibly a fair assess-ment, given Wallace's support for 'progressive capitalism' and his assertion that capitalism is 'the most efficient system of organ-izing production and distribution on principles of freedom and equal opportunity yet devised by man', and that rather than being overthrown it 'should be modernized and made to work'.[89] The two men went head-to-head at the 1948 election, Thomas for the Socialist Party and Wallace for the Progressive Party. Whether or not Wallace himself was socialist, the newly formed party, which served as a vehicle for his campaign, certainly attracted the atten-tion of socialists – including communists and fellow travellers who were unable or unwilling to support the Socialist Party – and it acted as a left-wing alternative to the Democratic candidacy of Harry S. Truman.[90] It may seem poor tactics for two left-wing candidates to have run against Truman, but in the end it mattered little: Wallace received only 2.4 per cent of the vote and Thomas a mere 0.3 per cent. Wallace's contentment to work slowly towards a long-term spiritual change simply did not translate into an effective electoral programme to compete with the Democratic campaign of Truman.[91]

Spiritual Socialists

Wallace's commitment to long-term spiritual change marks him out as part of a group known as 'spiritual socialists'. The term is used by historian and political theorist Vaneesa Cook to designate a section of the Christian Left who emphasised the importance of working through small groups and local communities to a greater extent than electoral campaigns and large-scale political change. From these grassroots, localised efforts would come the spiritual change that society needed.[92] These spiritual socialists were different from Social Gospellers, who too often held paternalistic attitudes, focused on what the state or large charities could do for oppressed communities rather than what they could do for themselves, and were overly cautious or sometimes merely reformist.[93] They were also different from Christian Socialists, as represented by Debs, focusing on 'the inherent dignity of all individuals' rather than a class-based politics that pitted proletariat against bourgeoisie, and – again – on small-scale, community change rather than the seizure of political power as advocated by the Socialist Party.[94] Wallace was the exception among the spiritual socialists in that he did enter politics with both the Democratic and Progressive parties. His vision, though, remained one of spiritual change, as demonstrated in his fears that New Deal reforms would falter without a new spirit to support them. Cook explains that for the spiritual socialists, 'the ideal socialist society, in which peace, love, and justice become practical realities' must be developed first 'in local communities and then extrapolated to more complex social environments at the national and international levels'.[95]

A.J. Muste (1886–1967) – a key figure at the outset of the spiritual socialist movement – exemplified this perspective in criticising earlier movements of the Christian Left for failing to recognise that their vision of a socially righteous society required 'revolutionary living and action', not just external change brought about by government, charities or co-operative societies.[96] Muste was not necessarily averse to political change – he voted for Debs in 1912 on the grounds that Debs, unlike the Democratic candidate Woodrow Wilson, aimed at the total change of society rather than mere reform – but for Muste the process of gradual, spiritual change was itself the goal: 'We cannot foresee the society which is to be and we must finally accept the fact that we are dealing with a process and it is in the process that we find our success rather than in the realization of a static plan for society.'[97] Muste came from a Dutch Reformed background, but later became a Quaker minister.[98] He put his ideas of building socialism from the ground up into practice as a union organiser with the Amalgamated Textile Workers of America and then as a teacher at Brookwood Labor College. Brookwood was exactly the kind of community spiritual socialists wished for. It sought to put Christian social values into operation, building the Kingdom of God, yet was involved in the practical day-to-day struggle of the working class and labour unions.[99]

Muste became frustrated with the Socialist Party in the 1930s, giving his support instead to the Trotskyist Workers Party USA. The revolutionary zeal of the communists was attractive to Muste, who began to view church-based socialism as passive and unable to succeed. Eventually, though, he became disillusioned with the communist belief in achieving revolution through violence, taking instead the view that both socialist and pacifist commitments were required in order to achieve fellowship and brotherhood.[100] Norman Thomas later described him as someone who made a 'remarkable effort to show that pacifism was by no means passivism and that there could be such a thing as a non-violent social revolution'.[101] Muste was a founder member of the Fellowship of Reconciliation in 1915, a Christian pacifist organisation of which Thomas for a time served as president. Thomas' faith in pacifism left him along with his faith in Christianity, but he retained an admiration for Muste: 'I wanted to be like A.J. Muste. He was a remarkable man.'[102]

Another key figure was Sherwood Eddy (1871–1963), an evangelist and missionary. Eddy came to his socialism during the First World War and the years that followed. It was in this period that he developed a belief that it was external conditions rather than inherent depravity that led to immoral behaviour, and that capitalism in particular was the system that led to selfishness and greed. A change in conditions, therefore, could lead to a change in behaviours, to righteousness and justice.[103] Such change was necessary for, Eddy argued, the 'teachings of Jesus clearly and repeatedly forbid the selfish accumulation of wealth'.[104] Eddy came to the view that small-scale communities were the way in which a more co-operative form of life could be exampled and cultivated, gradually overcoming the atomistic individualism of the capitalist system. This view was rooted in Eddy's experience as a missionary in China and India, where he found that such communities operated in a spirit of brotherhood quite unlike the individualistic West.[105] Although Eddy voted for Eugene Debs and Norman Thomas he was never a committed supporter of the Socialist Party, preferring to focus on change initiated from the bottom rather than seeking the levers of power.[106] He borrowed from Marxist analysis – for example arguing that capitalism fell into inevitable crises of overproduction – but Eddy's criticism of capitalism remained primarily spiritual. Eddy's 'American Seminar' was his attempt to 'build a socialist alternative to both American capitalism and Soviet Communism', which would 'restructure human relations into the Kingdom of God on earth', while the co-operative farm he founded in Mississippi was an alternative to both Communist organising and New Deal welfare reforms during the depression era.[107]

Among the best known of these spiritual socialists is Dorothy Day (1897–1980), co-founder of the Catholic Worker Movement. Day was a communist before she had any religious faith but gradually became disillusioned with the class warfare and violence of the Marxist Left and, as a Roman Catholic convert, she argued that '[i]t is only through religion that communism can be achieved'.[108] In place of the top-down methodology of the Social Gospel and socialism Day advocated what she called 'the Little Way' – small-scale social transformation rather than large-scale political reform or revolution.[109] Along with her collaborator Peter Maurin (1877–1949), a French Roman Catholic socialist, Day developed a three-step process for bringing about social transformation: firstly the founding of a newspaper, *The Catholic Worker*, to disseminate ideas; secondly the opening of houses of hospitality to provide for the poor; thirdly the organisation of communal farms, much as Eddy had attempted before. The purpose of *The Catholic Worker* was, according to John C. Cort, himself a member of the Catholic Worker Movement, 'to expound the ideas about social justice contained in the papal encyclicals [...] It espoused a pacifist, communal, anarchist-leaning Catholicism devoted to feeding the hungry, clothing the naked, providing a home for the homeless, and seeing Christ in the poor and vulnerable'.[110] As Day described them, the houses of hospitality were 'a twentieth-century version of the ancient notion of a hospice, a place where "works of mercy" were offered and acknowledged in a person-to-person fashion, as opposed to the faceless, bureaucratic procedures of the welfare state'. For Day and Maurin 'works of mercy' should not be merely charitable acts to ameliorate the poverty and misery of capitalism, but a revolution of individual lives, which would bring about a revolution of the whole social, economic and political order.[111] This reflected Day's belief in 'cultivation', that the seeds of a new society would take time to grow, in a process largely mysterious and unseen, so long as God gave grace and people did the work He commanded.[112] If people would pray for 'an increase of love in our hearts' said Day, this would 'vitalize and transform all our individual actions, and [we] know that God will take them and multiply them, as Jesus multiplied the loaves and the fishes'.[113]

A potential danger in this small-scale, localised approach was noted by Myles Horton (1905–90), a socialist and civil rights activist from a Presbyterian background. Horton saw that the cultivation of these small-scale communities might become a means of escaping from, rather than changing society, arguing: 'you couldn't withdraw into a utopian community. To deal with injustice you had to act in the world.'[114] Horton nevertheless saw the value in the creation of such co-operative communities for, '[s]ince I know those things can happen on a small scale, I assume that if we ever get wise enough and involved enough people, it could happen on a bigger scale'.[115] Horton, like Muste before him, emphasised that the process of spiritual change was not just a means to a goal but had itself an intrinsic value, explaining that '[t]he goal I'm talking about is one that can never be reached. It's a direction, a concept of society that grows as you go along.' 'If you want love and brotherhood, you've got to incorporate them as you go along, because you can't just expect them to occur in the future without experiencing them before you get there.'[116] Horton's Highlander Folk School would go on to play an influential role in the formation of the civil rights movement, and he probably spoke for all spiritual socialists, and for the Christian Left in general, when he declared: 'From Jesus and the prophets I had learned about the importance of loving people, the importance of being a revolutionary, standing up and saying that this system is unjust.

Jesus to me was a person who had the vision to project a society in which people would be equally respected, in which property would be shared.'[117]

Conclusion

Although the division between Social Gospellers, Christian Socialists and spiritual socialists is a helpful one to organise our thoughts and appreciate the nuances of Christian Left thinking, we would do well not to overly emphasise the differences between them. We have already seen in this chapter some of the overlap: Henry Wallace as a spiritual socialist who sought political power as the head of the left-wing Progressive Party; Norman Thomas' background in the Fellowship of Reconciliation; Vida Scudder's willingness to work with both Walter Rauschenbusch and W.D.P. Bliss on the one hand and Eugene Debs on the other. There are certainly differences: some Social Gospellers called for little more than reform and none, Scudder excepted, gave enthusiastic support to the Socialist Party; Debs and others of the 'secular' Left as represented by the Socialist Party and the IWW favoured a working-class revolution; spiritual socialists advocated for the 'cultivation' of new spiritual values in local communities and small-scale co-operatives and works of mercy, which would flower into a renewed society. Yet the big-picture concepts, values and ideas remained the same. The Gospel of Christ, the Christian religion, calls us to renounce selfishness and individualism and live in a manner that reflects the Fatherhood of God and the consequent brotherhood of all people. In so doing, the Kingdom of God will, at least in part, be realised here on earth.

5

Moral Minority:
The Christian Left in the Age
of the Christian Right

By the 1950s Myles Horton's Highlander Folk School had become a powerful force in the development of the civil rights movement. Horton himself was an advocate of racial justice and equality; he set up workshops on desegregation at Highlander in anticipation of the Supreme Court's ruling in Brown v Board of Education (1954). Rosa Parks (1913–2005) attended one of these workshops prior to her celebrated protest against the segregated bus system in Montgomery, Alabama, in 1955. Parks – a committed Christian and member of the African Methodist Episcopal Church (AMEC) – later explained: 'At Highlander, I found out for the first time in my adult life that this could be a unified society [...] I gained there the strength to persevere in my work for freedom, not just for blacks, but for all oppressed people.'[1] She also declared that 'the only reason I don't hate every white man alive is Highlander and Myles Horton'.[2] Parks' courageous actions led to the Montgomery Bus Boycott led by Martin Luther King, Jr, as well as the broader campaign against segregation and for African-American civil rights.

Parks certainly would have had reason to feel hatred towards white people in general. She had grown up fearful of the Ku Klux Klan, had seen her father cheated in business by white men and, like other African-Americans, had been denied the right to vote throughout her life.[3] Furthermore the response of the Christian Left to such racial injustice was inconsistent. While Horton was committed to achieving civil rights, the issue of racial discrimination and oppression was not often touched upon by Social Gospellers such as Charles Sheldon, W.D.P. Bliss or Walter Rauschenbusch; Rauschenbusch was at best naive when it came to racial justice and at worst could produce some racist views of his own.[4] Thankfully this situation began to improve. Eugene V. Debs had shown xenophobic and racist attitudes towards foreign-born workers in his early years as a trade unionist, but had rejected these after coming to embrace socialism.[5] Debs attacked 'white supremacy', especially when it derived from members of the white working class, arguing that the 'Socialist Party is the party of the working class, regardless of color – the whole working class of the whole world.'[6] This socialist opposition to racism was continued by Norman Thomas, who was a keen supporter of King and the civil rights movement.[7]

The civil rights movement demonstrates that the Christian Left continued to operate, even though in the latter part of the twentieth century Christianity became more associated with the political Right. Fundamentalists,[8] who had to a large extent stayed out of the public sphere since the failure of anti-evolution statutes and the humiliation of the Scopes trial in 1921, took renewed interest in politics in the post-Second World War period. This included anti-communism, campaigns against 'feminism, abortion, pornography and gay rights', and in some cases opposition to civil rights legislation.[9] The initial period of closeness between evangelicalism and the Republican Party came in the 1950s, and that relationship was solemnised with the 1980 presidential campaign of Ronald Reagan; since Reagan, Republican candidates for the presidency have been able to rely on a majority of white evangelical voters – including Donald J. Trump, who won 75 per cent of white evangelical votes in the 2020 presidential election.[10] We should not, however, fall into the trap of assuming that the religious Left disappeared as the religious Right came to the fore. As Vaneesa Cook observes, 'the religious Left has never disappeared from American politics or culture. It remained strong among progressives throughout the twentieth century and continues to shape political and social action'.[11] In this chapter, we will consider three expressions of the American Christian Left in the second half of the twentieth century: the civil rights movement, of which Martin Luther King is the key figure; the 'black power' liberation theology of James H. Cone; and the 'red-letter Christianity' movement of evangelicals such as Tony Campolo and Jim Wallis.

Martin Luther King and civil rights

Black churches and black Christians have played an important role in left-wing and radical politics throughout the history of the United States.[12] We have already noted the significance of abolitionists such as Frederick Douglass and Sojourner Truth, but African-American spirituality continued to underpin the post-bellum fight against oppression. W.E.B. Du Bois, though not himself an orthodox Christian, viewed the black churches as a means of developing black consciousness, radicalism and anti-racist activism; in *The Souls of Black Folk* (1903) De Bois described the experience of attending a service at which the black congregation, those who outside the church were disempowered and disenfranchised, were fully empowered by the Holy Spirit.[13] Reverdy C. Ransom (1861–1959) was a pastor and bishop in the African Methodist Episcopal Church – the same church of which Rosa Parks would later be a member – who emphasised the function of the church in bringing about racial justice and became an ally of Du Bois and a supporter of the National Association for the Advancement of Colored People (NAACP).[14] Ransom's vision of a new society in which brotherhood and co-operation have replaced discrimination and oppression prefigures that of Martin Luther King, as well as marking Ransom out as a Christian Socialist: 'a new civilization rising – a civilization which shall neither be Anglo-Saxon, Asiatic nor African, but one which, recognizing the unity of the race and the brotherhood of man, will accord to each individual [...] the right to stand upon an equal plane and share all the blessings of our common heritage'.[15]

These themes were also present in the activism of Asa Philip Randolf (1889–1979), a Baptist and socialist considered to be 'the nation's preeminent black labor leader'.[16] Randolf campaigned against racial discrimination in industry following a Gandhian method of non-violence, planning a peaceful march on Washington DC in 1941 to draw attention to the plight of black workers. The march never took place, as President Roosevelt responded with an executive order banning racial discrimination

in the war industry (though this symbolic act had little effect) but
the idea found its fulfilment in Martin Luther King's 1963 March
on Washington for Jobs and Freedom.[17] Another major influence
on King and the civil rights movement was the Baptist pastor
and theologian Howard Thurman (1899–1981). Thurman, in a
similar manner to Rauschenbusch and others of the Social Gospel
tradition, moved beyond an understanding of the Gospel as
merely individual reconciliation with God, arguing that the Good
News should, in Lisa Sharon Harper's phrasing, 'be applied to
every facet of life – economic, political, social, and personal'.[18]
In his seminal work *Jesus and the Disinherited* (1949) Thurman
'called all those who said they believed in Jesus to follow their
disinherited leader into the revolutionary practice of sacrificial
love not just in words, but in actions'.[19] Thurman's emphases on
sacrifice, love of enemy and racial reconciliation are reflected in
King's commitment to non-violent action and description in the
'Letter from Birmingham Jail' of Jesus Christ as 'an extremist for
love, truth and goodness'.[20] Thurman's identification of Christ
with the downcast and oppressed of the world also prefigures the
black liberation theology of James H. Cone, to which we shall
return.

Martin Luther King, Jr, (1929–68) was a Baptist pastor and
theologian, and perhaps an unlikely leader of the civil rights movement. The kind of black spirituality lauded by Du Bois was at
first alien to King, who favoured a more cerebral faith, 'a God of
ideas', rather than the faith of southern black Christianity, which
he viewed as being primitive.[21] It was the strain of fighting for civil
rights and enduring the threats of violence against himself and his
family that pushed King towards a deeper faith in a personal God,
one who would be a real source of help and encouragement in
the lengthy struggle against oppression.[22] King had only recently
taken up the pastorate at Dexter Avenue Baptist Church when
Parks' protest sparked the Montgomery bus boycott; at first he
was reluctant to lend his support but soon overcame his doubts,
being elected as president of the campaign's coordinating committee owing to his reputation as 'a strong social gospel preacher'.[23]
At a meeting early in the campaign King declared that 'we are not
wrong in what we are doing'. If we are wrong, he argued, 'God
Almighty is wrong. If we are wrong, Jesus of Nazareth was merely
a utopian dreamer that never came down to earth.'[24]

King's philosophy took time to develop. In a manner similar to the later liberation theology method of practice preceding reflection – indeed, out of necessity – King found himself taking action and forming his thoughts and ideas as he went along. At the outset he relied on the theology of Paul Tillich (see Chapter 3) – the subject of his doctoral dissertation – who had argued that love and justice must complement each other. Yes the African-American community was called to love its white oppressors, but this was not a passive love which overlooked wrong; rather, it was a love in action which sought to correct that which was sinful and wicked and establish justice, so that the quest for justice was itself an expression of Christian love.[25] In this way King shared in the broader emphasis of the Christian Left, for 'the civil rights movement was not just about black rights. It was about integrating all members of the human family into a society that reflected the Kingdom of God'.[26] King took the view that '[t]his is not a war between the white and the Negro but a conflict between justice and injustice [...] We are determined to make America a better place for all people'.[27] King also came to the view that achieving legal or political rights for African-Americans would be a futile effort without the development of such fellowship and brotherhood between blacks and whites; 'King was convinced that justice without reconciliation was nearly worthless, sowing the seeds of future hatred and hostility'.[28] This reconciliation was for King a realistic possibility. In *Souls of Black Folk* Du Bois had posited a 'double-consciousness' in African-Americans in which their identity as blacks and their identify as Americans led to an irreconcilable tension. As a Hegelian, King believed that these two facets of the African-American identity could be synthesised into a tool for emancipation and reconciliation.[29]

Most famously King developed a philosophy of non-violence which he referred to as 'soul force', Gandhi's translation of his Sanskrit phrase *satyagrahi*.[30] King was not at first an absolute pacifist, but in time he came to a total commitment to non-violence forged out of 'an amalgam of Gandhian nonviolence and black Christian faith'.[30] Among the first glimpses of this commitment are King's remarks to the crowd who gathered after the bombing of his home in 1956: 'We are not advocating violence. We want to love our enemies. I want you to love our enemies. Be good to them. Love them and let them know that you love them.'[32] It was more fully developed in the 'Letter from Birmingham Jail' seven years later, by which time king was the head of the Southern Christian Leadership Conference (SCLC) across the southern US. Here King outlines four steps to any nonviolent campaign. Firstly comes 'collection of the facts' to determine if injustice exists and whether action is necessary. Secondly is 'negotiation' – an attempt to resolve the issue through discussion and mediation without recourse to civil disobedience or direct action. Thirdly is 'self purification' – the making of the self ready to do battle with injustice without retaliating to violent provocation. Fourthly and finally comes 'direct action' itself.[33] Here King made clear the Christian basis for his philosophy, citing the view of Augustine of Hippo Regius and Thomas Aquinas that an unjust law should not be considered a law, and adding:

> Of course, there is nothing new about this kind of civil disobedience. It was evidenced sublimely in the refusal of Shadrach, Meshach and Abednego to obey the laws of Nebuchadnezzar, on the ground that a higher moral law was at stake. It was practiced superbly by the early Christians, who were willing to face hungry lions and the excruciating pain of chopping blocks rather than submit to certain unjust laws of the Roman Empire [...] But the Christians pressed on, in the conviction that they were 'a colony of heaven', called to obey God rather than man.[34]

It was in this letter that King declared his willingness to be labelled an 'extremist', for 'the question is not whether we will be extremists, but what kind of extremists we will be. Will we be extremists for hate or for love? [...] Perhaps the South, the nation and the world are in dire need of creative extremists.'[35]

This creative extremism took the form of bus boycotts and 'freedom rides' in an attempt to desegregate public transport, sit-ins at shops and restaurants in order to combat segregationist policies there, and marches such as those at Birmingham in 1963 and from Selma to Montgomery in 1965.[36] This latter march, led by Hosea Williams of the SCLC and John Lewis of the Student Nonviolent Coordinating Committee (SNCC), took place despite the order of Alabama Governor George Wallace making it illegal and ended with police attacking non-violent protestors as they tried to cross Edmund Bettus Bridge over the Alabama River.[37] The Selma march was part of a campaign for voting rights with the aim of allowing disenfranchised African-Americans to vote for the first time. One of the key figures in the voting rights movement was Fannie Lou Hamer (1917–77), a devout Christian and relentless campaigner. In 1965 she was among a group of women who were arrested in Mississippi for attending an SCLC workshop on voter registration, then beaten and sexually assaulted while in police custody. 'Fired up by righteous anger, Hamer was out registering voters in the cotton fields as soon as she could walk, heedless of her limp.'[38] A year later, as vice-president of the Mississippi Freedom Democratic Party (MFDP), she appeared on television to recount her experiences of discrimination and demand the right to vote, the right for African-Americans 'to become first-class citizens'.[39] A friend of Hamer's later recalled: 'I have never met or read about anyone else who so lived the doctrine of her Christianity. Her talks at community meetings were always peppered with biblical parables to emphasize her points.'[40]

As the 1960s went on, King's focus widened from African-American civil rights to a broader emphasis on human rights. This shift was exemplified by his opposition to the war in Vietnam, the expansion of his idea for a 'Negro Bill of Rights' into a 'Bill of Rights for the Disadvantaged', and his Poor People's Campaign against poverty, of which Myles Horton was an enthusiastic supporter.[41] This in turn was linked to a growing radicalism in King, a growing commitment to socialism. While he repudiated Marxist and Soviet communism, King came to believe that '[i]f we are going to achieve real equality the United States will have to adopt a modified form of socialism' similar to the social democracy of the Scandinavian states.[42] King called for 'a radical revolution of values. We must rapidly begin the shift from a thing-oriented society to a person-oriented society. A nation that continues year after year to spend more on military defence than on programs of social uplift is approaching spiritual death.' There must be a declaration of 'eternal hostility to poverty, racism and militarism'.[43] King, argues Vaneesa Cook, is part of the tradition of spiritual socialism.[44]

King did not support the violence with which some African-Americans, especially in urban areas, responded to their sense of oppression, but neither did he condemn it. 'The turmoil of the ghetto is the externalization of the Negro's inner torment and rage', he argued. The crimes of rioters and looters were 'derivative crimes.

They are born out of the great crimes of white society'.[45] King had previously argued against the 'hatred and despair of the black nationalist' and, while he was not opposed to the ideas underpinning 'black power', he was concerned that the phrase itself can 'give the impression that we are talking about black domination rather than black equality'.[46] For King, 'the movement was about more than securing civil rights. He wanted to transform society into a brotherhood of man.'[47] He argued that '[b]eyond the calling of race of nation or creed is the vocation of sonship and brotherhood'.[48] This was a particularly Christian vocation: 'The only hope for mankind upon this globe is the true fostering – not only speaking, but living – the kind of life Jesus Christ lived, non-violently.'[49]

Black power

Martin Luther King was convinced that non-violence, 'extremism' for love and justice, and 'soul force' were not only more ethical than violent struggle but also more practical.[50] In this he was followed by many – for example, Barbara Demming, feminist activist and advocate of non-violent direct action, explained: 'We can put more pressure on the antagonist for whom we show human concern […] We put upon him two pressures – the pressure of our defiance of him and the pressure of our respect for his life.'[51] Yet not everybody agreed. After the murder of three civil rights activists in Mississippi in 1964, some of those who had committed to non-violence, such as Dave Dennis of the SNCC, began to reject King's philosophy of soul force.[52] When King himself was assassinated four years later, over a hundred cities across the US erupted into violence.[53] This, argues Lisa Sharon Harper, was

> a great retreat from the vision of the kingdom […] The antagonisms of us versus them began to prevail between blacks and whites in the movement and soon after, SNCC voted to excise all white leaders. The black power movement was born and the vision of King's beloved community was swallowed up by the violence and confusion of the late 1960s.[54]

The ideas of the black power movement are exemplified in the work of theologian and activist James H. Cone (1938–2018).

Cone was 'the founder of Black theology', an African-American liberation theology, which developed in parallel to but separately from the Latin American liberation theology of Gustavo Gutiérrez (see Chapter 6).[55] He was an admirer of King who, Cone argued, 'preached black liberation in the light of Jesus Christ and thus aroused the spirit of freedom among black people'; King's non-violent philosophy, however, did not meet the needs of black people or the black power movement.[56] White America, said Cone, loved King not for his efforts to free black people but because his pacifism was less threatening and less effective than a black power philosophy that would truly emancipate black people and destroy white privilege.[57]

While King was ambivalent on the concept of black power, Cone argued that it was necessary to free black people from racist oppression, for African-Americans must be empowered to liberate themselves rather than appealing to whites to do it for them.[58] Cone defined black power as the 'complete emancipation of black people from white oppression by whatever means black people deem necessary'.[59] Cone would not have the liberating activity of the black community restricted by any commitment to non-violence, for violence was an appropriate and necessary response to the systemic violence meted out by whites.[60] Cone was scornful of those who would view the recourse to violence as unchristian: 'Their Christ is a mild easy-going American who can afford to mouth the luxuries of "love", "mercy", "long-suffering" and other white irrelevancies.'[61] Taking aim at the Social Gospellers of previous decades, Charles M. Sheldon in particular, Cone denies 'that ethical questions dealing with violence can be solved by asking: "What would Jesus do?" We cannot solve ethical questions of the twentieth century by looking at what Jesus did in the first. Our choices are not the same as his. Being Christian does not mean following "in his steps" (remember that book?).'[62] The process of emancipation and liberation must go hand-in-hand with a rediscovery and assertion by black people of their own being and worth, these having been denied by white society.[63]

Cone was dubious about the possibility of integration and reconciliation. If integration involved a meeting between whites and blacks 'on equal footing' this would be acceptable but, in reality, integration involved forcing the black community to accept the dominant values and culture of whites.[64] African-Americans must remain suspicious of all whites who want to be 'friends' with black people. While racial reconciliation is the ultimate hope, 'the biblical doctrine of reconciliation can be made a reality only when white people are prepared to address black men as *black* men and not as some grease-painted form of white humanity'.[65] A reconciliation that aims to be 'color-blind' or to 'transcend color' in reality means that black people are expected to become white; this form of reconciliation is no more than another form of white supremacism, and black people must be prepared to destroy it.[66] 'They will not let Whitey make an It of them, but will insist, with every ounce of strength, that they are people.'[67] Cone's writing is surprisingly and tragically relevant to our contemporary situation. These words, though written half a century before, could refer to the racist murder of George Floyd in Minnesota in 2020: 'Black people live in a society in which blackness means criminality, and "law and order" means "Get blacky" [...] To breathe in white society is dependent on saying Yes to whiteness, and black people know it.'[68]

There is something of a double meaning in Cone's references to 'black' and 'white'. These terms can refer literally to skin colour, race or ethnicity, yet they can also be used in an ontological rather than a literal sense; hence those whites who truly identify and suffer with oppressed blacks become 'black men in white skins'.[69] Blackness, explains Cone, is 'an ontological symbol and a visible reality which best describes what oppression means in America [...] Blackness then, stands for all victims of oppression who realize that their humanity is inseparable from man's liberation from whiteness.'[70] Man must be liberated from whiteness, for whiteness is the ontological symbol denoting oppression and wickedness, 'the expression of what is wrong with man', 'a symbol of man's depravity'.[71] While, therefore, a reconciliation that aims to turn blacks into whites must be rejected, true reconciliation 'makes us all black'.[72] Cone denies that this terminology is itself racist, but questions remain. While the terms 'white' and 'whiteness' may be employed in an ontological sense, this does not prevent Cone from referring to whites as 'honkies' who must recognise that they cannot be 'white and human at the same time', or asserting that black people must 'get about the business of cleaning up this society by destroying the filthy manifestations of whiteness in it'.[73] Yes this is an *ontological* whiteness generated by *ontological* honkies; but to use 'blackness' and 'whiteness' as markers for that which is normatively good and normatively bad can itself be interpreted as racist.

Cone's role as a theologian is to repudiate a white theology that does not serve the needs of black liberation and instead declare black power as 'Christ's central message to twentieth-century America.'[74] He also seeks to defend black Christianity from those such as Malcolm X and Frantz Fanon who identified the Christian religion as an expression of oppression and white supremacism.[75] For Cone, a Christianity that focuses on a world beyond our own is indeed a 'white lie'.[76] An understanding of salvation as being cleansed from sin and justified before God by Christ's atoning sacrifice is merely a 'white' understanding.[77] When theologians and evangelists speak of sin, wickedness or iniquity, what they really mean is a failure to live according to the values and norms of white society.[78] Yet Cone did not allow that this was the proper understanding of Christianity, for 'Christianity is essentially a religion of liberation' in which God is not a God who saves from sin but, rather, a God who identifies with and liberates from oppression.[79] These themes, Cone argues, are found consistently in scripture: the freeing of the Israelites in Exodus; the preaching of 'ethical prophets' such as Amos, Hosea, Micah and Isaiah, all of whom were concerned with 'social justice'; the promise of liberation delivered by Christ in the Gospel of Luke.[80] 'The God of the oppressed,' concludes Cone, 'is a God of revolution who breaks the chains of slavery.'[81]

This view of God as the 'God of the oppressed' leads Cone to identify God as being black, for 'God is identified with the oppressed to the point that their experience becomes his.'[82] This identification with the oppressed is most clearly seen at the incarnation, at which Christ did not 'become a universal man but an oppressed Jew [...] Christ is not a man for all people; he is a man for oppressed people whose identity is made known in and through their liberation.'[83] Christ 'is God himself coming into the very depths of human existence for the sole purpose of striking off the chains of slavery, thereby freeing man from ungodly principles and powers'.[84] By contrast, the 'white God is an idol, created by the racist bastards, and we black people must perform that iconoclastic task of smashing false images'.[85] 'If God is not for us and against white people, then he is a murderer, and we had better kill him.'[86] The work of black power, of black liberation, represents the continuing presence of Christ with those who are fighting against oppression and injustice. Cone, echoing a sentiment widely shared across the Christian Left, believed that this work would lead naturally to the Kingdom of God on earth. This kingdom was the realisation of Cone's vision of reconciliation: whiteness would be destroyed, all people would be black, and all the black people would be free from oppression. The 'Black Revolution is God's kingdom becoming a reality in America.' It is 'the reality of God's historical liberation of the oppressed [...] The kingdom of God is a black happening. It is black people saying No to whitey.'[87]

Although Cone's ideas have been linked to the development of intersectional theory,[88] the early Cone was prone to overlook forms of oppression other than that of race. Cone – like others in the civil rights and black power movements – did not take seriously enough the oppression of women. Pauli Murray (1910–85) was a civil rights and feminist activist who coined the term 'Jane Crow' to describe the system of oppression against women, especially black women, in the United States.[89] Murray experienced racist discrimination first-hand growing up in the segregated South, and she later suffered sexist discrimination as a student at Howard University, which led her to adopt a feminist position 'long before I knew the meaning of the term "feminism"'.[90] She held that combating gender injustice must be a priority for anybody who claimed to be fighting for justice, democracy or God's kingdom, and was critical of Martin Luther King and others in the civil rights movement for not making this battle part of their mission.[91] Indeed the staff of the SCLC – 'mostly men with large egos' – could be themselves guilty of sexism and misogyny.[92] Ella Baker, the director of the SCLC, was often ignored and sidelined by the men, including King; Dorothy Cotton, the SCLC director of citizenship education, was asked by King to get coffee at staff meetings; and there were other men within the movement who expected women 'to be the movement secretaries and "shit workers" as well as to service their sexual needs'.[93]

King did not regard oppression of women as being on a par with oppression of African-Americans. He was unlikely to understand the focus of second-wave feminism on oppression in the home and within the family given 'his background and his patriarchal assumptions'.[94] Cone was also dismissive of feminist arguments, especially the claims of white women to be oppressed, later admitting: 'Unfortunately, my early reflection on women's liberation was so completely controlled by black males' fears that I could not think straight regarding the complexity of the problem.'[95] Cone has argued that black women are oppressed by black men, warning black men to avoid acting as oppressors. 'Most of us have not even thought about the unique suffering of black women. We have not allowed ourselves to be taught by black women so that our theological reflections can more adequately reflect the whole black community.' Cone, however, did not believe that white women are in any way oppressed by black men.[96] Murray, though, did not accept that sexist discrimination was less important than racist discrimination. African-Americans could not, she believed, achieve full civil rights without also working for women's rights; the reverse was also true. Identity was multifaceted – an insight Murray derived in part from her own background, which included black, white and Native American – and she declared her belief in the 'interrelation of all human rights'.[97]

For Murray, this also included economic oppression. Attending Brookwood Labor College in the 1930s, Murray came to believe that the oppression of the white working class had 'echoes of the black experience', explaining: 'The study of economic oppression led me to realize that Negroes were not alone but were part of an unending struggle for human dignity the world over.'[98] This aspect of oppression was also overlooked by the early Cone, a key difference between his liberation theology and that of Gutiérrez. Cone later came to accept the need for socialism, declaring that the black churches must 'take a stand against capitalism and for democratic socialism, for Karl Marx and against Adam Smith, for the poor in all colors and against the rich of all colors, for the workers and against the corporations'.[99] In this, Cone was influenced by the work of philosopher and activist Cornel West (b.1953), whose *Prophecy Deliverance!* describes Christianity as 'a religion especially fitted to the oppressed. It looks at the world from the perspective of those below' and cites 'the fundamental role of economic structures and institutions in subjugating peoples and individuals'.[100] William J. Barber II (b.1963), a pastor and political activist, is another who has recognised the need to consider multiple indices of oppression, including the economic.

Barber has founded a new Poor People's Campaign in honour of the campaign founded by King and the SCLC.[101]

West, though insisting that he well understand Cone's anger at the outrages committed against African-Americans, has nevertheless criticised Cone's black theology and the black power movement in general, fearing that it serves to create division rather than reconciliation. 'Love breaks down barriers,' argues West, 'even when black rage and righteous indignation have to look white supremacy in the face [...] the language of love still allows black brothers and sisters to recognize that it's not all white people.'[102] Murray too was sympathetic to Cone, even while voicing her concern that his ideas led to a deepening of racial divisions rather than racial reconciliation: 'This emerging racial rhetoric smacked of an ethnic "party line" and made absolutely no sense to me. I was uncomfortable in any environment that was not inclusive.'[103] Barber, like Murray, calls for a recognition that there are different forms of oppression and different elements of individual identity, with the aim that these should lead to 'fusion' rather than division. He concludes: 'We must learn how our issues intersect in a comprehensive moral agenda that demands transformation of everyone.'[104]

Red-letter evangelicalism

It was at the end of the 1970s when evangelical Christians, disappointed in the administration of President Jimmy Carter, began to firm up the growing alliance between evangelicalism and the Republican Party. Viewing politics as 'a battleground between secular humanists and true believers', evangelical leaders came together as a Religious Right, determined to 'transform their movement into an influential voting bloc within the GOP'.[105] Organisations such as Jerry Falwell Sr's Moral Majority played a significant role in the election of Ronald Reagan in 1980 and – despite the lack of a constitutional amendment outlawing abortion and Reagan's appointment of the pro-choice Sandra Day O'Connor to the Supreme Court in 1981 – his re-election in 1984.[106] 'Evangelicals gave Reagan and the Republican Party even stronger support in 1984 than they had in 1980 [...] striking was the degree to which evangelicals had become loyal to the entire

Republican Party.'[107] There is the perception that the Christian Left disappeared at this stage, the tradition of Rauschenbusch, Debs, Horton and King obliterated by the marriage of evangelicalism and the American Right. This, however, is a mistake. The tradition once labelled the 'Moral Minority' is still active in American politics.[108] One key strand has been the evangelical movement known as red-letter Christianity.

Red-letter Christians tend to be evangelicals who repudiate the notion that evangelicalism must go hand-in-hand with conservative or right-wing politics, instead emphasising and seeking to reassert the tradition of the Christian Left. This tradition incorporates such strands as Christian Socialism, the Social Gospel, the Catholic Worker Movement, anti-abolitionism, the campaign for African-American civil rights, and liberation theology.[109] The term 'red-letter' is a reference to Bibles in which the words of Christ are printed in red, emphasising these evangelicals' desire to live out the commands and instructions of Jesus, as Tony Campolo explains: 'when we reflect on all Jesus had to say about caring for the poor and oppressed, committing ourselves to His red-letter message just might drive us to see what we can do politically to help those He called "the least of these"'.[110] Campolo (b.1935), a Baptist pastor and evangelist, is something of a father figure to the red-letter movement. In *Red Letter Christians* (2008) he denounces a false view of evangelicals as 'anti-gay, anti-feminist, anti-environmentalists, anti-gun-control, pro-war, right-wing ideologues', citing abolitionists such as Charles Finney as examples of a more progressive evangelical faith.[111] Yet Campolo places himself and his allies squarely within catholic and evangelical Christianity, citing a commitment to the historic creeds and confessions, an understanding of the Bible as 'an infallible guide for faith and practice', and a belief that it is possible for each individual to be saved by a personal encounter with Jesus Christ.[112] The only difference between red-letter Christians and other evangelicals is 'our passionate commitment to social justice'.[113]

Campolo is very much echoing Walter Rauschenbusch and W.D.P. Bliss when he criticises the church for having forgotten that the Gospel is both individual and social.[114] The message of Christ was the announcement that the Kingdom of God is at hand, a kingdom which represented a 'new social order' on earth, 'a new kind of society, wherein the effects of poverty and physical suffering would be no more'.[115] This announcement is itself the Gospel. Campolo's emphasis is on the biblical condemnation of economic injustice and oppression, such as that of Isaiah: 'Woe to those who decree iniquitous decrees, and the writers who keep writing oppression, to turn aside the needy from justice and to rob the poor of my people of their right.'[116] Considering the words of the Apostle James – 'Come now, you rich, weep and howl for the miseries that are coming upon you [...] Behold, the wages of the labourers who mowed your fields, which you kept back by fraud, are crying out against you' – Campolo argues:

> These verses are a warning against those who embrace laissez-faire capitalism without question and declare that workers should be paid whatever the market value of labor establishes. Those who pay wages determined solely by the law of supply and demand, leaving workers with an unfair share of the profits from their labor, will one day have to face God's judgement and answer for their injustices. Workers created in the image of God cannot be exploited.[117]

'We ought,' he concludes, 'to look for men and women who dare to point Americans away from our self-centred, consumeristic values so that we might be a light on a hill, modelling something of God's Kingdom here on earth.'[118]

Another passage emphasised by Campolo comes from the Gospel of Luke, where Christ in the words of Isaiah declares:

> The Spirit of the Lord is upon me,
>   because he has anointed me
>   to proclaim good news to the poor.
> He has sent me to proclaim liberty to the captives
>   and recovering of sight to the blind,
>   to set at liberty those who are oppressed,
> to proclaim the year of the Lord's favour.[119]

Campolo views this declaration as being of the new social order, the Kingdom of God upon earth.[120] This passage, with its emphasis on liberty from oppression, injustice and poverty, and its reference to the Old Testament Year of Jubilee in which debts would be forgiven and freedom restored, is a key one for the Christian Left. It is cited by Rauschenbusch, by John C. Cort and, as we have seen, by James Cone.[121] Lisa Sharon Harper views a renewed focus on this passage among evangelicals as 'the good news of

Christianity' – rather than, for example, John 3:16: 'For God so loved the world, that he gave his only Son, that whoever believes in him should not perish but have eternal life' – as the evidence that evangelicals are developing their understanding of the Gospel beyond simply individual salvation and towards a social understanding of the Kingdom of God.[122]

Harper (b.1969) is another prominent red-letter evangelical who gradually expanded her own understanding of the Gospel in this way. Evangelicals, Harper believes, are starting to see that the Gospel is not 'a limited message, focused exclusively on individual sin and salvation' but 'a vision of a transformed world, focused on the good news of the coming of the kingdom of God'.[123] This includes an emphasis on the year of jubilee, as described by Christ in Luke's Gospel, not as a future eschatological event but as an illustration of what society should be in the here and now. Harper rejects the neo-liberal capitalist system as irredeemable, for the 'premises upon which it stands are inherently in direct opposition to the purposes of God'.[124] The biblical worldview does not expect nor allow unrestricted, unlimited economic growth; rather, 'God imposes regulations on the business sector' in order to preserve 'the well-being of workers and the land [...] God's regulations limit exploitation and offer conditions conducive to flourishing'.[125] One key way this principle should be implemented is in a state-provided healthcare system as a means of ensuring full and equal access to healthcare for all people regardless of their financial situation.[126] Harper's view here is essentially a social democratic one, in which the economy must be regulated and managed to prevent exploitation and allow the state to provide social goods which the market either cannot or will not.

Harper is also committed to combating racial injustice, criticising Social Gospellers such as Rauschenbusch for remaining silent on racism and drawing on the legacy of civil rights activists such as Martin Luther King and John M. Perkins (b.1930), another evangelical who came to believe that '[s]ocial action fleshes out the Lordship of Christ'.[127] Perkins' three 'R's, in Harper's estimation, 'laid down key foundations for evangelical American understanding of social justice in the late twentieth century': 'relocation', in which Christians should be those who give up the comforts of privilege and draw near to the poor and oppressed, the opposite of the 'white flight' seen in the twentieth-century US; 'redistribution', meaning not just financial redistribution but that Christians must use all their resources – skills, abilities, contacts, platform – to create a more equitable society; and 'reconciliation', by which Christians of different racial and social-economic backgrounds should be neighbours to each other, taking the Good Samaritan as their example.[128]

Harper has been sharply critical of 'white evangelicals [who] don't believe in systemic oppression' and a Religious Right, which she argues has its origins in white supremacism and opposition to de-segregation. 'Evangelicalism,' she argues, 'has been hijacked by the religious right' to the extent that the church has become 'toxic'.[129] Yet red-letter Christians are among those evangelicals who 'understand it and we can offer a solution'. That solution – expressed most clearly in *The Very Good Gospel* (2016) – is a recognition that the Gospel requires a commitment to building *shalom*, a peace achieved when people and communities are in right relationships with each other, not separated by distrust, domination or exploitation.[130] While the Gospel of individual salvation has too often been neglected by liberal Christians, the message of God's Kingdom on earth bringing *shalom* has been forgotten by twentieth-century evangelicals.[131] The recovery of this message will loosen 'the death grip of the Religious Right's agenda on the soul of evangelical America' and bring about a day when 'vibrant peace will prevail between people and God, men and women, families, ethnic groups, nations, and humans and the rest of creation, and oppressive systems and structures will be transformed to serve humanity and help each person thrive'.[132]

Another key figure in the red-letter movement is Jim Wallis (b.1948), a pastor and founder of Sojourners, an evangelical ministry focusing on peace, justice and reconciliation. Wallis, originally from a Plymouth Brethren congregation, began radical activism at Trinity Evangelical Divinity School, arguing that 'the Christian response to our revolutionary age must be to stand and identify with the exploited and oppressed'.[133] This included opposition to the war in Vietnam and identification with the oppressed African-American community; indeed, Wallis stepped away from Christianity after an elder in his childhood church told him that Christianity had nothing to say about racism, because that was a political issue and the Gospel was solely personal. Wallis' response is to argue that 'God is personal, but never private.'[134] He criticises the Religious Right for focusing 'only on sexual and cultural issues while ignoring the weightier matters of justice' and calls for a return to 'a historic, biblical, and genuinely evangelical faith'.[135]

Like Harper – who previously worked for Sojourners – Wallis emphasises Christ's jubilee vision of liberation in Luke's Gospel.[136] 'Jubilee,' he explains, 'is a call for a regular "levelling" of things, necessary because of the human tendency towards overaccumulation by some while others lose ground.'[137] This then, in a manner similar to Harper and Campolo, is a social democratic vision of a market economy bounded and regulated in order to prevent oppression and injustice. While the Bible does not give a blueprint for what the economy must look like, it is clear that it must conform to biblical principles of fairness and justice in a manner which cannot be achieved under pure *laissez-faire* capitalism.[138]

> The entrepreneurial spirit and social innovation fostered by a market economy has benefited many and should not be overly encumbered by unnecessary or stifling regulations. But left to its own devices and human weakness (okay, let's call it sin), the market will too often disintegrate into greed and corruption [...] Capitalism needs rules, or it easily becomes destructive.[139]

Wallis appears to be describing what we might term a mixed economy, in which the benefits of free enterprise must not be diminished by excessive state ownership or regulation, but neither must Christians buy into the neo-liberal assumption that free economic decisions within an unguided, unbounded economy will by definition result in just outcomes. This, Wallis argues, applies as much to a global economy in which developing countries are often exploited by the wealthier and more powerful nations.[140]

Wallis remains committed to combating racial prejudice. Slavery, he argues, represents 'America's original sin', a sin that, even after slavery's abolition, ensures that African-Americans and other communities of colour have remained the victims of oppression.[141] Like Perkins and King, Wallis advocates a racial reconciliation based on biblical values, such as those expressed by the Apostle Paul in the Second Epistle to the Corinthians: 'The old has passed away; behold, the new has come. All this is from God, who through Christ reconciled us to himself and gave us the ministry of reconciliation.'[142] Responding to the death of George Floyd and the disproportionate impact of the COVID-19 pandemic on black, Latinx and indigenous communities, Wallis argues that race was the defining issue of the 2020 US presidential election, criticising the Religious Right for misusing issues such as abortion and religious freedom in order to drown out calls for racial and economic justice.[143] 'Until white Christians understand that loving their neighbors as themselves means fighting unrelentingly for justice for Black and brown people and dismantling the oppressive structures of white supremacy, white American Christian claims to understand the heart of the gospel ring exceedingly hollow.'[144] Christians must vote against racism, must 'treat racism as a political deal breaker for their support', instead of 'ignoring racial justice' in order to vote for candidates who cosy up to the evangelical Right.

Sojourners has been among a movement of evangelicals which, in the United States and elsewhere, has sought to prioritise ecological issues and take action against climate change. Wallis has argued that a focus on 'creation care', as well as persuading Christians to take seriously the need to preserve the environment and achieve justice for those communities most affected by climate change, is a means of shifting the agenda away from those issues touted by the Religious Right as those about which Christians should be exclusively concerned. Wallis has also taken the view that, as with economic justice, individual action alone is insufficient; rather, governments must take action to avert ecological disaster.[145] It was the historian Lynn White, Jr, who argued in his 1967 article 'The Historical Roots of Our Ecological Crisis' that Christianity is 'the most anthropocentric religion the world has seen', viewing in contrast to other religions the environment as something to be exploited, and that therefore Christianity could only lead to further environmental damage.[146] Several Christian groups and individuals have recognised an element of truth to this critique – such as the Sri Lankan liberation theologian Tissa Balasuriya, who attributed the problem to the Western-centrism of Christianity (see Chapter 7) – and sought to develop a theology of creation care. Among these has been Anglican theologian Sallie McFague (1933–2019), Lutheran theologian H. Paul Santmire (b.1936), co-directors of the Forum on Religion and Ecology at Yale University John Allen Grim (b.1946) and his wife Mary Evelyn Tucker (b.1950), and Roman Catholic feminist Rosemary Radford Ruether (see Chapter 7).[147]

Among Protestants – especially those in the US – concern for the environment appears in three broad, possibly overlapping, strands. The first of these is an emphasis on stewardship, linked to a biblical mandate to care for God's creation. This is most appealing to evangelicals who are theologically conservative but nevertheless reject a fundamentalist disregard for creation.[148] Secondly, mainline churches, including those with a prior commitment to the Social Gospel or similar Christian Left positions, are more likely to emphasise 'eco-justice' as part of a broader conception of social justice. Sociologist Laurel Kearns explains that 'eco-justice advocates assert that being in right relation to each other is part of being in right relation to the natural world'.[149] Finally, what Kearns refers to as 'creation spirituality' draws on non-Christian, panentheistic spiritualities in common with the broader ecologist movement.[150] The fear of panentheism and New Age ideas, along with a concern that the ecological focus on population reduction may undermine a pro-life position, has perhaps prevented wider acceptance among evangelicals of the need to protect the environment. Christian concern for the environment does, though, go far beyond evangelicalism, as demonstrated by Pope Francis' 2015 encyclical *Laudato si'* (see Chapter 3) and the 2008 publication of the 'Green Bible' – a New Revised Standard Version text printed on recycled paper with verses relevant to creation care highlighted in green – endorsed by Desmond Tutu (see Chapter 7) and Pope John-Paul II.

It should be noted that Wallis disavows the label Christian Left, arguing that a politics based on biblical values should not be tied to either end of the ideological spectrum. 'I think Left and Right are political categories and not religious ones', he argues. 'Religion doesn't fit those categories of Left and Right [...] We're not a Religious Left to counter a Religious Right, but rather a moral center, often challenging the selective moralities of both the Right and the Left.'[151] Campolo takes the same view – that a biblical political worldview will not be aligned to one ideology or one political party.[152] Indeed, red-letter evangelicalism does at times appear to lean conservative on issues of medical and sexual ethics. This appears most clearly when it comes to abortion, with the red-letter Christians – in a similar manner to the Catholic Worker Movement – taking a 'pro-life' or anti-abortion stance.[153] Harper argues that 'to abort a pregnancy is an affront against

God', while for Campolo 'the issue comes down to whether or not a human fetus is a sacred human being created in God's image. If the answer to that question is yes, then abortion must be regarded as murder.'[154] Campolo's reference here to 'God's image' demonstrates that the same reasoning behind opposition to racism – that, as Wallis puts it, racial prejudice is an affront to 'the image of God – *imago dei*' – is behind the opposition to abortion.[155]

Both Wallis and Campolo draw on the idea of a 'seamless garment' developed by Roman Catholic Cardinal Joseph Bernardin, a position that can also be termed 'consistent pro-life'[156] The argument here is that there should be more to a biblical understanding of the importance of life; as Campolo argues, a pro-life commitment 'requires that there be commitments to stop wars, end capital punishment and provide universal healthcare for all our citizens – in addition to stopping abortions'.[157] On this interpretation Christians who oppose abortion but do nothing to prevent racist violence, ensure state provision of social goods such as healthcare and welfare, or combat the life-limiting effects of climate change and ecological damage might be regarded as hypocritical. At the same time, Wallis criticises 'a left-wing political correctness, which now includes a rigid litmus test of being pro-choice on abortion' and does not allow for those who are opposed to abortion, while nevertheless being committed to social justice. Despite this, it has been argued that criticism of the conservative positions adopted by Sojourners and by red-letter evangelicalism in general comes not from the secular Left as Wallis alleges, but from more radical Christians of the Left.[158] In addition, conservative Christians might make the argument that the 'seamless garment' or 'consistent pro-life' position is something of a dodge, allowing red-letter evangelicals to adopt the pro-life label, while de-emphasising the issue of abortion. It does seem as though, while the answer to issues of economic injustice, racial oppression and environmental damage is always for the federal government to do more, a policy of making abortion illegal is always beyond the pale.

The Christian response to the Religious Right goes far beyond the red-letter movement. John Lewis (1940–2020), noted above as a key figure within the SNCC, was a determined fighter for racial justice. At the Washington Rally of 1963 he declared to the crowd of protestors: 'By the force of our demands, our determination and our numbers, we shall splinter the segregated South into a thousand pieces and put them together in the image of God and democracy.'[159] Lewis went on to serve as the Democratic representative for Georgia's fifth district from 1987 until his death, bringing a Bible-based sense of justice to his tenure in Congress. Lewis, for example, opposed the 1996 welfare reforms passed by the Clinton administration, which had their origins in Republican Party policy, asking rhetorically: 'Where is the sense of decency? What does it profit a great nation to conquer the world, only to lose its soul?'[160]

Another major figure from the civil rights movement to enter mainstream politics was Jesse Jackson (b.1940), the head of the SCLC's Operation Breadbasket, a campaign to improve the economic circumstances of impoverished black communities, who was ordained a Baptist minister in 1968. Jackson ran twice in the Democratic presidential primaries, in 1984 and 1988, on a platform far more progressive than any other Democratic candidate.[161] The Jackson campaign drew inspiration from the Mississippi Freedom Democrats movement of Fannie Lou Hamer, yet Jackson's aim in forming what would become known as the Rainbow Coalition was also to show that he represented not just African-American interests but the interests of all marginalised and oppressed peoples, in a similar manner to Martin Luther King's Poor People's Campaign in which Jackson had also played a key role.[162] In a campaign speech Jackson declared: 'Our flag is red, white, and blue, but our nation is a rainbow – red, yellow, brown, black, and white – and we are all precious in God's sight.'[163] Later he reflected:

> Most poor people are not black or brown; they are white, female and young, and unspoken for. If whites begin to vote their economic interests and not racial fears, and blacks vote their hopes and not despair, we can change America. We have the numbers and the need; if we have the will, we can win.[164]

Jackson's campaign provided a left-wing alternative for those within the Democratic Party who eschewed the neo-liberal policies that were in the ascendancy during the Ronald Reagan years and opposed those Democrats who wanted their party to accept *laissez-faire* Reaganomics.[165] Ultimately, Jackson did not win the nomination – and, arguably, a more pro-free market approach triumphed in the Democratic Party with the presidency of Bill Clinton, whose Third Way philosophy pre-empted that of Tony Blair (see Chapter 2) – but the campaigns did help to preserve a left-wing current within the Democratic Party, which has arguably come to fruition in the ongoing revival of 'democratic socialism' within the party.

When Bernie Sanders came to speak at Liberty University – the university of Jerry Falwell, Jr, a staunch supporter of Donald Trump – he set out a vision of social justice based on the words of Amos, 'let judgment run down as waters, and righteousness as a mighty stream', adding that this was not possible 'in a nation and in a world which worships not love of brothers and sisters, not love of the poor and the sick, but worships the acquisition of money and great wealth'.[166] Sanders' speech caused one pastor and Liberty graduate to endorse the senator for president, for Sanders 'declares justice for the poor. He declares Good News for "the least of these". He has come to bring Gospel.'[167] One of Sanders' allies, Alexandria Ocasio-Cortez (b.1989), is herself a representative of the Christian Left, drawing her political vision including the Green New Deal from her Roman Catholic faith and declaring in the House of Representatives that 'if Christ himself walked through these doors and said what he said thousands of years ago – that we should love our neighbor and our enemy, that we should welcome the stranger, fight for the least of us, that it is easier for a camel to go through the eye of a needle than for a rich man to get into a kingdom of heaven – he would be maligned as a radical and ejected from these doors'.[168] Raphael Warnock (b.1969), a Democrat elected the first black senator from Georgia in January 2021, is the pastor of Ebenezer Baptist Church in Atlanta, the church pastored by Martin Luther King from 1960 until his death in 1968.[169] The ecumenical Institute for Christian Socialism was founded in December 2019 in order to 'support US churches, their members, and institutions in confronting the world's captivity to capitalism and in claiming, embodying, and promoting the radical socialism of the Christian faith and life'.[170] The US Christian Left – the tradition of Rauschenbusch and Bliss, Debs and Wallace, King and Cone – is still active today.

Conclusion

In the latter part of the twentieth century the Christian Left has taken on a number of different forms, ranging from the civil rights and racial reconciliation sought by Martin Luther King and the Southern Christian Leadership Conference, to the 'black power' liberation theology of James H. Cone, to the red-letter Christianity movement which allows space for social conservatism, while advocating for economic, racial and environmental justice. There are differences and disagreements: King's 'soul force' strategy is antithetical to Cone's willingness to turn to physical force; Pauli Murray's feminism was not shared by either the civil rights or black power movements, which failed to see the importance of combating sexism and misogyny; the social conservatism and moderate economic vision of Tony Campolo and Jim Wallis falls short of that advocated by more radical Christians, including the Institute for Christian Socialism. Yet there remains a consistent emphasis on the Kingdom of God, whether expressed using the language of liberty, justice or *shalom*, and an understanding that the Gospel must bring social reconciliation and harmony rather than being restricted to a message of individual sin and salvation.

6

Preferential Option for the Poor: Liberation Theology in Latin America

In 1970, in a highly controversial speech, the Bishop of Cuernavaca, Mexico, Sergio Méndez Arceo (1907–92), declared: 'Only socialism can enable Latin America to achieve true development [...] I believe that a socialist system is more in accord with the Christian principles of true brotherhood, justice and peace [...] for myself, I believe it should be a democratic socialism'.[1] Nicknamed 'The Red Bishop', Arceo was a supporter of liberation theology, a variant of the Christian Left which developed in Latin America in the 1960s and 1970s. His words demonstrate for us that liberation theology is a commitment to 'true development' rather than development along capitalist lines; that liberation requires 'a socialist system'; and that liberation theology is drawn out of an interpretation of 'Christian principles'. Liberation theology is not exactly the same as the Christian Socialism of Britain, the religious socialism of Europe, or the Social Gospel of the United States – but here we can see an undeniable link between these varieties of the Christian Left.

Liberation theology, as we shall see, emerged in a particular context: as an attempt to apply Catholic social teaching and the declarations of Vatican II to the Latin American situation; as a means of overcoming the dependence of Latin American nations on the former colonial powers which now represented the centre of globalised capitalism; and as a critique of the programme of development that assumed colonial, capitalist values and perpetuated the dependence of Third World communities. Out of this context emerged the Medellín conference of 1968 and the work of Gustavo Gutiérrez, as well as many other liberationist thinkers and theologians. Base Ecclesial Communities – small groups of Christians encouraged to act, think and reflect for themselves – provided a real link between the theological thinking of the clergy and the needs and desires of the impoverished. These communities were a genuine expression of liberation theology's commitment to the preferential option for the poor, its methodology of developing truth out of the perspective of the oppressed, and its focus on action or 'praxis' which precedes rather than emerges out of reflection and theory. Liberation theology provided a radical critique of capitalism and argued forcefully for the need for radical change. In drawing on the Bible, church teaching and sacraments, focusing on brotherhood as a key concept, and emphasising the Kingdom of God as something to be sought in the political and economic structures of society, liberation theology shares much in common with other strands of the Christian Left.

Theological, cultural and political context

As with other strands of the Christian Left – indeed, of all political ideologies – elements of liberation theology can be identified long before the advent of the movement itself. One figure who serves as a precursor of liberationist thought is Bartolomé de Las Casas (1484–1566), whom Gustavo Gutiérrez refers to as 'a prophetic forerunner of the church's radical "option for the poor"'.[2] Las Casas spoke out against the mistreatment and oppression of the indigenous population of the Americas during the early colonialism of the *conquistador* era, arguing that Christ identified with the subjugated native peoples rather than with the European Christian invaders.[3] Las Casas was in 1516 granted the title 'Defender of the Indians', and in his *A Short Account of the Destruction of the Indies* (written in 1542 and published 1552) he sought to fulfil this role by appealing to Prince Philip II of Spain on behalf of the indigenous people who found themselves under Spanish rule. Modern critics, however, while acknowledging that Las Casas did much to protect the indigenous Americans from violence and bloodshed, argue that he remained complicit in the imposition of alien European culture and values – 'complicit', says one, 'in cultural genocide, extinguishing and substituting indigenous culture with European centered value systems'.[4] It would await the full emergence of liberation theology for European – latterly, North American – norms to be repudiated in an attempt to develop a contextualised Latin American approach to combating oppression.

There are three key elements to the mid-twentieth-century context in which liberation theology emerged: (1) the ideas of the Second Vatican Council, 1962–5, and the broader sweep of Catholic social teaching; (2) dependence theory; (3) developmentalism.[5] The overwhelming majority of liberationists were Roman Catholics, with some exceptions, such as the Argentine Methodist minister José Miguez Bonino (1924–2012), who called liberation theology 'the response of a generation of young Catholics and evangelicals to the call of the Holy Spirit for a renewed spiritual, ethical and social commitment to the poor'.[6] The Second Vatican Council – also known as Vatican II – led to a change in focus from otherworldly salvation to human flourishing in the here and now, as well as creating an atmosphere in which the proper role of the church became a matter for open discussion.[7] The council 'called the Church to identify with the hope, joy, grief, and trials of humanity'.[8] These emphases reflect those of Pope Paul VI, who oversaw the conclusion of Vatican II, and his predecessor Pope John XXIII who had opened the council, as well as the overarching themes of Catholic social teaching (see Chapter 3), which as far back as Pope Leo XIII's *Rerum novarum* (1891) had imbued Catholic social teaching with an understanding of the oppression resulting from the exploitation of labour as well as a concern for the restoration of justice. These themes flowed into liberation theology.[9]

Yet liberation theology would grow to be more radical than Catholic social teaching, which, as we have seen, offers a critique of capitalism without necessarily endorsing socialism as an alternative; indeed, in some interpretations socialism and communism are condemned, while capitalism is merely chided. Where Catholic social teaching implied reform, liberation theology would stipulate structural and systemic – indeed, revolutionary – change. An illustration of this is that Christian Democracy, that political ideological manifestation of Catholic social teaching which at one time was viewed in Latin America as an alternative to free-market capitalism, came to be seen as allied to that very system. The Federation of Christian

Peasants in El Salvador is just one example of a group that began aligned to Christian Democracy, only to jettison that ideological alignment in favour of liberation theology.[10] Similarly, in Chile, where Salvador Allende and the Popular Unity left-wing coalition came to power, there developed a 'Christians for Socialism' movement of which some members were former Christian Democrats.[11] Nevertheless, the Medellín conference of 1968 – to which we shall return – can be viewed as the Latin American church's 'ratification' of Vatican II and Catholic social teaching.[12] Medellín represented 'a contextualized reception of Vatican II, and thereby gave substance to what had previously been marginal concepts: the church of the poor, and a church committed to the liberation and full flourishing of the needy and the abandoned'.[13]

The sociological theory of dependence is the second element in the emergence of liberation theology. Dependence theory held that countries of the global centre – most obviously the United States, as well as others of the European and Anglophone worlds – had created an international division of labour in which it was the role of peripheral regions such as Latin America to produce raw materials and agricultural products for export rather than producing what was needed by their own people. This situation resulted in peripheral states being forced into dependence, for the 'Third World countries cannot develop autonomously in accordance with their own needs; they are dependent on decisions taken elsewhere'.[14] In such circumstances the peoples of Latin America remained colonised – albeit in supposedly free-market rather than feudal conditions – by both the old European powers of empire and the new US power behind global capitalism. Dependence came as a result of the global division of labour but was rooted in the colonial past, a kind of learned helplessness, which had taken hold over the centuries.[15] 'Oppression is institutionalized to maintain the privileged position of the so-called developed.'[16] Yet the response of these peripheral countries, including those of Latin America, was too often a commitment to developmentalism; 'virtually all the countries of the ex-colonial or dependent part of the globe [...] were committed to economic independence and "development".'[17] The critique of this 'developmentalism' provides the third element in the emergence of liberation theology.

A key flaw of developmentalism was that it did little to consider the needs and desires of the people themselves. As long as trade increased, production became more efficient, and GDP per capita went up (notwithstanding awkward questions about distribution), Third World countries were considered to be developing successfully. Yet the proponents of liberation theology argued that despite improvements in economic metrics the people remained impoverished and oppressed. Furthermore, the focus on economic development required that countries of the global periphery remain part of the capitalist system that had perpetuated the dependence of them and their people. They must continue to provide for the needs of the global centre, to build an economy based on production for export rather than production for use – to remain, in short, colonised and dominated by alien economic forces.[18] Developmentalism was, says one writer, 'modernity with a colonial face'.[19] Among those who favoured developmentalism were both social democratic and Christian Democratic parties, such as those in Brazil, a fact that contributed to the rejection of centre-Left and Christian Democrat politics and the reinterpretation of Catholic social teaching into something more radical, more revolutionary.

Liberation theology emerged in part as an alternative response to the problem of dependence. The answer could not be capitalist development – more of the same – but a genuine liberation from the economic and political forces of oppression. Hugo Assmann (1933–2008), the Brazilian Catholic theologian, argued that most countries undergoing 'development' under the auspices of capitalism 'are being kept undeveloped; they are not in reality "developing" countries but rather countries that find themselves on a path that is not at all progressive; rather, it is increasingly regressive. We must not let ourselves be deceived by phony progress.'[20] Assmann's answer was a revolution, which would lead communities into real development and liberate them from dependence. Manuel Larraín Errázuriz (1900–66), a Chilean bishop, set out an alternative vision of developmentalism in *Development: Success or Failure in Latin America?* (1965). True development, he said, should 'respond to the threefold hunger – physical, cultural, and spiritual – that torments both individual persons and modern society. It is a question not only of having more but of being more [...] The flourishing of each and every individual is what gives development its true purpose and meaning.'[21] Pope Paul VI concurred, writing in his 1967 encyclical *Populorum progressio* that 'development which is good and genuine does not consist in wealth that is self-centred and sought for its own sake, but rather in an economy which is put at the service of humankind, the daily bread which is distributed to all, as a source of brotherhood and a sign of Providence'.[22]

Foundations of liberation theology

It was the Second General Conference of Latin American Bishops – convened with the blessing of Pope Paul VI – in Medellín, Colombia, in 1968 that drew these currents and ideas together into the beginning of a coherent response to the problems of Latin America and the need for liberation. Those who attended declared that the 'Latin American bishops cannot remain indifferent in the face of the tremendous social injustices existent in Latin America, which keep the majority of our people in dismal poverty, which in many cases becomes inhuman wretchedness.'[23] Medellín described 'liberation' as an act of 'genuine development', and called for a 'transition from less human to more human conditions for each and every person' in a movement similar to the Exodus liberation of the Israelites from slavery.[24] In statements such as this Medellín broadened an understanding of the Gospel beyond personal holiness or individual salvation to include transformation for the poor and oppressed, itself a Vatican II emphasis.[25] The bishops declared: 'It is the same God who, in the fullness of time, sends his Son in the flesh so that He might come to liberate all men from the slavery to which sin has subjected them: hunger, misery, oppression, and ignorance, in a word, that injustice and hatred which have their origin in human selfishness.'[26]

The church's evangelical mission was no longer to win converts, but to aid in bringing salvation from the oppressive and brutal conditions to which the children of God were subjected by unfettered economic forces. The bishops therefore committed themselves to 'defending, according to the Gospel mandate, the rights of the poor and the oppressed'.[27] The Brazilian cardinal Avelar Brandão Vilela (1912–86) and Argentine cardinal Eduardo Francisco Pironio (1920–98) explained in their introduction to the published papers of Medellín that:

salvation – offered by the Church as sign and instrument – requires that human beings be totally liberated from the slavery of sin and its consequences (ignorance, oppression, poverty, hunger, and death) and incorporated into a new life by means of grace, the principle and kernel of eternity. The Kingdom of God is already present among us, and it is moving forward, intimately entwined with human progress, toward the consummate eschatological fullness.[28]

Vilela and Pironio here set out unequivocally that salvation has a social aspect and that society must progress in likeness to the Kingdom of God. These themes, including Cardinal Pironio's view that 'the Christian message of love and justice shows its effectiveness through action for justice in the world', were reiterated in the apostolic exhortation *Evangelii nuntiandi* published by Pope Paul VI in 1975.[29]

Among the most influential figures at Medellín was Peruvian theologian Gustavo Gutiérrez (b.1928), who helped to draft a key chapter among the published documents, which condemned institutionalised violence against the poor.[30] Three years after the conference Gutiérrez published *A Theology of Liberation*, a full exploration of liberation theology's contextualised, experience-based approach to the economic and political issues faced by Latin America. This would quickly become a key text of the movement. Gutiérrez is clear in his denunciation of developmentalism, arguing that the attempt to seek economic and social development through the capitalist system caused the Latin American countries to adopt an oppressive capitalist perspective. Those nations seeking development on the terms of the global centre were forced to accept 'the political structures of domination', allowing themselves to remain 'dependent' on the so-called developed world. Under developmentalism, therefore, Latin America remained 'a dominated and oppressed continent'.[31] As such, developmentalism had no adequate response to the 'untenable circumstances of poverty, alienation, and exploitation in which the greater part of the people of Latin America live', which instead 'urgently demand that we find a path toward economic, social, and political liberation'.[32]

Gutiérrez equated this liberation with salvation. Sin is 'the ultimate cause of poverty, injustice, and the oppression in which men live', and therefore the biblical concept of salvation from sin includes freedom from these degrading consequences of sin.[33]

This perspective came in part because theologians were rejecting the exclusivity of salvation, adopting instead a universalism that denied that humanity was divided into saved and unsaved, or that salvation belonged to one faith or to one church. Universal reconciliation to God was, in this view, an established fact. Priests and theologians who adopted such a view began to see their role not as freeing individuals from personal culpability for sin – there was no need – but instead freeing them from the sinful circumstances that oppressed so many.[34] Because salvation is universal, Gutiérrez argued, it is not the purpose of the church to convert people into Christians; therefore, 'the Church must cease considering itself as the exclusive place of salvation and orient itself towards a new and radical service of people'.[35]

The church, however, had thus far focused too much on an individualistic, personal understanding of salvation, neglecting that the Gospel called for liberation and that therefore the Gospel has a political dimension.[36] Realising this, the church must move beyond its idea of individual redemption to embrace a fuller concept of 'liberation from all that limits or keeps man from self-fulfilment, liberation from all impediments to the exercise of his freedom'.[37] In Latin America this was already beginning to happen – Gutiérrez quotes from the Peruvian Episcopal Conference of 1969: 'We recognise that we Christians for want of fidelity to the Gospel have contributed to the present unjust situation through our words and attitudes, our silence and inaction.'[38] This perspective, maintains Gutiérrez, is not a theological novelty but the very Gospel itself:

> In the Bible, Christ is presented as the one who brings us liberation. Christ the Savior liberates man from sin, which is the ultimate root of all disruption of friendship and of all injustice and oppression. Christ makes man truly free, that is to say, he enables man to live in communion with him; and this is the basis for all human brotherhood.[39]

This is a Gospel in which salvation encompasses 'the whole man' – man in society, man in relationship with those around him. Sin breaks communion with God and between men in the here and now; salvation therefore cannot be something just 'otherworldly, in regard to which the present life is merely a test', but must incorporate radical, liberative changes, which will banish oppression and repair the broken vertical relationship between God and men as well as the broken horizontal relationship among men.[40] 'Sin demands a radical liberation, which in turn necessarily implies a political liberation.'[41]

This radical liberation, argues Gutiérrez, cannot be achieved through mere reform to the existing system – whether the phony reform promised by capitalistic developmentalism or any other sincere but flawed approaches proffered by social democracy or Christian Democracy. Liberation requires 'a social revolution', for oppression is 'rooted in the structures of capitalist society'.[42] This mention of a social revolution to overcome the structural wickedness of capitalism necessarily implies a socialist alternative. Gutiérrez does not go into detail about what any alternative society would look like, but it is clear that it would be a form of socialism, which for Gutiérrez 'represents the most fruitful and far-reaching approach' to liberation.[43] Society, at present 'structured to benefit a few who appropriate to themselves the value of the work of others', must be transformed so as to collectivise the means of production and ensure that the worker receives the value he creates.[44] This, however, must be an indigenous Latin American theory of socialism rather than a slavish adherence to Marxism or any other imported doctrine. The problems of Latin America required solutions tailored to the needs of that continent; the oppressed of Latin America must be the agents of their own liberation.[45]

This position represents the commitment of Gutiérrez, and of liberation theology in general, to a contextualised approach to resolving the problem of oppression, rather than the application of predigested theories, especially those originating from outside Latin America. Liberation, in whatever form it takes, 'must be undertaken by the oppressed people themselves and so must stem from the values proper to these people'.[46] Revolutionary change, says Gutiérrez, 'requires the active participation of the oppressed', a position that automatically rejects the vanguardism of Marxism–Leninism and the high-handed paternalism which at times characterised Catholic social teaching.[47] 'The whole climate of the Gospel is a continual demand for the right of the poor to make themselves heard, to be considered preferentially by society, a demand to subordinate economic needs to those of the deprived.'[48]

Key concepts of liberation theology

The bishops at Medellín and Gutiérrez in *A Theology of Liberation* therefore fashioned a new and distinct approach drawn from the context of Vatican II and Catholic social teaching, the theory of dependence, and a critique of developmentalism for perpetuating dependence. That approach contains a number of key concepts, among them: the preferential option for the poor; the experience of oppressed peoples as the necessary context for understanding of what is true and right; action, or 'praxis', as the basis for theology rather than the other way round; capitalism as a form of idolatry; revolution or radical change as a necessary step in order to achieve liberation. These concepts represent melding together of the theological (scripture, Catholic social teaching), the political (Marxist) and the experiential (the lived experience of the poverty-stricken).

It was at Medellín that the bishops affirmed what was to become perhaps liberation theology's best-known concept, the 'preferential option for the poor'.[49] This, explains Gutiérrez, 'means solidarity with the poor and rejection of poverty as something contrary to the will of God', and he has also described it as 'the option for the oppressed'.[50] Although it was only with the emergence of liberation theology that this concept rose to prominence, we have seen (Chapter 3) that it was present in Catholic social teaching as early as *Rerum novarum*, Pope Leo XIII declaring: 'Still when there is a question of protecting the rights of individuals, the poor and helpless have a claim to special consideration.'[51] The option for the poor, says Gutiérrez, is something demonstrated by God – throughout scripture, but most clearly in Christ – which is then imitated by his people; Christians must 'take sides' with 'the poor and oppressed', as did God in the Old Testament and Jesus Christ in the Gospels.[52] 'Entering history and standing in solidarity with the oppressed means that God takes sides over and against the rich and powerful, not because the marginalized are somewhat holier, but because they are oppressed. God makes a preferential option for the poor and oppressed, over and against the pharaohs of this world.'[53]

A key section of the Bible for liberationists is the Exodus, which represents God's identification of himself with the oppressed and the liberating power of his message: 'Yahweh is the Liberator', says

Gutiérrez.[54] 'The Exodus,' says former priest Phillip Berryman (b.1938), is 'not simply an event but a pattern of deliverance that provides a key for interpreting the Scriptures and for interpreting present experience.'[55] Gutiérrez argues that the laws given to Israel relating to proper use of land and social justice reflect this same pattern. The prohibition of usury, the command not to reap a field to the very edge to allow the landless poor a portion of the harvest, the cancellation of debts at the year of jubilee – these were given because the Israelites had been liberated from slavery and must not be allowed to fall back into it.[56] The denunciations by prophets such as Amos, Micah and Isaiah again follow the same pattern, for they call Israel back to these laws and seek to sustain and renew liberation.[57] This pattern is fulfilled in Christ, who appeared in poverty in order to proclaim 'liberty to the captives' as recorded in the synagogue sermon of Luke 4:16–20. 'Latin Americans see this as a kind of manifesto', explains Berryman. 'Jesus is saying that the age of liberation foretold by the prophets is present in him.'[58] The teaching of Christ, says Gutiérrez, proclaims both 'a head-on opposition to the rich and powerful and a radical option for the poor'.[59] This, argues Cardinal Pironio, demonstrates that 'in salvation history the divine work is an action of integral liberation'.[60]

It also demonstrates that God's people should commit themselves to the work of liberation. The church, says Gutiérrez, must take sides in a society divided between the victims and the beneficiaries of economic oppression.[61] 'To know Yahweh, which in biblical language is equivalent to saying to love Yahweh, is to establish just relationships among men, it is to recognize the rights of the poor,' argues Gutiérrez, and '[t]o be converted is to commit oneself to the process of the liberation of the poor and oppressed.'[62] God's revelation, it is argued, shows us that poverty is not a natural or a legitimate phenomenon, but one which results from human sin and selfishness; 'poverty', says Gutiérrez, 'is a scandalous condition inimical to human dignity and therefore contrary to the will of God'.[63] This view was reiterated by a 1979 conference of Latin American bishops in Puebla, Mexico, which declared: 'We see the growing gap between rich and poor as a scandal and a contradiction to Christian existence.'[64] If proof were needed for this perspective on poverty, the judgement of the sheep and the goats in Matthew 25 seems to suggest, in Berryman's words, that 'practical material aid for one's neighbour is the criterion of a just life'. The criterion is not being a Christian – 'one might even be an atheist' – but whether you have helped and provided for the poor and sought to liberate the oppressed.[65]

In liberation theology the experience of oppressed peoples is the necessary context for understanding what is true and right, for 'the experience of poverty and oppression [...] is as important a text as the text of Scripture itself'.[66] For some liberationists, 'the vantage point of the poor is particularly, and especially, the vantage point of the crucified God and can act as a criterion for theological reflection, biblical exegesis, and the life of the Church'.[67] The Dutch theologian Carlos Mesters (b.1931) explains that, when interpreting the Bible, 'the emphasis is not placed on the text's meaning in itself but rather on the meaning the text has for the people reading it [...] the common people are putting the Bible in its proper place, the place where God intended it to be. They are putting it in second place. Life takes first place!'[68] This is because theological truth is not absolute but subjective; it emerges in a particular context and cannot claim to be universally useful or universally applicable. Latin American clergy began to view the theology they had learned in seminary as being not universal but a theology of the first world, which did not serve the needs of communities at the dependent global periphery.[69] All varieties of liberation theology 'represent reactions against a European and North American theological establishment that unconsciously assumed that its theology was simply "Christian" theology'.[70] The 'history of Christianity,' says Gutiérrez, 'has been written by a white, western, bourgeois hand' which excludes the experiences and perspectives of 'all the poor, the victims of the masters of this world.'[71]

One example of this, Gutiérrez explains, concerns the 'problem' that prompts the development of new theological reflection. Post-enlightenment theology has to do with responding to the challenge raised by unbelief, working out ways in which Christian theology might respond to the growth of scepticism and rationalism.[72] A theology worked out in this context is clearly not relevant to Latin America, argues Gutiérrez, as a majority of people remain committed to Christianity.[73] The problem of Latin America is not that of unbelief, but that of the 'non-person' – one who has been robbed of their humanity, their dignity as an image-bearer, by

poverty and oppression. 'The question we face, therefore, is not
so much how to talk of God in a world come of age, but how to
proclaim God as Father in an inhuman world? How do we tell the
"non-persons" that they are the sons and daughters of God?'[74]
This is the context in which a theology suited to the needs of Latin
America must be developed.

Connected to this view of contextual theology is that theology
must emerge from action, or 'praxis', rather than being worked
out in the abstract prior to any action. 'Theology *follows*', says
Gutiérrez; 'it is the second step'.[75] Action comes first, then reflection; this combination of action with reflection is the source of
theology. This again is different from traditional or 'Western'
theology, in which the theological system is developed first in
order to provide a basis for practice, whether the practice of the
church or the life of the individual believer. A key setting for this
theological reflection, which emerges from praxis, is the Base
Ecclesial Community (BEC, otherwise known as a Christian Base
community or Church Base Community). These are 'small lay-led
communities, motivated by Christian faith, that see themselves as
part of the church and that are committed to working together to
improve their communities and to establish a more just society'.[76]

The significance of BECs was affirmed at Medellín, but they
began to develop years earlier, beginning at first in Brazil as a
means for parishioners to hold a service – referred to as a 'priest-
less mass' – when an ordained minister was not able to preside.[77]
The BEC meeting was originally highly constrained – a lay reader
would deliver only homilies that were prepared and approved
by diocesan authorities – yet these groups became places where
Christians could come together to commit themselves to action
and develop ideas through reflection on that action.[78] They also
provided a format in which people were given the opportunity
through reflection and discussion to synthesise their experience of
oppression and poverty with scripture or church teaching, linking
with liberation theology's option for the poor and commitment to
contextualised theology.[79] Indeed, it has been argued that it is only
through BECs

> that Latin American liberation theology was fully enabled to root
> itself within the lived experiences of the masses at the base. Without
> this praxiological grounding, liberation theology would neither

have been able to articulate the sufferings of the poor, nor been allowed to claim the representative status upon which so much of its credibility continues to rest.[80]

These communities were also vital to the clergy who engaged with them, for in interacting more closely with the poor they began to realise that poverty was a result of oppression rather than the will of God.[81] BECs became an important source of praxis to support oppressed communities – for example, members may be involved in direct action against unjust employers or landowners – and they could also result in radicalisation – in Nicaragua, for example, the Sandinistas would recruit from the BECs.[82] This role became especially important in Brazil during the years of military dictatorship, and in the Latin American countries that fell under military rule in the 1970s, including Chile, Bolivia, Uruguay and Argentina.[83]

A key part of liberation theology's critique was that the capitalist system represented a form of idolatry. Proponents of this theory include the German theologian Franz Josef Hinkelammert (b.1931) and Hugo Assmann. Both Hinkelammert and Assmann draw on the Marxist concept of commodity fetishism, in which objects that have little or no intrinsic value are fetishised and worshipped in the manner of pagan deities for their exchange value; such worship is a form of false consciousness generated by the capitalist system. These commodities become as gods, before which human beings must sacrifice and obey, while capital itself takes on the role of a capricious deity.[84] This view links to the Old Testament denunciation of gods – idols – who enslave their people and are linked to power and oppression. By contrast the living God chooses a nation of slaves to liberate from captivity. The 'gods' expect rituals and sacrifice – even human sacrifice; God, by contrast, demands justice and love.[85] Hinkelammert in particular draws upon the Latin American conception of God as the God of Life in order to characterise liberation as a 'theology of life' in sharp contrast to capitalism as a 'theology of death'.[86] Linking back to the arguments of Gutiérrez regarding contextual theology, this idolatry is another 'problem' in which theology must develop.[87]

This critique of capitalism demonstrates the radicalism at the heart of liberation theology. It was not enough to provide charity or make some superficial alterations to the system; the system itself

needed to be changed. The classic expression of this is the apho-
rism of Brazilian Archbishop Dom Hélder Câmara (1909–99):
'When I give food to the poor, they call me a saint. When I ask
why the poor have no food, they call me a communist.'[88] Less
famously but just as straightforwardly, Câmara also argued that
'superficial, perfunctory reform will simply not be sufficient [...]
What is needed is a structural revolution.'[89] The same emphasis is
found in the *Manifesto of the Third World Bishops*, which argued
that where the system itself produces poverty and injustice, the
church must not only call for reform but must withdraw from
a system which is opposed to the will of God.[90] Richard Shaull
(1919–2002), a Presbyterian missionary and among the rare
Protestant contributors to the liberation theology of Latin America,
held that 'it became undeniable that the causes of poverty were
structural and would require basic structural changes'.[91] The
Latin American Church, said Gutiérrez, 'must make the prophetic
denunciation of every dehumanizing situation, which is contrary
to brotherhood, justice, and liberty [...] the Church must go to the
very causes of the situation and not be content with pointing out
and attending to certain of its consequences'.[92]

     This radical critique, argues Berryman, was that of Christ.
'Liberation theologians have not tried to recast Jesus as a social
revolutionary', says Berryman, yet the message of Christ does
contain 'the seeds of a critique of any use of power that would
bring death to human beings', and liberation theology 'insists that
faith cannot be neutral when the life and death of the people are in
question'.[93] Jesus' death resulted from this radical critique. Yet, in
the death of Christ, God became identified with the oppressed and
suffering, and in His resurrection the God of life had triumphed
over the forces of death – the idols, the false gods of oppression
and capitalism.[94] As such, many Christians have found themselves
becoming radicalised – we have already noted the shift from
Christian Democracy to liberation theology, and that members
of BECs in Nicaragua went on to join the Sandinistas. Christians
such as those of the Workers' Catholic Action Movement were
supportive of the socialist government of Chile, and the international conference of Christians for Socialism in Santiago declared,
in a phrase borrowed from Che Guevara, 'When Christians dare
to give full-fledged revolutionary witness, then the Latin American
revolution will be invincible.'[95]

Camilo Torres Restrepo (1929–66), a Colombian priest, is just one example of this radicalism. Torres in the 1960s was something of a precursor to the liberationist ideas that would be fleshed out in the late 1960s and early 1970s. He sought to bring together the oppressed of the capitalist system – peasants, workers, people who lived in slums and shanty towns, along with intellectual critics of the system – to form a revolutionary United Front, arguing that revolution was 'the way to bring about a government that feeds the hungry, clothes the naked, teaches the ignorant, puts into practice the works of charity, and love for neighbour, not just every now and then, and not just for a few'.[96] Torres fought with the Colombian guerrillas and died in combat. Óscar Romero (1917–80), archbishop of San Salvador and canonised as a saint by Pope Francis in 2015, was another whose radical critique of the forces of oppression resulted in the loss of his life. Romero was a trenchant opponent of El Salvador's military dictatorship, and eventually he was assassinated by the nascent *contras* movement while saying mass.[97] These were not isolated incidents – in Latin America between 1964 and 1978, 41 priests were killed, 11 went missing, 485 were arrested, 46 suffered torture, and 253 were expelled from their countries.[98] This repression came upon those who, like the Brazilian bishops in 1973, declared that capitalism was 'the greatest evil, sin accumulated, the rotten root, the tree that produces fruits we have come to know: poverty, hunger, sickness, death', and demanded that society move 'beyond private property of the means of production', for:

> We want a world where the fruits of work will belong to everyone. We want a world where people will not work to get rich but so all will have what they need to live on: food, health care, housing, schooling, clothes, shoes, water, electricity. We want a world where money will be at the service of human beings and not human beings at the service of money [...] We want a world in which the people will be one, and the division between rich and poor will be abolished.[99]

Liberation theology, Marxism and Christian Socialism

This radical vision brings us to a charge often levelled at liberation theology, that it is nothing more than a form of Marxism. This was, for example, the fear of both Pope John-Paul II and Cardinal

Joseph Ratzinger – the future Pope Benedict XVI – when head of the Congregation for the Doctrine of the Faith.[100] Yet while liberation theology had, in the words of Gutiérrez, 'fruitful confrontation with Marxism', it was never slavishly Marxist.[101] Christians (such as Workers' Catholic Action Movement) were supportive of the socialist government of Chile; many in Nicaragua supported the Sandinistas; others, as we have seen, quoted Che Guevara, called for revolution, and fought alongside communist guerrillas.[102] Yet these radical acts were undertaken out of a Christian understanding rather than a Marxist one – as one writer put it: 'The liberationist is more influenced by the Gospel of Mark than the Gospel of Marx.'[103]

Liberation theology, explains Berryman, is primarily biblical and theological. It draws on some tools and concepts of Marxist analysis but is not itself Marxist – at most it could be described as 'Marxist in the more limited sense of utilizing some Marxist concepts'.[104] Two key examples in the work of Gutiérrez illustrate the use of Marxist concepts to support rather than replace theological ideas. Brotherhood, argues Gutiérrez, is a theological fact, which should be the basis for a properly organised society; however, a Marxist analysis demonstrates that this brotherhood is disregarded in 'the division of humanity into oppressors and oppressed, into owners of the means of production and those dispossessed of the fruit of their work, into antagonistic social classes'.[105] Again, Gutiérrez argues from Genesis that work should be fulfilling; yet, as Marx pointed out, work under capitalism is alienating, and 'instead of liberating man, enslaves him even more'.[106] Berryman further argues that liberation theology's key idea – the preferential option for the poor – is not based on Marxism, for the liberationist concept embraces all the impoverished, not just the industrial proletariat.[107]

Liberation theology, furthermore, rejects the view of Marx and Engels that religion is a driver of false consciousness, a product of the economic base seeking to maintain the capitalist mode of production (see Chapter 3). The church, it was argued, has too often perpetuated false consciousness and maintained the oppression of capitalism, but rather than 'the Marxist move of dismissing religion as an opiate, the liberationist's task is to raise consciousness through faith convictions, calling for radical praxis that can transform political structures responsible for repression'.[108]

This much is evident in the *Manifesto of the Third World Bishops*:

> God does not want there to be rich people who enjoy the goods of this world at the expense of the poor. No, God does not want there to be poor people living forever in misery. Religion is not the opium of the people. Religion is a force that lifts up the poor and brings down the proud, that gives bread to the hungry and leaves hungry those who are sated.[109]

Liberation theology employs the analytical tools of Marxism – the relations of production, exploitation, alienation, false consciousness – when they are useful, but is entirely comfortable with rejecting or modifying them if they are not helpful or valid.

John Cort argues that liberation theology is effectively a form of Christian Socialism, while another writer calls it 'Latin America's most well-known social gospel strain'[110] – though we can certainly see in liberation theology a perspective much more radical than anything offered by Walter Rauschenbusch or W.D.P. Bliss (see Chapter 4). It would be overly simplistic to fully equate liberation theology with other strands of the Christian Left, but there are some overlaps and common emphases with Christian Socialism, especially insofar as liberation theology is based upon an interpretation of the Bible, the sacraments and church teaching.[111] Like Christian Socialism, liberation theology holds brotherhood as its ideal, for God calls us to what Gutiérrez refers to as a 'brotherhood among men'.[112] This brotherhood is represented in the Eucharist – the same emphasis placed on the sacrament by Anglo-Catholics such as Stewart Headlam (see Chapter 1) – to the extent that Gutiérrez argues that '[w]ithout a real commitment against exploitation and alienation and for a society of solidarity and justice, the Eucharistic celebration is an empty action'.[113] The Bible and the sacraments, says Berryman, provide a picture of 'what life should be – a society of brothers and sisters, a life of sharing and equality'.[114]

Liberation theology also shares the general Christian Left emphasis on the Kingdom of God as something which should shape society in the here and now. For Gutiérrez, 'the coming of the Kingdom [is] historical, temporal, earthly, social, and material [...] The struggle for a just world in which there is no oppression, servitude, or alienated work will signify the coming of the Kingdom.'[115] This Kingdom 'is realized in a society of brotherhood and justice', a society in which the values of the Kingdom are recognised in earthly politics: 'The political is grafted into the eternal.'[116] Liberation theology takes a view similar to that of Paul Tillich (see Chapter 3) and Shailer Mathews (see Chapter 4), and different to that of the British Christian Socialists of the late nineteenth and early twentieth centuries, in making a distinction between the Kingdom to be realised on earth and the eternal Kingdom, which is yet to be revealed.[117] The Kingdom, says Gutiérrez, is manifested in history through acts of liberation, yet neither the process of liberation nor the achievement of a truly fraternal society is 'the fullness of the Kingdom which is beyond history'; society must reflect the Kingdom and, insofar as society does this, it can be regarded as the appearing of the Kingdom, but the true Kingdom remains outside of time and space.[118] Nevertheless, says Berryman, the Kingdom 'is drawing near wherever human beings are achieving justice and love'.[119]

Conclusion

Liberation theology emerged in a particular context: as an attempt to apply Catholic social teaching and the declarations of Vatican II to the Latin American situation; as a means of overcoming the dependence of Latin American nations on the former colonial powers that now represented the centre of globalised capitalism; and as a critique of the programme of development that assumed colonial, capitalist values and perpetuated the dependence of Third World communities. It was the Medellín conference of 1968 and the work of Gustavo Gutiérrez that perhaps did the most to shape liberation theology and develop its key concepts, among them the preferential option for the poor, the development of truth out of the perspective of the oppressed, that action or praxis precedes reflection and theory, that capitalism is idolatrous, and that radical change is necessary to bring about a society of justice and brotherhood. In drawing on the Bible, church teaching and sacraments, focusing on brotherhood as a key concept, and emphasising the Kingdom of God as something to be sought in the political and economic structures of society, liberation theology shares much in common with other strands of the Christian Left. Liberation theology remains relevant today for three reasons. Firstly, as Gutiérrez argued in 2007, despite the claims of global capitalism to have delivered the goods, 'poverty has increased dramatically. The gap between the rich and poor nations is today wider than two decades ago. The same is the case within each Latin American country.'[120] Secondly, liberation theology provides a critique of populist government based on an appeal to religious values, such as that of Jair Bolsonaro in Brazil.[121] Thirdly – as we shall explore in the following chapter – liberation theology has proved adaptable enough to be applied to many other contexts all across the world.

7

Liberty to the Captives: Liberation Theology Across the World

In August 1989, at the height of the struggle against apartheid in South Africa, Archbishop Desmond Tutu held an 'Ecumenical Defiance Service' at St George's Cathedral in Cape Town as part of a campaign of non-violent civil disobedience. As Tutu was speaking, South African Security Police marched into the cathedral, lining the walls and surrounding the congregation. Some held notepads or tape recorders in order to take as evidence anything the Archbishop said against the South African government or the apartheid regime. Tutu turned to address them: 'You are powerful – very powerful – but you are not God. I serve a God who cannot be mocked. So since you have already lost, I invite you today to come and join the winning side.'[1] For Tutu, like other proponents of liberation theology, the demise of injustice and oppression is inevitable. Jim Wallis, who was in the cathedral and recounts these events, argues that it was Tutu's 'Christian belief that kept him going during so many difficult times', through 'the heat of South Africa's oppression and the heart of apartheid's despair'.[2]

We have already examined in detail the liberation theology that emerged from Latin America in opposition to dependence, developmentalism and the oppression of capitalism, and the liberation theology that emerged from the United States in opposition to racial oppression, injustice and inequality. Liberation theology, however, has spread across the world, being applied to many different circumstances and contexts. As in Latin America, other parts of the Third World that had suffered colonialism and dependence upon the global economic centre developed their own theologies of liberation, often in conversation with other religions and theology. The apartheid system of South Africa led to the emergence of a black liberation theology similar to that developed by African-Americans in the United States. Feminists and womanists began to develop their own liberation theology in response to the lack of focus on patriarchy, misogyny and gender-based oppression in these other forms. Liberation theology has proved to be perhaps the most adaptable and ubiquitous tradition of the Christian Left.

Liberation theology in Asia and the Middle East

Liberation theology's rootedness in time and place, it is argued, shows that it cannot simply be transplanted from one context to another.[3] The theology of Gustavo Gutiérrez was fashioned out of the lived experience of poverty in Peru and across Latin America; the theology of James Cone arose from the fierce oppression meted out against African-Americans; neither can simply be extrapolated to another situation. Yet, despite this, liberation theologies have indeed emerged across the world. This is because, while a specific liberation theology cannot be imported into another culture or context, the methodology of liberation theology can be. The commitment to praxis as the necessary precondition to theological reflection, the development of truth in conjunction with the experience of the oppressed, the commitment – broadly conceived – to liberation, all represent a framework that aids in the development of ideas and that can be transferred to another setting. An example of this methodological portability is found in the work of Hannah Lewis of the All Saints Centre for Mission and Ministry in Liverpool, who has used the principles of liberation theology in order to 'develop and teach and spread Deaf Liberation Theology as a means of promoting social justice for deaf people within the church'.[4]

Liberation theologies developed in different contexts do not always complement each other; rather, they can appear in opposition to one another. Latin American liberationists were critical of African-American liberation theology for failing, at least at first, to see that economic inequality led to the oppression of impoverished whites. Feminist and womanist theologians have criticised both of these for being clouded by patriarchy and therefore insufficiently sensitive to the oppression of women.[5] Over time, however, there has been a developing understanding that individuals and groups can suffer from multiple forms of oppression and disadvantage simultaneously:

> A Dalit girl working in a factory in an export-processing zone in India is exploited as an underpaid worker – like other workers around the globe – and suffers from a lack of protection by trade-union rights, while as a woman she suffers from male domination and violence – as other women do – whereas she shares her plight as an 'untouchable' suffering from caste oppression with other out-castes, male and female, in India.[6]

Insofar as liberation theology has developed such an understanding, committing itself to liberation from multiple and varied forms of oppression, it links well with the intersectional theory of political philosophers such as Kimberlé Crenshaw.[7]

Perhaps the most natural context for variants of liberation theology to develop are in those countries and regions of the world which, like Latin America, have suffered from both colonialism and the neo-colonialism of the global division of labour. Liberation theology has become well rooted in various Asian contexts. Samuel Rayan (1920–2019), an Indian Jesuit priest and theologian, has developed an approach that draws upon indigenous Asian spirituality, arguing for example that the Asian sense of a closer connection to creation is a possible basis, lacking in Western theology, for a liberationist approach to ecological threats.[8] This view is also articulated by the Sri Lankan theologian Tissa Balasuriya (1924–2013). For Balasuriya, the lack of respect for the natural environment within Christianity is the symptom of a European and latterly North American theology, 'fashioned within the framework of Western capitalism', posing as universal theology. Such a theology fails to see how capitalism oppresses both the working-class of the Western world and the global periphery that is the Third World, as well as leading to a male-dominated, patriarchal religion, which cannot serve for the liberation of women; Western theology is therefore irrelevant to the needs of the oppressed and marginalised.[9] This openness to non-Western perspectives leads also to an interfaith approach, drawing upon the liberationist insights of other religions. An example of this is the work of Choan-Seng Song (b.1929), who has drawn together Christianity and Buddhism – 'the cross and the lotus' – to develop a liberation theology suited to the Asian context. Christians, argues Song, should 'see the mission of the church as consisting not of conquering members of other faiths but growing with them in the knowledge and experience of God's saving work in the world'.[10]

Rayan takes a liberationist view of the caste system of India, arguing: 'We do not accept the idea that some are low-born while others are high-born, for all are born of God through Jesus Christ in the Holy Spirit.'[11] Yet, while Rayan's use of the Asian respect for nature and his liberationist critique of the caste system are rooted in his particular context, he – like other Asian liberation theologies – draws general conclusions that are not distinct from the theology of Latin America. Society, Rayan argues, should reflect that God is a God of love and justice. 'The only adequate response to God's unconditional love in Jesus Christ is to make our own God's concern for people and to give all we have for their total liberation and wholeness as God gave the Son for the world's salvation.' This Christ-like giving of self means 'securing bread for the breadless, recognition for the marginalised, dignity for the despised, liberation for captives, and freedom for the downtrodden'.[12] Geevarghese Mar Osthathios (1917–2012), a senior bishop of the Orthodox Church in India, does similarly, arguing that '[t]he church, following in the footsteps of the Nazarene, must become poor and preach the gospel to the poor, not only in words, but also in liberating them from the oppression of the mighty'.[13] Like Gutiérrez and others in the Latin American context, Osthathios draws upon Marxist tools of analysis but also refashions them to his purpose. An example of this is his likening of Marx's dictatorship of the proletariat to God throwing down the rich and powerful, as recounted in the *Magnificat*, but concluding: 'The classless society we dream of is not the dictatorship of any class, but a democratic, socialist rule.'[14]

One area in which fruitful interaction has taken place is South Korea, in which a liberative theology of *minjung* has developed. *Minjung* is a tricky concept to define, but does overlap somewhat with liberation theology's concept of the oppressed. Kim

Yong-Bok (b.1938) explains: 'Woman belongs to *minjung* when she is politically dominated by man. An ethnic group is a *minjung* group when it is politically dominated by another group. A race is *minjung* when it is dominated by another powerful ruling race. When intellectuals are suppressed by the military power elite, they belong to *minjung*.'[15] On this understanding Jesus Christ, born in poverty and identifying with the oppressed, was himself *minjung*. *Minjung* theology – which can loosely be translated as 'people's theology' or perhaps theology of the oppressed – emerged out of the suffering (*han*) of the Korean people in the mid twentieth century. It represents an 'act of protest against *han*, as it has served to legitimize political struggle and social action'.[16] While, unlike the countries of Latin America, South Korea has developed into an economic powerhouse and appears to have benefited greatly from free-market capitalism, *minjung* theologians still recognise that there are many oppressed and disadvantaged people within society, and call for, as Yong-Bok phrased it, a society built on 'justice, *koinonia* (participation), and *shalom*'.[17]

Among the more recent liberation theologies to be developed is that of the Christian community in Palestine, deriving from the sense of being part of an oppressed minority. 'Christian leaders in Palestine held that an indigenous theological response to the conflict was necessary in order to challenge the Jewish and Western-Christian theological justifications for the seizure of the land.'[18] Among these leaders is Naim Ateek (b.1937), an Anglican priest and founder of the Sabeel Ecumenical Liberation Theology Center in East Jerusalem, which aims to bring together Palestine's Protestant and Orthodox Christian communities as well as facilitating dialogue with Palestinian Muslims.[19] Sabeel was among the formative influences on the 2009 document *Kairos Palestine* which 'emphasizes a vision of the Holy Land – with Jerusalem as its crown jewel – inclusive of all humanity, as an exemplary space of coexistence and reconciliation'.[20] The document – endorsed by the World Council of Churches, the Middle East Council of Churches, and the All Africa Council of Churches – places love and justice at the centre of its theology: 'love invites you to resist, love puts an end to evil by walking in the ways of justice [...] love liberates both perpetrator and victim'.[21]

Like other forms, Palestinian Liberation Theology focuses on the development of theology out of praxis and context, disavowing that Western-style theology is universal. It represents 'a passionate indictment of state-run oppression and a call for justice and liberation'.[22] There are, however, contextual differences. The Exodus account, central to black liberation theology in the United States and important for all varieties of the Christian Left, poses a difficulty for Palestinian Christians who wish to refute Israel's claims to the 'Promised Land'. One result of downplaying the biblical conquest of Canaan is that Palestinian Liberation Theology is more committed to pacifism, as well as being more committed to reconciliation with than victory over their opponents. Theologian Luis Rivera-Pagan argues: 'Palestinian theology, maybe more than other liberation theologies, emphasizes the intertwining of justice and reconciliation, truth-telling and forgiveness, prophetic denunciation and peacemaking annunciation. The ultimate goal of the prophetic denunciation is neither the destruction nor humiliation of the enemy but the fulfilment of Isaiah's prediction of a new creation; a world free of bellicose violence and devastation.'[23]

Tissa Balasuriya, as noted above, demonstrates that Western theology cannot serve the needs of the oppressed and should not claim universality. Yet Balasuriya also argues that other context-dependent theologies, such as the liberation theology of Latin America, may also be deficient insofar as they lack a holistic, global understanding of oppression. For this reason, 'even the best of contextual theologies, related to a limited group or region, must be counterbalanced by more universal perspectives relating to the world as a whole'.[24] This does not mean a return to taking North American and European theology as normative – 'the false universalisms of the past' – but that 'the whole planet earth, as an entirety must also be seen as a context for theology'.[25] This Balasuriya refers to as a 'planetary theology', one derived not from the dominance of one context or another, but from dialectical interaction between various contextualised theologies and an overarching theology, which understands that, just as oppression is globalised, so must liberation be globalised.

Liberation theology in Africa

African liberation theology emerged from the anti-colonial movements and the experience of de-colonisation in sub-Saharan Africa in the mid twentieth century. There was, therefore, 'a close affinity between African theology and the movement towards freedom in Africa'.[26] Figures such as Julius Nyerere (1922–99), President of Tanzania from its founding in 1964 until 1985, drew together anti-colonial African nationalism and socialism. Nyerere's philosophy of *ujamaa* was a non-Marxist, contextualised, African socialism. African people, he argued, did not require a Marxist analysis to know that land was a gift from God and should therefore belong to the community rather than to private individuals. Prior to colonisation, 'the African's right to land was simply the right to use it; he had no other right to it, nor did it occur to him to try and claim one. The foreigner introduced a completely different concept – the concept of land as a marketable commodity.' This resulted in a class of landlords – 'loiterers' and 'parasites' – who lived from the labour of others.[27] Post-colonial Africa, Nyerere argued, should be characterised by an 'African socialism' based on 'the extended family. The true African socialist [...] regards all men as his brethren – as members of his ever-extending family.'[28] Nyerere concludes: 'We, in Africa, have no more need of being "converted" to socialism than we have of being "taught" democracy. Both are rooted in our own past.'[29]

At the 'All African Conference of Churches' (AACC) in 1963 in Kampala, Uganda, African Christian leaders began to undertake the development of a liberation theology developed in the African context.[30] One key figure was John Samuel Mbiti (1931–2019), the Kenyan Anglican priest and philosopher, who argued for the relevance of indigenous religion and philosophy in constructing African theology: 'African religious background is not a rotten heap of superstitions, taboos and magic; it has a great deal of value in it. On this valuable heritage, Christianity should adapt itself and not be dependent exclusively on imported goods.'[31] This theology was developed not only in the context of colonialism but also – as suggested by Nyerere – the neo-colonialism of global capitalism, as well as the repression of Africa's many corrupt and self-serving post-colonial leaders. These three factors taken together have left the continent in a state of 'abject material poverty that is characteristic of no other people in the world. These factors are almost identical from one African country to another.'[32]

Despite this essentially African context, African liberation theology nevertheless shares themes and ideas in common with the liberation theologies of other parts of the world. Jonathan Gichaara from the Urban Theology Unit in Sheffield gives an example:

> The biblical story of the children of Israel being held captive for over 400 years in Egypt resonates well with the African experience of colonialism [...] Liberation theologies from Africa are, so to speak, recoverers of the Moses heritage and memory. What they recover in this context is not merely Moses the law giver, but the liberator of the oppressed people. African liberation theology or theologies, as the case may be, calls to mind Moses the founder of a religious tradition that is at once political and radical.[33]

The interpretation here is rooted in the African context, but nevertheless shares much in common with, for example, Latin American liberation theology. This may be due in part to the similarity of the socio-economic context: colonialism, neo-colonialism, corrupt and oppressive government. In such a situation, as in Latin America, 'the hermeneutic of African theology can only be that of the poor'.[34]

African liberation theology has also drawn upon the black liberation theology of the United States, nowhere more so than in South Africa. While the experience of colonisation was one endured across the continent, South Africa endured the additional experience of systematic, institutionalised racism, analogous to the Jim Crow segregation of the southern United States; as a result, a South African black liberation theology developed, drawing upon but nevertheless distinct from the earlier pan-African liberation theology.[35] This theology was 'born in the context of the South African liberation struggle; it is synonymous with the apartheid struggle'.[36] Another key aspect of that struggle – again, in a similar manner to the US – was that churches and professing Christians, such as the Dutch Reformed Church, were often supporters of the apartheid system. There were exceptions – Christiaan Frederick Beyers Naudé (1915–2004), a white Dutch Reformed pastor, is just one example. Naudé founded the Christian Institute of South Africa, an ecumenical organisation committed to racial reconciliation, and helped to organise the 1960 Cottesloe Consultation, sponsored by the World Council of Churches, which issued an anti-racist statement that was subsequently rejected by the Dutch Reformed Church. Naudé therefore 'played an important and, at times, central role in the emergence of an indigenous liberation theology'.[37] Despite such exceptions, however, black theologians and church leaders were more likely to face hostility from their white co-religionists.

Albert John Lutuli (1898–1967), a minister in the United Congregational Church of South Africa, was an early key figure in the development of South African black liberation theology. Lutuli was the founder of the non-violent, anti-apartheid Defiance Campaign of the 1950s, and served as president of the African National Congress from 1952 until his death, the position later held by Nelson Mandela.[38] Later contributors to the liberationist opposition to apartheid were black Dutch Reformed pastor Allan Boesak (b.1946) and Archbishop Desmond Tutu (b.1931). Both have drawn from the 'black consciousness' philosophy of Steve Biko (1946–77) which aims at creating in black people a consciousness of their own value and worth that rejects the dehumanising nature of racism, particularly systemic racism.[39] Biko, something of an unorthodox Christian, was influenced by Frantz Fanon and James Cone, drawing like Cone a distinction between the 'white' God worshipped in institutional Christianity and the 'black' God who stands for the oppressed and subjugated of the world: 'If the white God has been doing the talking all along,' declared Biko, 'at some stage the black God will have to raise His voice and make Himself heard over and above the noises from His counterpart.'[40]

Boesak also recognised that sections of the Christian church – including his own Dutch Reformed denomination – did not provide the means to combat the evils of segregation, apartheid and racism. Apartheid, he argued, oppresses people simply for being born black; it therefore enshrines whiteness as normative and denies that black people are fully human. 'White' theology had failed to confront the de-humanising effects of racism – it required, as Biko had proposed, a 'black consciousness' through which 'black people discover that they are children of God and that they have rights to exist in God's world'.[41] The development of this consciousness in turn required a fuller and deeper understanding of the Gospel, grounded in the black African context. White Christians had sought to separate the Gospel from socio-economic matters; for 'black Christians, however, the gospel is the incomparable word of liberation'.[42] 'Black theology,' declared Boesak, 'is a theology of liberation.'[43] This much was evident from the incarnation in which God shares and identifies with the humanity of his creatures; it is seen in the year of jubilee, which demonstrates 'the wholeness of God's liberation'; it is seen in the Exodus and in the synagogue sermon where Christ, argued Boesak, places himself in that same Exodus tradition.[44] 'What we need,' said Boesak, 'is a spiritual and a political Exodus out of the situation of oppression towards a situation of liberation, out of the situation of inhumanity, darkness, and hatred, toward a situation in which we, both whites and blacks, can regain our common humanity and enjoy a meaningful life, a wholeness of life that has been destroyed.'[45]

The above demonstrates perhaps a difference between the black liberation theology of Boesak and that of James Cone. Boesak spoke of a 'common humanity' between blacks and whites, in a manner quite distinct from Cone's insistence that white people must repent of whiteness and, if it were possible, become black (see Chapter 5). Boesak, argues theologian Timothy van Aarde, 'did not advocate an American black theology that cast itself as a purely black–white struggle. The essence of the black theology that developed in South Africa was a struggle for human dignity, what it means to be human, and an identity which clearly set it apart from its American counterpart that focused on what it meant to be black.'[46] Indeed, Boesak criticised black liberation theology in the United States for focusing on black power rather than reconciliation, in his opinion moving the civil rights movement away from the ethos of Martin Luther King, Jr. He argued not that God was on the side of the oppressed but on the side of justice, and held that the oppressed of the world could easily become the oppressors if they did not commit to love and reconciliation.[47] Boesak also differed from the early Cone in emphasising economic as well as racial justice; black South Africans needed freeing from the 'stubborn refusal to respect the dignity of Black personhood', but all impoverished South Africans needed to be liberated from economic oppression.[48]

Desmond Tutu has been described as one of 'the leading protagonists of the liberation theology movement, particularly in the struggle against global racism'.[49] Tutu served as Archbishop of Cape Town from 1986 to 1994, General Secretary of the South African Council of Churches from 1979 to 1985 – he was succeeded by Bayers Naudé – and from 1996 to 1998 as chair of the post-apartheid Truth and Reconciliation Committee. More an activist than a theorist, he has nevertheless 'demonstrated in his life and ministry of practice [...] a model of theological resistance to the evil of racism in church and society'.[50] Tutu was influenced by the Community of the Resurrection, originally set up by Charles Gore (see Chapter 1), the organisation that founded St Peter's Theological College where Tutu trained. From here comes Tutu's emphasis on humanity in the image of God and the incarnate God sharing in that humanity, demonstrating the inherent dignity and worth of all people, as well as that all kinds of people are connected and should love and co-operate with each other. This perspective found its ultimate fulfilment in Tutu's vision of South Africa as a 'rainbow nation' for people of all races and ethnicities.[51] His vision was also underpinned by the Xhosa philosophical concept of *ubuntu*, which emphasises the interrelatedness of humanity.[52]

Like Boesak and others, Tutu was influenced by Latin American liberation theology, US black liberation theology, and African theology.[53] He did not regard African theology and black theology as strictly separate from each other, viewing himself as 'an exponent of black theology coming as I do from South Africa' and 'an exponent of African theology coming as I do from Africa', adding that black liberation theology is, in South Africa, African theology.[54] Tutu 'understood African Theology as indigenous theology, whereby Africans endeavour to express Christianity in an authentic African way, liberate Africans from bondage, and come to an African understanding of God'. As such, it was not altogether separate from a South African black theology that reasserts the dignity of black people and seeks the liberation of both whites and blacks.[55] That whites should also be liberated is a difference between Tutu and Cone, but Tutu was no opponent of US black liberation theology, rejecting a view that black theology is impoverished because it developed in the context of oppression and victimhood; rather, Tutu said, this gave black liberation theology in both the US and South Africa a welcome sense of urgency, which had not always been present in African theology.[56]

Tutu also drew upon the idea of black consciousness developed by Biko and elaborated by Boesak, arguing that the 'most violent form of colonialism' has been for whites to teach blacks 'self-disgust and self-hatred', and that both in Africa and the US, black people who wanted to be accepted as equals were forced 'to see themselves and be seen as chocolate-covered whites', a situation that denigrates their own humanity.[57] Blackness, however, is 'intractable'; black people 'cannot will it away', and nor should they. Indeed, the racism meted out in South Africa, the US, and elsewhere in the world provides for the black community 'the glorious privilege and opportunity to further the gospel of love, forgiveness, and reconciliation – the gospel of Jesus Christ – in a way that is possible to no other group'.[58] Black Christians, therefore, were well placed to fulfil the church's prophetic role of criticising and opposing the unrighteous actions of the state.[59]

Tutu did not deny that liberation could be achieved by violence, but he nevertheless 'encouraged negotiation instead of violence'.[60] More radical opponents of apartheid criticised Tutu's pacifism, but for him it was a necessary component of 'the ministry of reconciliation'.[61] This view served Tutu well in overseeing the Truth and Reconciliation Committee of the post-apartheid era. Tutu also took a broader view of liberation, including economic oppression and the oppression of women. Rejecting the individualism of both Western theology and political theory, he was a critic of free-market capitalism both for creating an unequal distribution of resources between blacks and whites, and for destroying the liberty of all the impoverished. Tutu held that the so-called free market was a myth, advocating instead a socialist economy based on co-operation, which would minimise inequality of outcome.[62] Tutu also recognised the need for women to be liberated from the oppression of patriarchy, adding that under apartheid black women were doubly discriminated against.[63] Tutu's vision of liberation was so broad and all-encompassing, that even when the apartheid system had been abolished he could not be wholly satisfied, arguing in 2010: 'It pains me to have to admit that there is less freedom and personality in most independent Africa than there was during the much-maligned colonial days.'[64] Nevertheless, Tutu's 'insistence on a sound spirituality, respect of dignity of human life, justice and reconciliation' has had a lasting impact in South Africa and around the world.[65]

Feminist liberation theology

As well as economic and racial oppression, theologies of liberation have been developed, which seek to oppose oppression based on sex, gender or orientation. Most notably, alongside Latin American and African/black liberation theologies, feminist theology has emerged with the aim of showing that Christianity's message of liberation frees women from the institutional misogyny of patriarchal society. At first, patriarchal oppression was not considered by male Latin American liberationists. The Argentine liberation theologian Marcella Althaus-Reid (1952–2009) criticised mainstream liberation theology for not viewing the oppressed poor, women in particular, as sexual beings in need of sexual liberation.[66] Among other feminist theologians who called the theology of Latin America to take the oppression of women into account were Beatriz Melano Couch (1931–2004) of Argentina, Julia Esquivel (1930–2019) of Guatemala, and Elsa Támez (b.1951) of Mexico.[67] From the 1980s onwards, liberation theology came to view women as 'doubly' oppressed – 'triply' oppressed if, in addition to being female and impoverished, they were also black or indigenous rather than white.[68] Here we perhaps see an early example of intersectional thinking in a Christian Left tradition.

Mary Grey (b.1941), the British Roman Catholic eco-feminist, has described the twofold task of feminist liberation theology as being 'to uncover the theologies and institutional practices which perpetuate the injustices inflicted on women and deny their full human subjectivity; and constructively, to create a liberated and liberating theology'.[69] This should be done, argued Grey, out of an awareness that 'the Christian churches failed to promote the full humanity of women in their structures of theology, and what was worse, legitimised the subordination and victimisation of women by recourse to Scripture and tradition to show that this was the part of God's plan for creation'.[70] Feminist liberation theology, however, may have had a more difficult task than other liberation theologies, which focused on economic inequality or racial discrimination. While the Bible contains many verses that can be interpreted to support economic collectivism and redistribution, argues Dan McKanan, the Bible also appears to support patriarchal power.[71] Gary Dorrien raises the same issue: 'Can any form of Christianity be liberating to women after feminist criticism has exposed the patriarchal character of Christian scripture and tradition?'[72]

One feminist scholar to respond to this challenge is the American theologian Rosemary Radford Ruether (b.1936). Like other Roman Catholic feminists, Ruether began her work in the post-Vatican II period, which had heralded, it seemed, a more liberating and progressive era.[73] Ruether's theology is based not on a denial that the Bible and church teaching reflect patriarchal norms – '[t]here is no question,' says Ruether, 'that patriarchy is the social context for both the Old and New Testament and that this social context has been incorporated into religious ideology on many levels' – but there is a liberative message within Christianity which can be applied to the emancipation of women.[74] Ruether calls this the 'prophetic-liberating tradition', which, she argues, is not a marginal theme in scripture but 'the central tradition, the tradition by which the biblical faith constantly criticizes and renews itself and its own vision'.[75] This tradition is seen in the Old Testament prophets such as Isaiah and Amos, in the *Magnificat* of Mary, in Christ's cleansing of the temple and denunciation of the religious authorities. These examples suffice to show that 'the God-language of the prophetic tradition is destabilising toward the existing social order' – and this includes the patriarchal order. The prophetic-liberating tradition may not be a set of 'ideas' or concepts, but it is a guide, a prompt, towards justice and liberation.[76]

Despite this prophetic-liberating tradition, the Bible, Ruether concedes, does not state explicitly the equality of women. This, she argues, is due to the patriarchal assumptions that prevented even those prophets who denounced injustice and oppression from seeing the full implications of their preaching. Male prophets of Israel saw clearly the oppression of the poor by the rich, but failed to see their own complicity in patriarchal oppression of women. Similarly in the New Testament, the Apostle Paul in his letter to the Galatians spoke of there being no male–female distinction in Christ, but was not able to fully unpack this revolutionary concept in order to support sexual equality and women's freedom from patriarchy.[77] This conceptual blindness is perpetuated by the church, which, says Ruether, 'suppresses the social justice dimension fundamental to the entire biblical prophetic tradition'.[78] Feminist theology, therefore, has the responsibility of making 'explicit what was overlooked in male advocacy of the poor and oppressed: that liberation must start with the oppressed of the oppressed, namely, *women* of the oppressed.'[79]

One way that this is accomplished is to emphasise the role of women in a manner that has been neglected by mainstream Christianity. Ruether cites the role played by oppressed women in the Gospels – the Samaritan woman at the well, the destitute widow, the prostitutes who seek the friendship of Jesus and the liberation revealed in His life and teaching – as part of this over-looked tradition.[80] Perhaps the clearest example is that of Mary, portrayed in Roman Catholicism as a submissive wife and mother, and ignored in Protestantism for fear of idolatry and superstition. Mary, argues Ruether, is liberated by the Gospel; yet, more to the point, her choice to place her faith in the message of God brought to her by the angel is a crucial element in bringing about liberation for the poor and oppressed throughout history. Furthermore, Mary did not consult with Joseph, her soon-to-be husband, before taking on this liberating role.[81] The *Magnificat* of Mary, important to many of the Christian Left, is especially important to feminist theology because it is the 'liberation language' of a woman who speaks in 'explicitly economic and political' terms.[82] The Indonesian Presbyterian theologian Henriette Marianne Katoppo (1943–2007) also holds up Mary as an example, declaring her 'the fully liber-ated human being'.[83] This is reflected in Mary, 'this Asian woman', bursting into a great song of joy and liberation, as well as in the vir-ginity of Mary, which Katoppo interprets as referring not to absti-nence from sex but to 'a woman who does not lead a "derived" life (as "mother of", "wife of", "daughter of"), a woman who matures to wholeness within herself as a complete person, who is subject of herself, and who is open for others, for God'.[84]

Feminist theology must also reckon with the historic Christian portrayal of God as male. Many Christians, argues Katoppo, are 'unaware of the feminine aspects of divinity [...] For so long masculine imagery has dominated the text; the feminine images have been conveniently overlooked.'[85] This creates a problem, not just that women are alienated from God – 'it is', says Katoppo, 'oppression to force people to relate to an all-male Trinity' – but that men hold a divine characteristic: as Mary Daly (1928–2010) phrased it: 'If God is male, then the male is God.'[86] The answer, Mary Grey suggests, is not to simplistically begin to view God as Mother instead of Father, but rather to view the Godhead as rela-tional via characteristics that we may think of as female as well as male.[87] God is not male, argues Ruether, but a spirit who is analo-gised using both male and female names, male and female char-acteristics.[88] This includes, according to Katoppo, Old Testament references to God's mercy or compassion as *rahamin*, which is literally translated as 'movements of the womb' and suggests a feminine, motherly relationship between God and creation. The New Testament word for the Holy Spirit, *ruach*, Katoppo suggests is also a feminine word. Katoppo also cites the Hebrew *hokmah* and Greek *sophia* as feminine words for the wisdom of God, adding that in the early church the word *hokmah* was associated with Jesus Christ.[89]

The incarnation presents something of a difficulty for feminist theology. Unlike the other persons of the Trinity, who remain purely spiritual and unseen, the second person of the Trinity was incarnated as a man. The response to this, suggests Grey, is to shift the focus from Christ's incarnation as a man to Christ's incarnation as a human being, the identification of God with all people, not just men.[90] Ruether agrees, arguing that Christ's message of liberation can be applied in the service of female liberation, even if this is not made explicit by the Gospel writers.[91] Ruether adds:

> His ability to speak as a liberator does not reside in his maleness but in the fact that he has renounced this system of domination and seeks to embody in his person the new humanity of service and mutual empowerment [...] Theologically speaking, then, we might say that the maleness of Jesus has no ultimate significance.[92]

This understanding can be applied to the whole Trinity, for here we have, says Grey, '[t]he concept of a God who suffers with the pain of women and all broken people'.[93] Liberation theology, Katoppo reminds us, is 'a philosophy and theology of the Other' – or as Gutiérrez termed it, the 'non-person' – and for Katoppo 'God is the absolute Other' who identifies with all the Others, liberating them from their non-personhood.[94]

As with mainstream feminism, feminist liberation theology has been criticised for adopting a white perspective that excludes the insights and experiences of women of colour. For this reason, there emerged womanist (African-American) and *mujerista* (Hispanic) theologies in the United States.[95] 'White women, say the womanist theologians, do suffer from oppression *qua* women; but *vis-à-vis* black women they are privileged because of the benefits which whiteness, and often class privilege, bring in a racist, unequal society.'[96] This denotes one of the key differences between womanism and some strands of feminist theology, as well as mainstream first- and second-wave feminism – namely intersectionality. This also stands as a difference between womanist theology and the black liberation theology of the United States, which in its earlier iterations was not open to the oppression suffered by black women as women, or by women in general. Another difference between womanism and white feminism – though this time a characteristic which black liberation theology shares – is its rootedness in the black church.[97]

Further criticism of feminist theology comes from LGBT+ or 'queer' theology, which argues that feminist thinking did not do enough to disrupt heteronormativity. LGBT+ theology at its most basic rejects that homosexuality is sinful, affirms that LGBT+ relationships are created good, and therefore sees gay communities as both liberating and in need of liberation. It is a project of 'debunking and countering the homophobia of the religious community by reclaiming resources within it, reframing religious narratives to include and even affirm LGBT members'.[98] In this sense then it is similar to feminist theology in arguing that the affirmation of LGBT+ is not stated explicitly in the Bible or church tradition, but is implicit in the biblical message of liberation. Gary David Comstock (b.1945) sums up this perspective by arguing: 'Christian Scripture and tradition are not authorities from which I seek approval; rather, they are resources from which I seek guidance and learn lessons as well [as] institutions that I seek to interpret, shape, and change.'[99] Like other liberation theologians, Comstock and Richard Cleaver (b.1954) focus on the Exodus and the resurrection as part of the liberation narrative of scripture. Cleaver argues that 'these events reveal that God is the one who saves through the creation of new types of people'. His primary theological point is that salvation is not an individual matter but rather is found in communal political action. It is about rejecting "bourgeois religion" and establishing a new type of family.'[100]

There is a tension between 'lesbian and gay liberation theologies that seek to normalize the homosexual on the one hand, and queer theologies that seek to undo the category of normal on the other'.[101] For the latter, 'queer' is linked to what Henriette Marianne Katoppo referred to as the 'Other' and Gustavo Gutiérrez called the 'non-person'. For this reason, 'queer theologians tend to argue that Christianity has long been queer, particularly evident in incarnational and Trinitarian reflections that show that Christ always stood outside the norm, troubled the categories, and essentially queered the world'.[102] While earlier gay liberation theology focused on sexual orientation to the exclusion of other matters, later LGBT+ theology was open to the need to consider different elements of oppression, again highlighting the intersectionality of more developed liberation theologies; for example, Virginia Ramey Mollenkott (1932–2020) and Justin Sabia-Tanis (b.1969) have focused on developing a theology of transgenderism.[103] Such theology aims at creating 'a Christian theology of affirmation'.[104]

Despite the various forms of feminist, womanist, gay, LGBT+ and queer theologies, there remain those who argue 'that Christian theology is not only rooted in heterosexism but is also patriarchal, racist, and classist'.[105] Among these are Mary Daly, for example, who argued that 'feminist liberation requires deeper critiques of Christianity and new forms of language and community', yet whose critical approach drew her out of the institutional church, away from an orthodox understanding of Christianity, and latterly to a rejection of Christianity altogether.[106] Even theologies such as Ruether's, developed within Christianity, draw upon Gnosticism and paganism in order to create feminist forms of religion.[107] Feminist theology has:

> embarked on what has been called a post-Christian direction. For example, goddess-based spirituality invokes the memory and active presence of the ancient earth-goddesses, in particular Isis, Cybele, Demeter, Astarte, Ceridwen, Aphrodite and so on. And these are merely to cite one tradition: African, Afro-Caribbean, Indian, Japanese, Chinese and Latin American women are actively reclaiming the goddess traditions of their own cultures as part of their own burgeoning spiritualities. In addition, the Wicca or witchcraft movement, often associated with the name of Starhawk, evokes the power of the ancient goddess as inspiration for its rituals of healing, celebration of the seasons, and ethical lifestyle based on respect for the earth and bodily rhythms.[108]

Feminist theology is not, as we have seen, the only liberation theology to draw upon non-Christian concepts and views of the world in order to sustain itself, but it arguably does rely on these to a greater extent than other liberation theologies and other strands of the Christian Left. This being the case, question marks are raised over whether feminist theology – and other Christian Left traditions such as the interfaith forms of liberation theology noted above – are actually Christian.

Some feminists, arguing that the institutional church is too misogynistic for their purposes, have set up their own church structures. The main example of this is the Women Church (originally the Woman Church), described by Mary Grey as 'an exodus, not from the institutional Church, but from patriarchy' in order to become 'a global movement of women seeking authentic ecclesial communities of justice'.[109] The movement was founded in 1983 at Grailville, a Christian community in Loveland, Ohio, at a conference of around 1,400 Catholic women. Over time this church movement has grown across the world, becoming interfaith and ecumenical in the process.[110] The Women Church seems to invite comparison with the early twentieth-century Labour Church in the UK, founded by Unitarian preacher John Trevor. In a similar manner the Labour Church emerged out of conviction that the existing church would not suffice for the needs of the working class. The Labour Church, however, soon moved away from specifically Christian language and doctrine. It represented more socialism as a religion rather than religious socialism; arguably the Women Church faces a similar danger of devolving into feminism as religion rather than religious feminism.[111]

Conclusion

Liberation theology has spread across the world, being applied to many different circumstances and contexts. This has proved possible because, while a specific liberation theology cannot be imported into another culture or context, the methodology of liberation theology can be. The commitment to praxis as the necessary precondition to theological reflection, the development of truth in conjunction with the experience of the oppressed, the commitment – broadly conceived – to liberation, all represent a framework that aids in the development of ideas and that can be transferred to another setting. As in Latin America, other parts of the Third World that had suffered colonialism and dependence upon the global economic centre developed their own theologies of liberation, often in conversation with other religions and theology. The apartheid system of South Africa led to the emergence of a black liberation theology similar to that developed by African-Americans in the United States. Feminists and womanists began to develop their own liberation theology in response to the lack of focus on patriarchy, misogyny and gender-based oppression in these other forms.

Liberation theology, however, is open to criticism insofar as it moved beyond a plain reading of the Bible to focus on a perceived 'prophetic-liberating tradition', to use Rosemary Radford Ruether's terminology. Feminist, womanist, LGBT+ and 'queer' theologies are perhaps the clearest examples of this, having to adopt a hermeneutic of suspicion and a rather loose method of exegesis when it comes to scripture, as well as historic church teaching. This much is suggested in the feminist reliance on non-Christian religions and traditions, including paganism, Gnosticism and Wicca, and in the argument of LGBT+ theologian Gary David Comstock that scripture itself should not be considered authoritative, but rather a resource for the construction of a more affirming theology. Similar criticisms can be levelled at all liberation theologies – indeed at all traditions that fall under the general heading of Christian Left (see Chapter 8). These, along with the growing secularism of the political Left, raise questions about the ongoing viability of the Christian Left.

8

Where Next for the Christian Left?

The foregoing chapters have focused on only a selection of examples from the Christian Left. While it is to be hoped that we have encountered a representative sample, at least of Western Christianity, there is certainly more that could be examined. Yet even with this caveat in place we have encountered a galaxy of Christian Left traditions: British Christian Socialism, European religious socialism, Catholic social teaching, liberation theology, black liberation theology, feminist and womanist theology, LGBT+ theology, the Social Gospel, spiritual socialism, and so on. These movements are all different, with ideological and doctrinal distinctives, which cannot be simplistically lumped together. British Christian Socialism is derived from a homegrown mix of largely Anglo-Catholic and Nonconformist piety, trade unionism, modern liberalism, and even Tory paternalism. Religious socialism, particularly in the German-speaking world, developed separately from the socialist mainstream, only latterly linking with the revisionism of Bernstein and the later SPD. The Social Gospel was a broad movement, at some points linking to socialism itself and at others being little more than Christian charity. The civil rights movement had aims and emphases which differ from the later black liberation movement. Liberation theologies in and of themselves differ according to time and place, whether holding one aspect of oppression – race, sex, orientation, class – as most important or embracing an intersectional understanding of how these various aspects overlap. Those that adhere to the progressive commitment to critical theory, intersectionality, and – even while rejecting economic individualism – a focus on the identarian and psychological needs of the individual are fully at odds with those that advocate post-liberal values of tradition and communitarianism.

Core concepts of the Christian Left

Despite this, it is striking how the same themes, concepts and ideas appear in vastly different contexts. Key among these is the concept of brotherhood. The language of brotherhood is used most clearly by the British Christian Socialists, especially those of the late nineteenth and early twentieth centuries, Anglo-Catholic and Nonconformist. It appears in central Europe, such as in the social democratic Brotherhood Movement of Sweden, as well as among the Social Gospellers and spiritual socialists of the United States. The concept of brotherhood also appears in the liberation theology of Latin America, though feminist, womanist, LGBT+ and intersectional theologies might regard such gendered language as problematic. Brotherhood is a theological concept with political implications. It derives from an understanding of God as a Father, as summed up succinctly in Stewart Headlam's assertion of 'the fact of the Fatherhood of God, implying as it does the Brotherhood of men' and is even more plainly stated by Washington Gladden: 'From the fact of the divine Fatherhood is derived the fact of human brotherhood.'[1] Brotherhood is also seen in the teaching and work of Christ. It is Christ, argued Charles M. Sheldon, 'who bids us all recognize the Brotherhood of the race'.[2] It is the liberation won by Christ which Gustavo Gutiérrez regards as 'the basis for all human brotherhood'.[3]

That these theological ideas have a practical, political outworking is expressed nowhere better than in a statement of the British Free Church Socialist League 'that the principle of Brotherhood as taught by Jesus Christ cannot adequately be wrought out under existing industrial and commercial conditions, and that the faithful and commonplace application of this principle must result in the Socialization of all natural resources, as well as the instruments of production, distribution and exchange'.[4] The capitalist system, it is maintained, fails to enshrine human brotherhood, encouraging instead exploitation, competition, and individualistic self-interest. In order to live as brothers, as children of God, it is necessary to create a society characterised by co-operation, equality, justice and liberty – to make, as Gutiérrez phrased it, 'prophetic denunciation of every dehumanising situation, which is contrary to brotherhood, justice, and liberty' and create 'a society of brotherhood and justice'.[5] Insofar as the Christian Left can be summed up in a configuration of concepts, we may view the brotherhood of man as the central concept, the organising principle, straddling the divide between the theological and the political. The Fatherhood of God is the theological basis for this, and the other concepts – co-operation, equality, justice, liberty – the political or socio-economic ideas that logically follow.

Co-operation was key to earliest Christian Socialists of Britain – F.D. Maurice, Charles Kingsley and John Ludlow. Maurice, despite the question marks that remain over his socialism, was convinced of the need for people to work together and support each other, rather than competing with and exploiting one another; Ludlow was even more firmly committed to this vision. Co-operation would continue to be at the heart of the Christian Socialist movement, often implying collectivism – whether that meant state ownership as some favoured, or other forms of joint ownership and management. Even Tony Blair, having abolished the Labour Party's constitutional commitment to collectivism in Clause IV, would continue to speak of collective duties and responsibilities. Blue Labour thinkers such as John Milbank and Adrian Pabst also have a vision of a cohesive, co-operative society, in which economic activity is governed by a Christian ethic. The concept of co-operation is in evidence elsewhere: it was also at the heart of the ethical socialism of Henri Saint-Simon and Philippe Buchez; it is emphasised, albeit shorn of any endorsement of state control, in Catholic social teaching; it emerges in the declaration of Latin American liberation theology for collectivisation of the means of production. Co-operation based on common brotherhood is at the heart of Desmond Tutu's black liberation theology and vision of South Africa as a 'rainbow nation'.

Brotherhood also implies equality – a moral or foundational equality, which needs to be translated into practice as formal equality, genuine equality of opportunity, and greater equality of outcome. The Christian Left – perhaps demonstrating its proximity to social democracy rather than Marxist socialism – has not always argued for full equality of outcome, but rather, as Tawney phrased it, that 'it is the mark of a civilized society to aim at eliminating such inequalities as have their source, not in individual differences, but in its own organization'.[6] Differences in outcome should reflect differences in people; inequality of outcome that exists because of an exploitative system cannot be justified. Some strands of the Christian Left held a greater commitment to equality of outcome, most notably liberation theology, partly due to its theoretical incorporation of Marxism; others, perhaps the Social Gospel of the United States, as well as the purportedly social democratic Third Way, as advocated by Blair, stand accused of neglecting anything like equality of outcome and advocating a conception of equality of opportunity which Tawney derided as 'obviously a jest, to be described as amusing or heartless according to taste'.[7]

For most of the period we have been examining, formal equality – that is, equal standing before the law – has not been an issue for white men. Christian Socialists, however, such as Margaret Bondfield and Ellen Wilkinson – supported by allies such as George Lansbury – were among those who had to fight for the right of women to vote, latterly on equal terms with men, formerly at all. In later decades the clearest examples of formal equality – and consequently the principle of equality itself – being denied are found in the segregated southern United States and apartheid South Africa. Reverdy Ransom's vision of 'a new civilization rising – a civilization which shall neither be Anglo-Saxon, Asiatic nor African', which, 'recognizing the unity of the race and the brotherhood of man, will accord to each individual [...] the right to stand upon an equal plane and share all the blessings of our common heritage', foreshadows not only the US civil rights movement of Martin Luther King, Jr, but also the South African black liberation theology of Tutu and Allan Boesak.[8] King's vision of a society of equality expressed at the Lincoln Memorial, and Fannie Lou Hamer's demand that African-Americans be viewed as 'first-class citizens', reflect a cry for formal equality based on a natural, God-given equality.[9]

The denial of these claims led in part to the rise of 'black power' and the black liberation theology of James H. Cone. Cone's view of equality paralleled that which we have discussed so far, but with

significant differences. The notion of a 'white' God, as represented
in mainstream Christianity, could not serve for the liberation from
oppression of the wretched of the earth. God is black, argued Cone,
'black' here being an ontological marker for identification with the
oppressed, with 'white' representing the role of the oppressor.[10] In
order therefore for the Fatherhood of God to mean universal equality, white people must repent of their 'whiteness', becoming 'black'
in order to have fellowship with the black God and the oppressed.
Cone's vision of an egalitarian society was one in which all people
were – if not physically, then ontologically – black. Cone's vision is
arguably different from that of King or Tutu for a 'rainbow nation'
of equals; it is certainly a long distance from Christian Socialist
discussions of equalising economic outcomes.

Feminist, womanist and *mujerista* theologies would here take
issue with the gendered nature of God's Fatherhood and human
brotherhood, arguing that these masculine, 'patriarchal' concepts
cannot serve for the realisation of sexual equality. This arguably
accounts in part for the ways in which British Christian Socialism,
European religious socialism, and Latin American liberation theology has often overlooked the oppression of women. The civil
rights and black power movements also neglected the issues faced
by women, both black and white, as argued by Pauli Murray.
Feminist theologians such as Henriette Marianne Katoppo and
Rosemary Radford Ruether have therefore sought to replace an
understanding of God as a father by emphasising that God relates
to humanity by means of revealed characteristics and attributes
that are both feminine and masculine. The formula of God as
Father leading to a brotherhood of man is therefore replaced with
God as relational leading to a family of persons.

The Christian Left is also committed to the concept of justice.
God – whether one conceives of a Father God or a relational
God – demands that his children behave justly to one another.
King's view of the civil rights movement was that '[t]his is not
a war between the white and the Negro but a conflict between
justice and injustice'.[11] Yes, the African-American community was
called to love its white oppressors – for they were, despite everything, brothers and sisters – but this was not a passive love that
overlooked wrong; rather, it was a love in action, which sought to
correct that which was sinful and wicked and establish justice, so
that the quest for justice was itself an expression of Christian love.

Ellen Wilkinson also linked justice to human fraternity, emphasising the need to combat 'injustice' wherever it afflicted 'human beings, the children of God'.[12] Sergio Méndez Arceo described his belief that 'a socialist system is more in accord with the Christian principles of true brotherhood, justice and peace'.[13]

The concept of liberty is also emphasised – children of God should be free, not enslaved by capitalism or by other forms of oppression. This perspective is given most clearly, of course, in liberation theology, but it is evident across the spectrum of Christian Left traditions. Wilhelm Emmanuel von Ketteler hoped for 'common ownership of the goods of this world', which would bring about 'maximum freedom in our social and political institutions'.[14] Lisa Sharon Harper and Tony Campolo both speak of the liberty that is to be realised in Christ. Gutiérrez called for 'liberation from all that limits or keeps man from self-fulfilment, liberation from all impediments to the exercise of his freedom'.[15] Martin Luther King dreamed of that day 'when we allow freedom to ring [...] that day when all of God's children, black men and white men, Jews and Gentiles, Protestants and Catholics, will be able to join hands and sing in the words of the old Negro spiritual: "Free at last. Free at last! Thank God almighty, we are free at last!"'[16]

For those on the Christian Left, the achievement of such a society – one characterised by co-operation, equality, justice and liberty – was linked to the Kingdom of God. For some, among them Paul Tillich, Shailer Mathews and Vida Scudder, this society would be the reflection of the Kingdom and its values, the reality of which would be realised outside of time. For Walter Rauschenbusch, such a society would be the actual fulfilment of the Kingdom, albeit only in part. For others it was to be the realisation of the Kingdom in full. Sherwood Eddy, Dorothy Day, Tony Campolo and others of the American Christian Left took this view. Gutiérrez straddled both views, acknowledging that the fullness of the Kingdom was an eschatological reality, but nevertheless viewing 'the coming of the Kingdom [as] historical, temporal, earthly, social, and material [...] The struggle for a just world in which there is no oppression, servitude, or alienated work will signify the coming of the Kingdom.'[17] Scott Holland spoke for many among the British Christian Socialists when he set out his vision of 'a Kingdom of earthly righteousness and social happiness [...] The Holy Jerusalem descends from heaven to Earth: the City of God.'[18]

Theological question marks

Despite the many differences and variations within the Christian Left, it does not appear that any Christian denomination or tradition is more likely than any other to espouse socialist or radical politics. In these pages we have encountered Roman Catholics from a variety of contexts; Anglicans and Episcopalians both Anglo-Catholic and evangelical; representatives of the black church and the white church; a whole range of Protestant denominations – Lutherans, Reformed, Methodists, Baptists, Congregationalists, Presbyterians and others; as well as those holding to more idiosyncratic, non-institutional forms of Christianity. What does seem to be the case – and even this is not a universal condition – is that whatever denomination or tradition is in view, it is those with a more liberal approach to the Bible, theology and church teaching who appear more likely to embrace political Leftism.

This is seen most clearly in feminist, womanist, LGBT+ and 'queer' theologies, as well as those other liberation theologies that take an intersectional view. Such is evidenced in the 'hermeneutic of suspicion' adopted by Rosemary Radford Reuther and other feminists, in which the plain reading of scripture is subjected to the reader's critique in order to strip away the 'patriarchal' assumptions of prophets and apostles, who allegedly themselves did not understand the 'prophetic-liberating' theme of the message they were delivering. Feminist theology, as we have seen, requires the insights of non-Christian traditions – paganism, Gnosticism, wicca – in order to sustain itself. Some, such as Mary Daly, find themselves moving away from Christianity altogether. The same issues are seen in LGBT+ and 'queer' theologies that have sought to build a theology of liberation around lifestyles that the Bible describes as sinful. This in part explains the methodology of Gary David Comstock, who argues 'Christian Scripture and tradition are not authorities from which I seek approval', but must be seen as 'resources from which I seek guidance and learn lessons as well [as] institutions that I seek to interpret, shape, and change'.[19]

The criticism of such an approach is that the Bible and church teaching are no longer the basis for a theological–ideological worldview, but the reverse – that the worldview is adopted first and allowed to shape an understanding of the Bible and church teaching. Yet this problem does not affect only those theologies which focus on sex, gender and orientation. The Christians who favour socialism, a collectivised order of society, also stand accused of reading their politics and economics into rather than deriving them from the Bible and church teaching. Stewart Headlam, for example, argued: 'All those ideas which we now express vaguely under the terms solidarity, brotherhood, co-operation, socialism, seem to have been vividly present in Jesus Christ's teaching.'[20] Gustavo Gutiérrez, for another, insisted: 'The whole climate of the Gospel is a continual demand for the right of the poor to make themselves heard, to be considered preferentially by society, a demand to subordinate economic needs to those of the deprived.'[21] Yet, a straightforward reading of the Gospel, while certainly picking up on the condemnations of economic injustice and oppression, does not obviously amount to an argument for socialist collectivism. To see these things arguably requires a hermeneutic, a method of exegesis, which has already assumed socialism, which goes to the Bible trying to find socialism, and which therefore finds both what it presupposes and searches for.

The concept at the very core of Christian Socialism – brotherhood – is itself contestable. To view brotherhood as applying to all people, each and every individual without distinction, relies on a universal understanding of God's Fatherhood, which is not sustained in scripture. A theologically conservative understanding is that only those who have been reconciled to God through faith in Christ are children of God. New Testament references to brotherhood are set in the context of a division between believers and unbelievers, saved and unsaved – Christ declares that his 'brothers' are those who follow him and do his will (Matthew 30:32), the 'brothers' in Acts of the Apostles are those who have turned to Christ in contrast to those who oppose the Gospel (Acts 14:2), and Paul declares in Romans: 'For those whom he foreknew he also predestined to be conformed to the image of his Son, in order that he might be the firstborn among many brothers' (Romans 8:29). The Catechism of the Roman Catholic Church (Article Four, Section Two, 2:II) affirms that it is those who have been reconciled to God who are brothers, quoting Cyprian of Antioch: 'The new man, reborn and restored to his God by grace, says first of all, "Father!" because he has *now begun to be a son*' [emphasis added]. The 1689 London Baptist Confession of

Faith (18:2–3) shares the same emphasis. Examples here could be multiplied, but it is clear that neither brotherhood nor God's Fatherhood is universal. Christ delivers a stark message to those who mistakenly claim to be children of God: 'If God were your Father, you would love me [but] you cannot bear to hear my word. You are of your father the devil, and your will is to do your father's desires' (John 8:42a, 43b–44).

The impact this has on Christian Left thought runs deep. If God is not a universal Father, as F.D. Maurice claimed all those years ago, then neither is there a universal brotherhood of man. If there is no universal brotherhood of man, then the central concept of the Christian Left – of Christian Socialism, of the Social Gospel, of liberation theology – collapses, and with it the basis for a message of co-operation, equality, justice and liberation. Take, for example, a passage often cited by the Christian Left, the judgement of the sheep and the goats, in which Christ declares to the sheep – the righteous – at his right hand:

> 'Come, you who are blessed by my Father, inherit the kingdom prepared for you from the foundation of the world. For I was hungry and you gave me food, I was thirsty and you gave me drink, I was a stranger and you welcomed me, I was naked and you clothed me, I was sick and you visited me, I was in prison and you came to me.' Then the righteous will answer him, saying, 'Lord, when did we see you hungry and feed you, or thirsty and give you drink? And when did we see you a stranger and welcome you, or naked and clothe you? And when did we see you sick or in prison and visit you?' And the King will answer them, 'Truly, I say to you, as you did it to one of the least of these my brothers, you did it to me.'

This parable of the final judgement has often been used to demonstrate the love that Christ demands to be shown to all people – all the exploited, oppressed and disadvantaged of the world. It is this parable, declared Stewart Headlam, which 'seems to compel every Christian to be a socialist'.[22] It proves, argues Phillip Berryman, that 'practical material aid for one's neighbour is the criterion of a just life'.[23] Yet the parable is not about one's neighbour, but specifically the 'brothers' of Christ. Minus a universal conception of brotherhood, it is clear that the hungry, impoverished and oppressed of this parable are not all such in all times and places, but specifically believers; they are Christ's brothers because they are those who have been reconciled to him. The parable therefore prompts consideration not of general economic justice, but of how those who profess to follow Christ serve and support the least of his followers, the least of his brothers, including the persecuted church across the world.

Christians, to be sure, are not limited to caring just for other Christians. The Apostle Paul taught the church, 'as we have opportunity, let us do good to everyone' – but even here immediately followed the instruction: 'and especially to those who are of the household of faith' (Galatians 6:10). There are many verses and passages that teach care and compassion for one's neighbour without distinction, including the Golden Rule: 'Love your neighbour as yourself' (Mark 12:31). Yet it is a conception of universal brotherhood that underpins not just help, support, care and charity, but an entire system of fraternal, familial collectivism and co-operation; take away the universal brotherhood, and the theological support for that system – especially where that system is conceptualised as God's Kingdom on earth rather than simply the most efficient way of showing practical love for one's neighbour – is severely damaged. If universal brotherhood is omitted, the Christian Socialist end-of-history or ultimate aim – Christian co-operation between all individuals – is unsupported by the Bible and church teaching, which view humanity, far from being united as one human family with common aims and objectives, as ultimately divided. More broadly, the Christian Left could be accused of downplaying the role of individual sin and the barriers which this places on those who wish to reorganise the world as more just, moral and righteous.

Other proof texts for socialism could be subjected to the same scrutiny from a theologically conservative perspective. Paul's discussion of a body in which all the members co-operate with each other (1 Corinthians 12:12–30) is a reference not to society as a whole, but to the church. The common ownership of Acts of the Apostles (Acts 2:44–5), so often taken as the clearest biblical injunction to collective ownership, points to the free sharing of resources and property within the community of believers, those who do share a common brotherhood in Christ. The same applies to the land laws – including the year of jubilee – given to Israel, which was the Old Testament church. The liberty proclaimed by Christ in the synagogue sermon (Luke 4:18–19), beloved of liberation theology and 'red-letter' evangelicalism, likewise becomes an exclusive message of salvation from sin rather than a general declaration that intersectional oppression will be ended. The Gospel is not, as Gutiérrez thought, about liberty from the consequences of institutional sin; it is, in fact, about salvation from one's own personal sin. None of this should be taken to mean that Christians should be indifferent to poverty, oppression and economic injustice – though some certainly are – but that the Bible and church teaching are not the clear and consistent socialist message that those of the Christian Left seem to think.

The future of the Christian Left

If Christianity is not as compatible with the Left as has often been supposed, it is also arguable that the contemporary Left is not compatible with Christianity. The incompatibility arises insofar as the contemporary Left has de-prioritised opposition to economic inequality in favour of opposition to identarian inequality. Policies which serve to overturn economic oppression, capitalist exploitation and working-class disadvantage have become secondary, with the priority now to dismantle 'repressive sexual codes' in order to achieve liberation from oppression.[24] For this reason 'the modern Left [...] will devote a wildly disproportionate amount of time and resources – almost to the point of obsession – campaigning in identarian causes', focusing on 'biological characteristics, sexual orientation or religion of a particular section of society' to the exclusion of economic class.[25] Neither the socialist mission to overturn capitalism nor the social democratic commitment to regulate capitalism is the core of today's left-wing politics; rather, politics is 'dominated by issues of identity' and oppression has become a psychological – not economic – category, in which non-recognition of (primarily sexual, but also racial) identity is the main issue.[26]

The issue for the Christian Left is not that it is necessarily unable to adapt to the progressivism of the modern age. Certainly, however, those of the Blue Labour, radical orthodoxy, post-liberal strand of Christian Socialism will not wish to, thereby sealing their separation from the mainstream Left. At one point in history it could be imagined that Christian Socialists might put differences of opinion about sexual ethics to one side in order to work together combating economic injustice and building a socialist or social democratic society; this is no longer conceivable in an age in which 'silence is violence' and tolerance just a more insidious form of oppression. Even modern liberation theologies, especially those which are feminist, womanist or *mujerista*, LGBT+ or 'queer', or which are otherwise open to an intersectional understanding of oppression, face this problem. For the New Left, Christianity enshrines the oppressive sexual codes which need to be dismantled,[27] embodying and perpetuating identarian, psychological oppression, raising doubts that Christianity can ever be recast as the bearer of a 'prophetic-liberating tradition'.

As such, Leftist antipathy to Christianity is increasing. In Britain, for example, the gatekeepers of the contemporary Left are, according to left-wing activist Paul Embery, 'disdainful of the early Labour tradition and the party's roots in Christian socialism'.[28] Those who have been traditionally regarded as heroes of the Left such as Keir Hardie and R.H. Tawney, along with those who have made a perhaps quieter but significant contribution, among them George Lansbury and William Temple, will come to be dismissed by the political Left of the twenty-first century as the bearers of 'white Christian privilege'. If this seems unlikely, consider how the US presidential campaign of Bernie Sanders was dogged by accusation from the progressive Left that Sanders and his supporters were merely misogynistic, bigoted, angry white men. This, one left-wing activist argues, is the result of a progressive political movement in which 'personal identity has become a shorthand for "progress" and "white man" has become an epithet'.[29] The faith-based socialism of Hardie, Lansbury, Tawney and Temple, even resulting as it did in the social democratic achievements of 1945–51, might today be unacceptable – the Bible-centred and theologically rich political views of these men an example of 'Christian hegemony' or 'Christian normativity'.[30] According to intersectional scholar Khyati Y. Joshi, after all, we must today 'recognize the long presence of White Christian supremacy'.[31] Can there be a future for the Christian Left now that Christianity is itself viewed as problematic?

Yet the Christian Left has been around for too long to disappear now, even if both non-socialist Christians and non-Christian progressives might throw theological and ideological obstacles in its path. We have seen that there has been a multiplicity of

Christian Left movements over the past century and a half. These movements draw on a tradition of religiously based egalitarianism, collectivism and denunciation of economic and other forms of injustice, which can be traced all the way back to the New Testament church – some would say all the way back to the Garden of Eden. Put simply, for however long there has been radicalism and socialism, there has been Christian radicalism and socialism. The Christian Left will certainly have to work harder to make its voice heard in a conversation increasingly dominated on the one hand by a secular-minded, identarian Left and on the other by the populist Right, which claims Christianity for itself, but it will continue – if it is allowed – to play an important role in demonstrating that Christianity need not belong to the conservative Right and making the ethical case for an economic system subject to fairness and the common good.

Notes

Introduction

1 Joseph Maybloom, 'President Donald Trump's photo op in front of St John's Church', *Ecumenica*, 13, 2 (2020): p. 231.

2 Ibid.

3 Harriet Sherwood, 'White evangelical Christians stick by Trump again, exit polls show', *Guardian*, https: //www.theguardian.com/ us-news/2020/nov/06/white-evangelical-christians-supported-trump.

4 Matthew Teague, '"He wears the armor of God": evangelicals hail Trump's church photo op', *Guardian*, https: //www.theguard ian.com/us-news/2020/jun/03/donald-trump-church-photo-op-evan gelicals.

5 Paul LeBlanc, 'Bishop at DC church outraged by Trump visit: "I just can't believe what my eyes have seen"', CNN, https: //edition.cnn. com/2020/06/01/politics/cnntv-bishop-trump-photo-op/index.html.

6 'New England Episcopal bishops respond with one voice to President's "cynical" photo-op' (2020).

7 Francis Johnson, *Keir Hardie's Socialism* (London: ILP, 1922), p. 12.

8 Rosemary Radford Ruether, *Sexism and God-Talk: Toward a Feminist Theology* (Boston MA: Beacon Press, 1983), p. 23.

9 Stewart D. Headlam, *The Socialist's Church* (London: G. Allen, 1907), p. 8.

10 James Keir Hardie, *From Serfdom to Socialism* (London: G. Allen, 1907), p. 38.

11 Gustavo Gutiérrez, *A Theology of Liberation: History, Politics and Salvation* (Maryknoll NY: Orbis Books, 1973), p. 35.
12 Jonathan Schneer, *George Lansbury* (Manchester: Manchester University Press, 1990), p. 1.
13 Robyn J. Whitaker, 'Trump's photo op with church and Bible was offensive, but not new', *The Conversation*, https: //theconversation. com/trumps-photo-op-with-church-and-bible-was-offensive-but-not-new-140053.
14 Woody Guthrie, 'Jesus Christ', https://www.woodyguthrie.org/Lyrics/Jesus_Christ.htm.
15 Samuel E. Keeble, *Christian Responsibility for the Social Order* (London: Epworth Press, 1922), pp. 39 and 41.
16 John C. Cort, *Christian Socialism: An Informal History* (Maryknoll NY: Orbis Books, 2020 [1988]), p. 52.
17 Samuel E. Keeble, *The Ideal of the Material Life and other Social Addresses* (London: C.H. Kelly, 1908), p. 227.
18 Cort, *Christian Socialism*, p. 56.
19 Chris Bryant, *Possible Dreams: A Personal History of the British Christian Socialists* (London: Hodder & Stoughton, 1996), p. 4.
20 Noah Shusterman, *The French Revolution: Faith, Desire and Politics* (Abingdon: Taylor & Francis, 2013), pp. 223–4.
21 Cort, *Christian Socialism*, p. 5.

1   The Spirit of Brotherhood: Foundations of British Christian Socialism

1 Chris Bryant, *Possible Dreams: A Personal History of the British Christian Socialists* (London: Hodder and Stoughton, 1996), pp. 81–2.
2 James Keir Hardie, 'Labour and Christianity: is the labour movement against Christianity?', in *Labour and Religion: by Ten Members of Parliament and Other Bodies* (London: n.p, 1910), p. 49.
3 Bryant, *Possible Dreams*, p. 41.
4 John C. Cort, *Christian Socialism: An Informal History* (Maryknoll NY: Orbis Books, 2020 [1988]), p. 159.
5 Bryant, *Possible Dreams*, p. 37.
6 Gary Dorrien, *Social Democracy in the Making: Political and Religious Roots of European Socialism* (Yale CT: Yale University Press, 2019), p. 43.

7 Cort, *Christian Socialism*, p. 161.
8 Jeremy Morris, 'F.D. Maurice and the myth of Christian Socialist origins', in Stephen Spencer, ed., *Theology Reforming Society: Revisiting Anglican Social Theology* (London: SCM Press, 2017), p. 5; Bryant, *Possible Dreams*, p. 43.
9 Morris, 'F.D. Maurice', p. 5
10 F.D. Maurice, 'Tracts on Christian Socialism, Tract 1 (1850)' in Ellen K. Wondra, ed., *Reconstructing Christian Ethics: Selected Writings of F.D. Maurice* (Louisville KY: Westminster John Knox Press, 1995), p. 196.
11 Ibid., pp. 202 and 205.
12 Alan Wilkinson, *Christian Socialism: Scott Holland to Tony Blair* (London: SCM Press, 1998), p. 18.
13 Jeremy Morris, *F.D. Maurice and the Crisis of Christian Authority* (Oxford: Oxford University Press, 2008), pp. 135 and 146.
14 Ibid., pp. 146, 158 and 67.
15 Ibid., p. 75.
16 Ibid., p. 78.
17 Ibid., pp. 159–60.
18 Steven Schroeder, *The Metaphysics of Cooperation: A Study of F.D. Maurice* (Atlanta GA: Rodopi, 1999), p. 53.
19 Paul Dafydd Jones, 'Jesus Christ and the transformation of English society: the "subversive conservatism" of Frederick Denison Maurice', *Harvard Theological Review*, 96, 2 (2003): pp. 225–6.
20 Morris, *F.D. Maurice*, p. 149.
21 Schroeder, *Metaphysics of Cooperation*, pp. 53 and 56.
22 Morris, *F.D. Maurice*, p. 147.
23 Dorrien, *Social Democracy*, p. 42.
24 Cort, *Christian Socialism*, p. 166.
25 Ibid., p. 160.
26 Ibid., p. 155; Dorrien, *Social Democracy*, pp. 40 and 42.
27 Maurice, 'Tract 1', pp. 196–7; Dorrien, *Social Democracy*, pp. 44–5.
28 Cort, *Christian Socialism*, p. 164.
29 Ibid., pp. 168–9; Dorrien, *Social Democracy*, pp. 6 and 46–7.
30 Maurice, 'Tract 1', p. 202.
31 Dorrien, *Social Democracy*, p. 46; Cort, *Christian Socialism*, p. 171.
32 Stewart D. Headlam, *Maurice and Kingsley: Theologians and Socialists* (London: George Standring, 1909), p. 5.
33 Ibid., p. 8.
34 Stewart D. Headlam, *Priestcraft and Progress: Being Sermons and Lectures* (London: John Hodges, 1878), pp. 19 and 21.

35 Peter d'A. Jones, *The Christian Socialist Revival 1877–1914: Religion, Class, and Social Conscience in Late-Victorian England* (Princeton, NJ: Princeton University Press, 1969), p. 146.

36 Stewart D. Headlam, *The Socialist's Church* (London: G. Allen, 1907), p. 5.

37 Stewart D. Headlam, *Christian Socialism – A Lecture: Fabian Tract No.42* (London: Fabian Society, 1899), p. 6.

38 Stewart D. Headlam, *The Meaning of the Mass: Five Lectures with Other Sermons and Addresses* (London: S.C. Brown, 1905), p. 83.

39 Headlam, *Meaning of the Mass*, p. 73; Headlam, *Priestcraft and Progress*, p. 7; John Richard Orens, *Stewart Headlam's Radical Anglicanism: The Mass, the Masses, and the Music Hall* (Chicago IL: University of Illinois Press, 2003), p. 24; Kenneth Leech, 'Stewart Headlam, 1847–1924, and the Guild of St Matthew', in Maurice B. Reckitt, ed., *For Christ and the People: Studies of Four Socialist Priests and Prophets of the Church of England* (London: SPCK, 1968), p. 78.

40 Headlam, *Meaning of the Mass*, p. 29.

41 Dorrien, *Social Democracy*, pp. 98–9.

42 Stephen Mayor, *The Churches and the Labour Movement* (London: Independent Press, 1967), p. 197.

43 Dorrien, *Social Democracy*, p. 99.

44 Henry Scott Holland, *Our Neighbours: A Handbook for the C.S.U.* (London: A.R. Mowbray, 1911), pp. 67–8.

45 Dorrien, *Social Democracy*, p. 100.

46 Jones, *Christian Socialist Revival*, p. 166.

47 Scott Holland, *Our Neighbours*, p. 9.

48 Ibid., pp. 10–11.

49 Ibid., p. 18.

50 Ibid., p. 81.

51 Ibid., p. 83.

52 Ibid., p. 91.

53 Ibid., pp. 84 and 127.

54 Wilkinson, *Christian Socialism*, pp. 71–2.

55 Scott Holland, *Our Neighbours*, p. 152.

56 Peter Wadell, *Charles Gore: Radical Anglican* (Norwich: Canterbury Press, 2014), p. xxii.

57 Ibid.

58 Ibid., p. 145.

59 Ibid., p. 145.

60 Ibid., p. 146.

61 Ibid., p. 147.

62 Ibid., p. 154.

63 Dorrien, *Social Democracy*, p. 107.
64 Jones, *Christian Socialist Revival*, p. 181; Mayor, *Churches and the Labour Movement*, p. 223.
65 Cort, *Christian Socialism*, p. 177.
66 Mayor, *Churches and the Labour Movement*, p. 229.
67 Dorrien, *Social Democracy*, pp. 8 and 312.
68 Arthur Burns, 'Beyond the "Red Vicar": community and Christian Socialism in Thaxted, Essex, 1910–84', *History Workshop Journal*, 75 (2013): p. 103.
69 Ibid., p. 108.
70 Mayor, *Churches and the Labour Movement*, p. 203.
71 John Clifford, *Socialism and the Teaching of Christ: Fabian Tract No. 78* (London: Fabian Society, 1898), p. 7.
72 Ibid., p. 11.
73 Samuel E. Keeble, *Industrial Day-Dreams: Studies in Industrial Ethics and Economics* (London: R. Culley, 1907 [1896]), p. 190.
74 Ibid., p. 53.
75 Ibid., pp. 90 and 133–4.
76 Ibid., p. 17.
77 Ibid., p. 92.
78 Dorrien, *Social Democracy*, p. 327; Stephen Spencer, 'William Temple and the "Temple Tradition"', in Stephen Spencer, ed., *Theology Reforming Society: Revisiting Anglican Social Theology* (London: SCM Press, 2017), p. 86.
79 Bryant, *Possible Dreams*, p. 180; Dorrien, *Social Democracy*, p. 368.
80 William Temple, *Christianity and the Social Order* (London: Penguin, 1976 [1942]), p. 36.
81 Ibid., p. 37.
82 Ibid., pp. 51 and 68.
83 Spencer, 'Temple Tradition', pp. 100–1.
84 Temple, *Christianity and the Social Order*, pp. 101–2.
85 Dorrien, *Social Democracy*, p. 396.
86 Ibid., p. 54.
87 Thomas L. Jarman, *Socialism in Britain: From the Industrial Revolution to the Present Day* (New York: Taplinger, 1972), p. 106.
88 James Keir Hardie, *Can a Man Be a Christian On a Pound a Week?* (London: ILP, 1905), pp. 13–14 and p. 3; James Keir Hardie, *From Serfdom to Socialism* (London: G. Allen, 1907), pp. 38 and 36.
89 Hardie, *Can a Man Be a Christian?*, p. 11.
90 James Keir Hardie, *My Confession of Faith in the Labour Alliance* (London: ILP, 1909), pp. 13 and 16.

91 Bob Holman, *Keir Hardie: Labour's Greatest Hero* (Oxford: Lion, 2010), pp. 132–3.

92 Dorrien, *Social Democracy*, pp. 370–1; Graham Dale, *God's Politicians: The Christian Contribution to 100 Years of Labour* (London: HarperCollins, 2000), p. 77.

93 Dale, *God's Politicians*, pp. 56 and 62.

94 Ian S. Wood, *John Wheatley* (Manchester: Manchester University Press, 1990), pp. 155–7.

95 Ian S. Wood, 'John Wheatley and Catholic Socialism', in A.R. Morton, eds, *After Socialism? The Future of Radical Christianity* (Edinburgh: CTPI, 1994), p. 20; John Hannan, *The Life of John Wheatley* (Nottingham: Spokesman Books, 1988), p. 11.

96 Wood, *Wheatley*, p. 24.

97 Wood, 'John Wheatley and Catholic Socialism', p. 21.

98 Wood, *Wheatley*, p. 18.

99 Tony Judge, *Margaret Bondfield: First Woman in the Cabinet* (London: Alpha House, 2018), pp. 30, 5 and 44.

100 Judge, *Bondfield*, p. 114; M. Bondfield, et al., *Trade Unions and Socialism* (London: ILP, 1926), p. 4, pp. 10–12.

101 Margaret Bondfield, *Socialism for Shop Assistants: Pass On Pamphlets No. 10* (London: Clarion Press, 1909), p. 14.

102 Bondfield, et al., *Trade Unions and Socialism*, p. 3.

103 Paula Bartley, *Ellen Wilkinson: From Red Suffragist to Government Minister* (London: Pluto Press, 2014), p. xi; Ellen Wilkinson, 'Slaves of machines', *Burnley News*, 28/11/30.

104 Interview with Lansbury from the Christian Commonwealth Newspaper, 11 August 1915, LSE archive, Lansbury/7 213.

105 George Lansbury, 'Back to the Galilean!', in *The Religion in the Labour Movement* (London: Holborn, 1919), p. 54.

106 Hobsbawm, *Age of Extremes*, p. 152.

107 Memorandum for interview with Hitler by Lansbury, 19 April 1937, LSE archive, Lansbury/16 145–7; Telegram from Lansbury to Hitler, 15 April 1939, LSE archive, Lansbury/17 88.

108 R.H. Tawney, 'The choice before the Labour Party', *Political Quarterly*, 3, 3 (1932): pp. 22–4.

109 Ibid., p. 25.

110 Ibid., pp. 26–7.

111 Dorrien, *Social Democracy*, pp. 370–1.

112 J.M. Winter and D.M. Joslin, eds, *R.H. Tawney's Commonplace Book* (Cambridge: Cambridge University Press, 2006), p. 67.

113 Gary Armstrong and Tim Gray, 'Three fallacies in the essentialist interpretation of the political thought of R.H. Tawney', *Journal of Political Ideologies*, 15, 2 (2010): pp. 161–74.

114 R.H. Tawney, *The Acquisitive Society* (London: Bell, 1921), pp. 185–6.
115 Matt Beech and Kevin Hickson, *Labour's Thinkers: The Intellectual Roots of Labour from Tawney to Gordon Brown* (London: I.B. Tauris, 2007), p. 28.
116 Wilkinson, *Christian Socialism*, p. 105.
117 Tawney, *Acquisitive Society*, pp. 27–8.
118 Ibid., p. 31.
119 Ibid., p. 114.
120 Ibid., p. 99.
121 Ibid., p. 151.
122 Ibid., pp. 42 and 46.
123 R.H. Tawney, *Religion and the Rise of Capitalism* (London: Pelican, 1922), p. 180.
124 R.H. Tawney, *Equality* (London: C. Tinling & Co., Ltd., 1938 [1931]), pp. 24 and 39.
125 Ibid., pp. 115–17 and p. 122.
126 Ibid., p. 141.
127 Anthony A.J. Williams, *Christian Socialism as a Political Ideology: The Formation of the British Christian Left, 1877–1945* (London: I.B. Tauris, 2021), p. 167.

2 Identity Crisis: Christian Socialism in Post-War Britain

1 Paul Bickley, *Building Jerusalem: Christianity and the Labour Party* (London: Bible Society, 2010), p. 56.
2 Anthony A.J. Williams, *Christian Socialism as Political Ideology: The Formation of the British Christian Left, 1877–1945* (London: I.B. Tauris, 2021), p. 183.
3 Bickley, *Building Jerusalem*, p. 64.
4 Gary Dorrien, *Social Democracy in the Making: Political and Religious Roots of European Socialism* (Yale CT: Yale University Press, 2019), p. 403.
5 Bickley, *Building Jerusalem*, p. 65.
6 Chris Bryant, *Possible Dreams: A Personal History of the British Christian Socialists* (London: Hodder and Stoughton, 1996), p. 262.
7 Graham Dale, *God's Politicians: The Christian Contribution to 100 Years of Labour* (London: HarperCollins, 2000), p. 162.
8 Bryant, *Possible Dreams*, p. 265.
9 Ibid.
10 Dale, *God's Politicians*, p. 163.

11 Alan Wilkinson, *Christian Socialism: Scott Holland to Tony Blair* (London: SCM Press, 1998), pp. 184–5; Bryant, *Possible Dreams*, p. 261.
12 Dale, *God's Politicians*, p. 152.
13 Wilkinson, *Christian Socialism*, p. 185.
14 Bryant, *Possible Dreams*, pp. 264 and 268; Dale, *God's Politicians*, p. 164.
15 Dale, *God's Politicians*, p. 152.
16 Bryant, *Possible Dreams*, p. 270.
17 Dale, *God's Politicians*, p. 155.
18 Dorrien, *Social Democracy*, p. 406.
19 Bryant, *Possible Dreams*, p. 270; Dorrien, *Social Democracy*, p. 404.
20 Dorrien, *Social Democracy*, p. 400.
21 Robert Leach, *Political Ideology in Britain* (London: Macmillan, 2015), pp. 115–16.
22 Ibid., pp. 74–5.
23 Bickley, *Building Jerusalem*, p. 40.
24 Dale, *God's Politicians*, p. 187.
25 'The New Declaration', *Social Democratic Party* (2018).
26 Williams, *Christian Socialism*, p. 5.
27 Dale, *God's Politicians*, p. 189.
28 Ibid., pp. 190–1.
29 Bryant, *Possible Dreams*, p. 282; Ronald H. Preston, 'The legacy of the Christian Socialist Movement in England', in Walter Block and Irving Hexham, eds, *Religion, Economics and Social Thought* (Vancouver BC: Fraser Institute, 1982), p. 193.
30 Preston, 'The legacy of the Christian Socialist Movement', p. 195.
31 Bryant, *Possible Dreams*, p. 282.
32 Ibid., p. 283.
33 Ibid., p. 278.
34 Dale, *God's Politicians*, p. 186.
35 Margaret Thatcher, 'Speech at St Lawrence Jewry' (1981).
36 *Faith in the City: A Call for Action by Church and Nation – The Report of the Archbishop of Canterbury's Commission on Urban Priority Areas* (London: Church House Publishing, 1985), p. xv.
37 Ibid., p. 22.
38 Ibid., p. 48.
39 Ibid., p. 49.
40 Dale, *God's Politicians*, p. 186.
41 *Faith in the City*, p. 51.
42 Ibid., pp. 59, 53 and 204–5.
43 Ibid., p. 51.

44 Ibid.
45 Ibid., p. 52.
46 Bryant, *Possible Dreams*, p. 293.
47 Leach, *Political Ideology in Britain*, p. 122.
48 Dale, *God's Politicians*, p. 207.
49 Ibid., p. 209; Williams, *Christian Socialism*, p. 1.
50 Andy MacSmith, *John Smith: A Life, 1938–1994* (London: Mandarin, 1994), p. 320.
51 John Smith, 'Reclaiming the ground: freedom and the value of society', in Christopher Bryant, ed., *Reclaiming the Ground: Christianity and Socialism* (London: Spire, 1993), p. 127.
52 Ibid., pp. 129 and 132.
53 Ibid., pp. 130 and 133.
54 Ibid., pp. 133 and 141.
55 Ibid., pp. 134–5.
56 Bryant, *Possible Dreams*, p. 296.
57 Andrew Connell, 'Tony Blair', in Nick Spencer, ed., *The Mighty and the Almighty: How Political Leaders Do God* (London: Biteback, 2017), pp. 89–90.
58 Wilkinson, *Christian Socialism*, p. 235.
59 Tony Blair, 'Foreword', in Christopher Bryant, ed., *Reclaiming the Ground: Christianity and Socialism* (London: Spire, 1993), pp. 9–11.
60 Ibid., p. 10.
61 Wilkinson, *Christian Socialism*, p. 237.
62 Ibid., p. 240.
63 Connell, 'Blair', p. 91,
64 Bryant, *Possible Dreams*, p. 297.
65 Leach, *Political Ideology in Britain*, p. 124; Andrew Vincent, *Modern Political Ideologies* (Oxford: Wiley-Blackwell, 2010), p. 93.
66 Bickley, *Building Jerusalem*, p. 67.
67 Hans Keman, 'Third ways and social democracy: the right way to go?', *British Journal of Political Science*, 41, 3 (2011): pp. 673–4.
68 Leach, *Political Ideology in Britain*, p. 128.
69 Paul Embery, *Despised: Why the Modern Left Loathes the Working Class* (Cambridge: Polity, 2021), pp. 22–3.
70 Bickley, *Building Jerusalem*, p. 60.
71 Laura Hood, 'New Labour 20 years on: assessing the legacy of the Tony Blair years', *The Conversation* (April, 2017).
72 Dale, *God's Politicians*, p. 222.
73 Ibid.
74 Bryant, *Possible Dreams*, p. 295.

75 Ibid., p. 270.
76 Wilkinson, *Christian Socialism*, pp. 185–6.
77 Bryant, *Possible Dreams*, pp. 290 and 272.
78 Anthony A.J. Williams, 'Christian socialism? A critical evaluation of Christian socialist theology', *Evangelical Review of Theology and Politics*, 1, 4 (November 2016): p. 42.
79 Bryant, *Possible Dreams*, pp. 273–4.
80 Wilkinson, *Christian Socialism*, p. 191.
81 Bryant, *Possible Dreams*, p. 279.
82 Wilkinson, *Christian Socialism*, pp. 193–4.
83 Bryant, *Possible Dreams*, p. 279.
84 'The 2019 election and beyond', *Ekklesia* (2019), pp. 1 and 3.
85 Bryant, *Possible Dreams*, pp. 286 and 288.
86 Wilkinson, *Christian Socialism*, pp. 231–2.
87 'Former Labour MP Frank Field to stand for Birkenhead Social Justice Party at next election', *Politics Home*, https: //www.politic shome.com/news/article/former-labour-mp-frank-field-to-stand-for-birkenhead-social-justice-party-at-next-election.
88 Adrian Pabst, 'Introduction: New Labour and the politics of the common good', in Adrian Pabst and Ian Geary, eds, *Blue Labour: Forging a New Politics* (London: I.B. Tauris, 2015), p. 6.
89 For Cruddas' contribution to contemporary debates, see Jon Cruddas, *The Dignity of Labour* (Cambridge: Polity, 2021).
90 Williams, *Christian Socialism*, p. 151; Matt Beech and Kevin Hickson, 'Blue or purple? Reflections on the future of the Labour Party', *Political Studies Review*, 12 (2014): p. 78.
91 John Milbank, Graham Ward and Catherine Pickstock, 'Introduction: suspending the material – the turn of radical orthodoxy', in John Milbank, Graham Ward and Catherine Pickstock, eds, *Radical Orthodoxy: A New Theology* (Oxford: Taylor & Francis, 1999), p. 2.
92 John Milbank and Adrian Pabst, *The Politics of Virtue: Post-Liberalism and the Human Future* (London: Rowman & Littlefield, 2016), p. 1.
93 Ibid., p. 3.
94 Maurice Glasman, 'Blue Labour and Labour history', conference paper presented at the Labour History Research Centre, November 2012. For a fuller statement of Glasman's ideas, see Maurice Glasman, *Blue Labour: The Politics of the Common Good* (Cambridge: Polity, 2021).
95 Ibid., p. 1.
96 Ibid., p. 5.
97 Milbank et al., *Radical Orthodoxy*, p. 3.

98 Milbank and Pabst, *Politics of Virtue*, p. 3.
99 Pabst, 'New Labour and the common good', pp. 1 and 6.
100 Adrian Pabst, 'Civil economy: Blue Labour's alternative to capitalism', in Adrian Pabst and Ian Geary, eds, *Blue Labour: Forging a New Politics* (London: I.B. Tauris, 2015), pp. 101–2.
101 Ibid., pp. 102–4.
102 Ibid., p. 98.
103 Ibid., pp. 108–9 and 114.
104 Pabst, 'New Labour and the common good', pp. 8 and 4.
105 Pabst, 'Civil economy', pp. 112 and 104.
106 Ibid., p. 110.
107 Ibid., p. 99.
108 Ibid., p. 112.
109 Ekaterina Kolpinskaya and Stuart Fox, *Religion and Euroscepticism in Brexit Britain* (London: Routledge, 2021).

3   A Hostile Environment: Religious Socialism in Europe

1 John C. Cort, *Christian Socialism: An Informal History* (Maryknoll NY: Orbis Books, 2020 [1988]), p. 150.
2 Ibid., pp. 150–1.
3 Ibid., p. 149.
4 Gary Dorrien, *Social Democracy in the Making: Political and Religious Roots of European Socialism* (Yale CT: Yale University Press, 2019), pp. 27–8.
5 Jeremy Morris, *F.D. Maurice and the Crisis of Christian Authority* (Oxford: Oxford University Press, 2008), pp. 10–11.
6 Eric Hobsbawm, *The Age of Extremes, 1914–1991* (London: Abacus, 2010 [1994]), pp. 76–7.
7 Patrick Sookhdeo, *Hated Without A Reason: The Remarkable Story of Christian Persecution Over the Centuries* (McLean VA: Isaac Publishing, 2019), pp. 152–4.
8 Morris, *F.D. Maurice*, p. 12.
9 Friedrich Engels, 'Anti-Duhring', in Karl Marx and Friedrich Engels, *On Religion* (New York: Dover, 1964), pp. 147–8.
10 Karl Marx, 'Contribution to the critique of Hegel's Philosophy of Right', in Karl Marx and Friedrich Engels, *On Religion* (New York: Dover 1964), pp. 41–2.
11 Karl Marx and Friedrich Engels, *The Communist Manifesto* (Oxford: Oxford University Press, 1994) [1848]), pp. 27–8.
12 Ibid., pp. 28–30.

13 Andrew Vincent, *Modern Political Ideologies* (Oxford: Wiley-Blackwell, 2010), pp. 84 and 90.
14 Dan McKanan, *Prophetic Encounters: Religion and the American Political Tradition* (Boston MA: Beacon Press, 2011), p. 66.
15 Vincent, *Modern Political Ideologies*, p. 175.
16 McKanan, *Prophetic Encounters*, p. 69.
17 Cort, *Christian Socialism*, p. 107.
18 Ibid., p. 109.
19 Vincent, *Political Ideologies*, p. 97.
20 Cort, *Christian Socialism*, p. 121.
21 Ibid., p. 122.
22 Ibid., pp. 134–8.
23 Ibid., pp. 124–6.
24 Ibid., p. 131.
25 Ibid.
26 Ibid., p. 132.
27 Ibid., p. 204.
28 Ibid. pp. 203–6.
29 Dorrien, *Social Democracy*, p. 132.
30 Cort, *Christian Socialism*, p. 219.
31 Dorrien, *Social Democracy*, pp. 148–9.
32 Stefan Berger, 'Difficult (re-)alignments – comparative perspectives on social democracy and religion from late nineteenth-century to interwar Germany and Britain', *Journal of Contemporary History*, 53, 3 (2018): pp. 580–1 and 586.
33 Dorrien, *Social Democracy*, pp. 135–7.
34 Ibid., pp. 134–5 and 223.
35 Cort, *Christian Socialism*, pp. 214–15,
36 Ibid., p. 211.
37 Ibid., p. 213.
38 Ibid., p. 225.
39 Dorrien, *Social Democracy*, pp. 221–12; Cort, *Christian Socialism*, p. 225.
40 Dorrien, *Social Democracy*, p. 228.
41 Cort, *Christian Socialism*, p. 229.
42 Dorrien, *Social Democracy*, p. 226.
43 Ibid., p. 224; Cort, *Christian Socialism*, p. 229.
44 Dorrien, *Social Democracy*, p. 224.
45 Ibid., p. 231.
46 Cort, *Christian Socialism*, p. 233.
47 Dorrien, *Social Democracy*, p. 262.
48 John Marsden, 'Paul Tillich and the theology of German religious socialism', *Political Theology* 10, 1 (2009): pp. 32–3.

49 Dorrien, *Social Democracy*, p. 301.
50 Ibid; Gary Dorrien, *Soul in Society: The Making and Renewal of Social Christianity* (Minneapolis MN: Augsburg Fortress, 1995), p. 89.
51 Dorrien, *Social Democracy*, p. 289.
52 Paul Tillich, *Political Expectation* (New York: Harper & Row, 1971 [1930]), p. 44; Marsden, 'Paul Tillich', pp. 32–4.
53 Tillich, *Political Expectation*, p. 44.
54 Dorrien, *Social Democracy*, p. 286; John R. Stumme, 'Introduction', in Paul Tillich, *The Socialist Decision* (New York: Harper & Row, 1977 [1933]), p. xvii.
55 Stumme, 'Introduction', p. xix.
56 Marsden, 'Paul Tillich', p. 34.
57 Ibid., pp. 34–5.
58 Cort, *Christian Socialism*, p. 243.
59 Marsden, 'Paul Tillich', p. 36.
60 Tillich, *Political Expectation*, p. 50.
61 Dorrien, *Social Democracy*, p. 275.
62 Marsden, 'Paul Tillich', p. 36.
63 Ibid.
64 Tillich, *Political Expectation*, p. 50.
65 Ibid., p. 52.
66 Marsden, 'Paul Tillich', p. 44.
67 Charles E. Curran, *Catholic Social Teaching 1891–Present: A Historical, Theological and Ethical Analysis* (Washington DC: Georgetown University Press, 2002), p. 5.
68 Cort, *Christian Socialism*, p. 221.
69 Ibid., p. 323.
70 Ibid., p. 325.
71 Curran, *Catholic Social Teaching*, pp. 147 and 188.
72 Ibid., p. 199.
73 Ibid., pp. 138 and 150.
74 Paul Pombeni, 'Christian Democracy', in Michael Freeden, Lyman Tower Sargent and Marc Stears, eds, *The Oxford Handbook of Political Ideologies* (Oxford: Oxford University Press, 2013), p. 313.
75 Cort, *Christian Socialism*, pp. 328–9.
76 Ibid., pp. 332 and 330.
77 Ibid., p. 332; Maurice Glasman, 'Blue Labour and Labour history', conference paper presented at the Labour History Research Centre, November 2012, p. 2.
78 Berger, 'Difficult (re)-alignments', p. 582.
79 Ibid., p. 328.

80 Gary Dorrien, 'Introduction', in John C. Cort, *Christian Socialism: An Informal History* (Maryknoll NY: Orbis Books, 2020 [1988]), p. xv.
81 Curran, *Catholic Social Teaching*, p. 200.
82 Ibid.
83 Ian S. Wood, *John Wheatley* (Manchester: Manchester University Press, 1990), p. 24.
84 Graham Dale, *God's Politicians: The Christian Contribution to 100 Years of Labour* (London: HarperCollins, 2000), p. 72.
85 Francesco Nitti, *Catholic Socialism* (New York: Macmillan, 1908 [1894]), p. 17, pp. 20–1 and 26.
86 Ibid., p. 29.
87 Ibid., pp. 23–4.
88 Ibid., p. 31.
89 Vaneesa Cook, *Spiritual Socialists: Religion and the American Left* (Pennsylvania PA: University of Pennsylvania, 2019), p. 150.
90 Hannah Arendt, *The Origins of Totalitarianism* (Boston MA: Houghton Mifflin Harcourt, 1973 [1951]), p. 392; Ignazio Silone, in Richard Crossman, ed., *The God That Failed* (New York: Harper & Brothers, 1949), p. 112.
91 Silone, *God That Failed*, pp. 113–14.
92 Cook, *Spiritual Socialists*, pp. 2–3.
93 Ibid., pp. 153–4.
94 Dorrien, 'Introduction', p. xviii.
95 Cort, *Christian Socialism*, p. 350.
96 Ibid.
97 Ethna Regan, 'The Bergoglian principles: Pope Francis' dialectical approach to political theology', *Religions*, 10, 12 (2019): pp. 3–4.
98 Ibid., p. 8.
99 Eoin O'Neill, 'The Pope and the environment: towards an integral ecology?', *Environmental Politics*, 25, 4 (2016): pp. 750–1.
100 Ibid., p. 753.
101 Ibid., p. 749.
102 Curran, *Catholic Social Teaching*, p. 183.
103 Dorrien, 'Introduction', p. xix; Cort, *Christian Socialism*, pp. 4–5.
104 Dorrien, *Social Democracy*, p. 461.
105 Cort, *Christian Socialism*, p. 320.
106 Ibid., p. 248.
107 Ibid.
108 Robert Michael Bosco, 'Religious socialism in post-secular Europe', *Politics, Religion and Ideology*, 20, 1 (2019): p. 126.
109 Ibid., p. 125.
110 Ibid.

111 Cort, *Christian Socialism*, p. 248.
112 Bosco, 'Religious socialism', p. 125.
113 Ibid., pp. 127–8.
114 Ibid., p. 130.
115 Ibid., p. 129.
116 Tony Blair and Gerhard Schroeder, *Europe: The Third Way/Die Neue Mitte* (Johannesburg: Friedrich Erbert Foundation, 1998), pp. 5–6.
117 Bosco, 'Religious socialism', p. 131.
118 Ibid., p. 133.
119 Ibid., p. 132.
120 'It is time to mobilise the religious left!', International League of Religious Socialists, http: //ilrs.net/2012/08/30/hello-world/.

4 What Would Jesus Do? Social Gospel and Socialism in the United States

1 Dan McKanan, *Prophetic Encounters: Religion and the American Political Tradition* (Boston MA: Beacon Press, 2011), p. 124.
2 Ibid., pp. 39 and 41.
3 Ibid., p. 53.
4 Ibid., p. 56.
5 Ibid., pp. 57–8.
6 John C. Cort, *Christian Socialism: An Informal History* (Maryknoll NY: Orbis Books, 2020 [1988]), p. 255.
7 McKanan, *Prophetic Encounters*, pp. 112 and 125.
8 Ibid., p. 112.
9 Charles M. Sheldon, *In His Steps: What Would Jesus Do?* (Chicago Il: Advance, 1897 [1889]).
10 McKanan, *Prophetic Encounters*, p. 125.
11 Cort, *Christian Socialism*, pp. 280–1.
12 Gary Dorrien, *Soul in Society: The Making and Renewal of Social Christianity* (Minneapolis MN: Augsburg Fortress, 1995), pp. 5–6.
13 Ibid., pp. 28–9.
14 Walter Rauschenbusch, *Christianity and the Social Crisis* (New York: Associated Press, 1917 [1907]), pp. 20–2, 50, 85.
15 Ibid., p. 57.
16 Ibid., pp. 64–5.
17 Ibid., pp. 70–1.
18 Ibid., pp. 246 and 249–52, 395, 345.
19 Ibid., p. 238.

20 Dorrien, *Soul in Society*, p. 41.
21 Walter Rauschenbusch, *Christianizing the Social Order* (New York: Macmillan, 1915 [1912]), pp. 313 and 333.
22 Ibid., pp. 338 and 343–5.
23 Ibid., p. 346.
24 Ibid., pp. 430–1.
25 Gary Dorrien, *The Making of American Liberal Theology: Idealism, Realism, and Modernity, 1900–1950* (Louisville KY: Westminster John Knox, 2003), p. 73.
26 Rauschenbusch, *Christianizing the Social Order*, pp. 397–8.
27 Dorrien, *Soul in Society*, p. 88; Rauschenbusch, *Christianizing the Social Order*, p. 454.
28 Dorrien, *Soul in Society*, pp. 37 and 40; Rauschenbusch, *Christianity and the Social Crisis*, p. 246.
29 Dorrien, *Soul in Society*, p. 37.
30 Shailer Mathews, *The Social Gospel* (Philadelphia PA: Griffith & Rowland Press, 1910).
31 Ibid., pp. 20–1.
32 Ibid., pp. 121–2.
33 Cort, *Christian Socialism*, pp. 255–7.
34 Washington Gladden, *Christianity and Socialism* (New York: Eaton & Mains, 1905), pp. 23 and 33.
35 Ibid., pp. 42–5.
36 Ibid., pp. 122 and 124.
37 Ibid., p. 122.
38 Ibid., pp. 185–7.
39 Cort, *Christian Socialism*, p. 263.
40 W.D.P. Bliss, *What is Christian Socialism?* (New York: Society of Christian Socialists, 1890), pp. 14 and 24.
41 Ibid., pp. 5 and 40.
42 Ibid., pp. 8 and 40–1.
43 Ibid., p. 41.
44 Elizabeth Hinson-Hasty, 'Solidarity and the social gospel: historical and contemporary perspectives', *American Journal of Theology and Philosophy*, 37, 2 (May 2016): p. 138.
45 Cort, *Christian Socialism*, p. 299.
46 Hinson-Hasty, 'Solidarity and the social gospel', p. 144.
47 Ibid., p. 145.
48 Vida D. Scudder, *Socialism and Character* (Boston MA: Houghton Mifflin, 1912), p. 400.
49 Ibid., pp. 353–7.
50 Ibid., p. 378.
51 Ibid., p. 393.

52 Paul Buhle, *Marxism in the USA: From 1870 to the Present Day* (London: Verso, 1987), pp. 63–6.
53 Cort, *Christian Socialism*, p. 269.
54 McKanan, *Prophetic Encounters*, p. 118.
55 Roland Boer, 'Father Thomas J. Hagerty: a forgotten religious communist', *Monthly Review* (2011), p. 1; John Newsinger and James Newsinger, '"As Catholic as the Pope": James Connolly and the Roman Catholic Church in Ireland', *Irish Labour History Society*, 11 (1986): p. 7.
56 James P. Cannon, 'Introduction: E.V. Debs: The socialist movement of his time – its meaning for today', in Jean Y. Tussey, ed., *Eugene V. Debs Speaks* (New York: Pathfinder, 1994), pp. 26–8.
57 Eugene V. Debs, 'The outlook for socialism in the United States' (1900), in Jean Y. Tussey, ed., *Eugene V. Debs Speaks* (New York: Pathfinder, 1994), p. 66.
58 Eugene V. Debs, 'The Socialist Party's appeal' (1904), in Jean Y. Tussey, ed., *Eugene V. Debs Speaks* (New York: Pathfinder, 1994), p. 110.
59 Dave Burns, 'The soul of socialism: christianity, civilization, and citizenship in the thought of Eugene Debs', *Labor: Studies in Working-Class History of the Americas*, 5, 2 (2008): p. 84.
60 Ibid., p. 83.
61 Eugene V. Debs, 'The Socialist Party's appeal', pp. 108–9.
62 Eugene V. Debs, 'Industrial unionism' (1910), in Jean Y. Tussey, ed., *Eugene V. Debs Speaks* (New York: Pathfinder, 1994), p. 122.
63 Ibid., p. 124.
64 Eugene V. Debs, 'Danger ahead' (1911), in Jean Y. Tussey, ed., *Eugene V. Debs Speaks* (New York: Pathfinder, 1994), p. 160.
65 Burns, 'Soul of socialism', p. 98.
66 Eugene V. Debs, 'Jesus the supreme leader', *Progressive Woman* (1914).
67 Ibid.
68 Ibid.
69 Ibid.
70 Burns, 'Soul of socialism', p. 91.
71 Eugene V. Debs, 'Homestead and Ludlow' (1914), in Jean Y. Tussey, ed., *Eugene V. Debs Speaks* (New York: Pathfinder, 1994), p. 220.
72 Ibid., p. 218.
73 Elizabeth Balanoff, 'Norman Thomas: socialism and the social gospel', *Christian Century* (1985): p. 101.
74 John R. Erickson, 'A disappointed man', *Faith and Religion* (2015).
75 Ibid.

76 Norman Thomas, *A Socialist's Faith* (New York: W.W. Norton, 1951), pp. 141, 146 and 312.
77 Ibid., pp. 182 and 187.
78 Ibid., p. 186.
79 Ibid., pp. 128 and 125.
80 Ibid., pp. 122 and 300.
81 Erickson, 'Disappointed man'.
82 Vaneesa Cook, *Spiritual Socialists: Religion and the American Left* (Pennsylvania PA: University of Pennsylvania, 2019), pp. 109–10.
83 Ibid., p. 144.
84 Ibid., p. 145.
85 Ibid., p. 112.
86 Debs, 'Outlook for socialism', pp. 65–6.
87 Balanoff, 'Norman Thomas', p. 102.
88 Thomas, *Socialist's Faith*, p. 179.
89 Cook, *Spiritual Socialists*, p. 115.
90 Ibid., pp. 133 and 142.
91 Ibid., pp. 132 and 145.
92 Ibid., p. 12.
93 Ibid.
94 Ibid., pp. 6 and 16.
95 Ibid., p. 17.
96 Ibid., p. 13.
97 Ibid., p. 17.
98 McKanan, *Prophetic Encounters*, p. 175.
99 Cook, *Spiritual Socialists*, pp. 30–1.
100 Cook, *Spiritual Socialists*, pp. 40–1; McKanan, *Prophetic Encounters*, p. 175.
101 Norman Thomas, 'On the death of A.J. Muste', *New America*, 6, 9 (1967): p. 2.
102 Erickson, 'Disappointed man'.
103 Cook, *Spiritual Socialists*, pp. 45–6.
104 Ibid., p. 52.
105 Ibid., p. 45.
106 Ibid., pp. 58 and 61.
107 Ibid., pp. 52–3 and 58.
108 Ibid., pp. 69–70 and 73.
109 Ibid., p. 70.
110 McKanan, *Prophetic Encounters*, p. 161; Cort, *Christian Socialism*, p. xiii.
111 Cook, *Spiritual Socialists*, pp. 77–8.
112 Ibid., p. 79.
113 Ibid., p. 103.

114 Ibid., p. 159.
115 Ibid., p. 165.
116 Ibid.
117 Ibid., p. 169.

5   Moral Minority: The Christian Left in the Age of the Christian Right

1 Vaneesa Cook, *Spiritual Socialists: Religion and the American Left* (Philadelphia PA: University of Pennsylvania, 2019), p. 168.
2 Kenneth Torquil MacLean, 'Origins of the southern civil rights movement: Myles Horton and the Highlander Folk School', *The Phi Delta Kappan*, 47, 9 (1966): p. 487.
3 Ibid.
4 Gary Dorrien, *Soul in Society: The Making and Renewal of Social Christianity* (Minneapolis MN: Augsburg Fortress, 1995), pp. 43–4.
5 Dave Burns, 'The soul of socialism: Christianity, civilization, and citizenship in the thought of Eugene Debs', *Labor: Studies in Working-Class History of the Americas*, 5, 2 (2008): p. 95.
6 Eugene V. Debs, 'The Socialist Party's appeal' (1904), in Jean Y. Tussey, ed., *Eugene V. Debs Speaks* (New York: Pathfinder, 1994), p. 95.
7 Elizabeth Balanoff, 'Norman Thomas: socialism and the social gospel', *Christian Century* (1985), p. 102.
8 The term 'fundamentalist' is often used in the pejorative sense. Here it simply applies to those Christians who adopted that title for themselves in the first half of the twentieth century and might today be described as conservative evangelicals.
9 Daniel K. Williams, *God's Own Party: The Making of the Christian Right* (Oxford: Oxford University Press, 2010), pp. 1–3; Lisa Sharon Harper, *Evangelical ≠ Republican ... or Democrat* (New York: New Press, 2008), pp. 75–9.
10 Williams, *God's Own Party*, pp. 3 and 193; Harriet Sherwood, 'White evangelical Christians stick by Trump again, exit polls show', *Guardian*, https://www.theguardian.com/us-news/2020/nov/06/white-evangelical-christians-supported-trump.
11 Cook, *Spiritual Socialists*, p. 7
12 Dan McKanan, *Prophetic Encounters: Religion and the American Political Tradition* (Boston MA: Beacon Press, 2011), p. 32.
13 McKanan, *Prophetic Encounters*, pp. 128–33; Stewart Burns, *To*

the Mountaintop: Martin Luther King Jr's Sacred Mission to Save America: 1955–1968 (New York: HarperSanFrancisco, 2004), p. 49.

14 John C. Cort, *Christian Socialism: An Informal History* (Maryknoll NY: Orbis Books, 2020 [1988]), p. 297.

15 Burns, *Mountaintop*, p. 66.

16 Ibid., p. 67.

17 Harper, *Evangelical ≠ Republican*, p. 40.

18 Ibid., p. 39.

19 Martin Luther King, Jr, 'Letter from Birmingham Jail' (1963).

20 Burns, *Mountaintop*, p. 52.

21 Ibid., p. 38.

22 Ibid., p. 25.

23 Ibid., p. 26.

24 Ibid., p. 27.

25 Cook, *Spiritual Socialists*, p. 171.

26 Burns, *Mountaintop*, p. 78.

27 Ibid., p. 221.

28 Ibid., pp. 218–19.

29 Ibid., p. 128.

30 Ibid., p. 91.

31 Ibid., p. 15.

32 King, 'Letter from Birmingham Jail'; see also John Hoffman and Paul Graham, *Introduction to Political Theory* (Harlow: Pearson Education, 2009), pp. 446–8.

33 King, 'Letter from Birmingham Jail'.

34 Ibid.

35 Hoffman and Graham, *Political Theory*, pp. 445–6.

36 Burns, *Mountaintop*, pp. 274–5.

37 Ibid., pp. 205–6.

38 Ibid., p. 249.

39 McKanan, *Prophetic Encounters*, p. 198.

40 Burns, *Mountaintop*, pp. 324, 236, 382 and 417.

41 Ibid., pp. 89 and 267.

42 Ibid., p. 300.

43 Cook, *Spiritual Socialists*, p. 186.

44 Burns, *Mountaintop*, pp. 337 and 340.

45 King, 'Letter from Birmingham Jail'; Burns, *Mountaintop*, pp. 292–3.

46 Cook, *Spiritual Socialists*, p. 186.

47 Ibid.

48 Burns, *Mountaintop*, p. 446.

49 Ibid., p. 457.

50 Ibid., pp. 398–8.
51 Harper, *Evangelical ≠ Republican ... or Democrat*, p. 43.
52 Burns, *Mountaintop*, p. 452.
53 Harper, *Evangelical ≠ Republican ... or Democrat*, p. 43.
54 Joseph W. Caldwell, 'A starting point for understanding James Cone: A primer for White readers', *Review and Expositor*, 117, 1 (2020), p. 27; James H. Cone, 'Liberation theology', in Colin A. Palmer, ed., *Encyclopedia of African-American Culture and History* (Detroit MI: Macmillan, 2006), p. 1285.
55 James H. Cone, *A Black Theology of Liberation* (Philadelphia PA: Lippincott, 1970), p. 77.
56 James H. Cone, *Black Theology and Black Power* (New York: Seabury Press, 1969), p. 56.
57 Ibid., p. 17.
58 Ibid., p. 6.
59 Ibid., p. 141.
60 Cone, *Black Theology of Liberation*, p. 198.
61 Cone, *Black Theology and Black Power*, p. 139.
62 Ibid., p. 7.
63 Ibid., p. 17.
64 Ibid., pp. 145 and 147.
65 Ibid., pp. 151 and 144.
66 Ibid., p. 150.
67 Cone, *Black Theology of Liberation*, pp. 42 and 36.
68 Cone, *Black Theology and Black Power*, p. 3.
69 Cone, *Black Theology of Liberation*, pp. 27–8.
70 Cone, *Black Theology and Black Power*, p. 150.
71 Ibid., p. 151.
72 Cone, *Black Theology of Liberation*, pp. 42 and 192–3.
73 Cone, *Black Theology and Black Power*, p. 1.
74 Caldwell, 'James Cone', p. 34.
75 Cone, *Black Theology and Black Power*, p. 121.
76 Cone, *Black Theology of Liberation*, p. 225.
77 Ibid., p. 191.
78 Ibid., p. 11.
79 Ibid., p. 226; Cone, *Black Theology and Black Power*, pp. 40 and 35.
80 Cone, *Black Theology of Liberation*, p. 112.
81 Ibid., pp. 120–1.
82 Ibid., p. 157.
83 Cone, *Black Theology and Black Power*, p. 35.
84 Cone, *Black Theology of Liberation*, p. 114.
85 Ibid., pp. 59–60.

86 Ibid., p. 220.
87 McKanan, *Prophetic Encounters*, p. 231.
88 Cook, *Spiritual Socialists*, p. 199.
89 Ibid., pp. 194–6.
90 Ibid., pp. 197 and 193.
91 Burns, *Mountaintop*, p. 332.
92 Ibid., p. 374.
93 Ibid.
94 Dorrien, *Soul in Society*, pp. 248–9.
95 Ibid.
96 Cook, *Spiritual Socialists*, pp. 197 and 199.
97 Ibid., p. 195.
98 Dorrien, Soul in Society, p. 245.
99 Cornel West, *Prophesy Deliverance! An Afro-American Revolutionary Christianity* (Louisville KY: Westminster John Knox Press, 2002 [1982]), pp. 35 and 7.
100 Cook, *Spiritual Socialists*, pp. 211 and 214–15.
101 Ibid., p. 206.
102 Ibid., p. 201.
103 Ibid., pp. 214–15.
104 Williams, *God's Own Party*, pp. 185 and 188. 'GOP' stands for 'Grand Old Party', the nickname of the US Republican Party.
105 Ibid., pp. 195 and 203.
106 Ibid., pp. 205–6.
107 Cook, *Spiritual Socialists*, p. 211.
108 Sharon Harper, *Evangelical ≠ Republican … or Democrat*, pp. 16 and 64.
109 Tony Campolo, *Red Letter Christians: A Citizen's Guide to Faith and Politics* (Ventura CA: Regal, 2008), p. 22.
110 Ibid., p. 15.
111 Ibid., p. 23.
112 Ibid.
113 Ibid., p. 33.
114 Ibid., pp. 31–2.
115 Isaiah 10:1–2a.
116 James 5:1 and 4a; Campolo, *Red Letter Christians*, p. 167.
117 Campolo, *Red Letter Christians*, p. 203.
118 Luke 4:18–19. See also Isaiah 61.
119 Campolo, *Red Letter Christians*, p. 157.
120 Walter Rauschenbusch, *Christianizing the Social Order* (New York: Macmillan, 1915), p. 352; Cort, *Christian Socialism*, p. 21.
121 Harper, *Evangelical ≠ Republican … or Democrat*, pp. 175–6.
122 Ibid., p. 10.

123 Lisa Sharon Harper and David C. Innes, *Left, Right, and Christ: Evangelical Faith in Politics* (Boise ID: Russell Media, 2011), p. 83. This book takes the form of a debate between Harper and David Innes, a supporter of free-market capitalism and social conservatism.

124 Ibid., p. 79.

125 Ibid., p. 98.

126 Harper, *Evangelical ≠ Republican … or Democrat*, p. 51.

127 Ibid., pp. 52–6.

128 Eliza Griswold, 'Evangelicals of color fight back against the religious Right', *New Yorker* (2018).

129 Lisa Sharon Harper, *The Very Good Gospel: How Everything Wrong Can Be Made Right* (New York: Crown Publishing Group, 2016), pp. 11–12 and p. 49.

130 Ibid. pp. 10 and 13.

131 Harper, *Evangelical ≠ Republican … or Democrat*, pp. 176 and 11.

132 McKanan, *Prophetic Encounters*, p. 239.

133 Jim Wallis, *God's Politics: Why the American Right Gets It Wrong and the Left Doesn't Get It* (Oxford: Lion, 2005), p. 34.

134 Ibid., p. 3.

135 Ibid., p. 15.

136 Ibid., p. 273.

137 Ibid., p. 274.

138 Ibid., p. 264.

139 Ibid., p. 279.

140 Ibid., p. 308.

141 Ibid., p. 319; 2 Corinthians 5:17b–18.

142 Jim Wallis, 'A moment of truth for white Christianity', *Sojourners*, https: //sojo.net/articles/moment-truth-white-christianity.

143 Ibid.

144 Sabrina Danielson, 'Fracturing over creation care? Shifting environmental beliefs among evangelicals', *Journal for the Scientific Study of Religion*, 52, 1 (2013): pp. 207 and 210.

145 Mark Stoll, 'Review essay: the quest for green religion, religion and American culture', *A Journal of Interpretation*, 22, 2 (2012): p. 265.

146 Ibid., p. 269.

147 Laurel Kearns, 'Christian environmentalism in the United States', *Sociology of Religion*, 57, 1 (1996): pp. 55–6 and 60.

148 Ibid., pp. 56 and 64.

149 Ibid., p. 56; Andrew Vincent, *Modern Political Ideologies* (Oxford: Wiley-Blackwell, 2010), p. 211.

150 Harper, *Evangelical ≠ Republican … or Democrat*, p. 66.

151 Campolo, *Red Letter Christians*, pp. 17 and 43.

152 McKanan, *Prophetic Encounters*, p. 262.

153 Campolo, *Red Letter Christians*, p. 123.

154 Wallis, 'Moment of truth'.

155 Campolo, *Red Letter Christians*, p. 121; Wallis, *God's Politics*, pp. 79–80

156 Campolo, *Red Letter Christians*, p. 121.

157 McKanan, *Prophetic Encounters*, pp. 263–5.

158 Katharine Q. Seelye, 'John Lewis, towering figure of civil rights era, dies at 80', *Washington Post* (2020).

159 'Social Programs: World Report. The wreck of the gravy train, *Canada and the World Backgrounder*, 62, 2 (1996).

160 Darryl S. Tukufu, 'Jesse Jackson and the Rainbow Coalition: working class movement or reform politics?', *Humanity and Society*, 14, 2 (1990): p. 159.

161 Robert Green, 'Jesse Jackson's Rainbow Coalition paved the way for the Biden–Harris ticket', *Washington Post* (2020).

162 Jesse Jackson, 'The rising American electorate is a rainbow', *Souls*, 14, 1–2 (2012): p. 68.

163 Ibid., p. 69.

164 Green, 'Jesse Jackson's Rainbow Coalition'.

165 'Bernie Sanders liberty university speech, annotated', *Washington Post* (2016). Sanders is referring to Amos 5:24.

166 'Biblical argument for Bernie', https: //clypit/eusxalwe.

167 'Alexandria Ocasio-Cortez: 'Jesus would be maligned as "radical" by today's congress', *HuffPost*, https: //www.huffingtonpost.co.uk/entry/alexandria-ocasio-cortez-faith_n_5e580e16c5b6450a30bbd0f7?ri18n=true.

168 Olivia B. Waxman, 'How one Atlanta church impacted Martin Luther King, Jr, the civil rights movement and incoming Sen. Raphael Warnock', *Time* (2021).

169 'About', Institute for Christian Socialism, https: //christiansocialism.com/about/.

6   Preferential Option for the Poor: Liberation Theology in Latin America

1 Gustavo Gutiérrez, *A Theology of Liberation: History, Politics and Salvation* (Maryknoll NY: Orbis Books, 1973), p. 111.

2 Miguel A. De La Torre, 'Liberation theology', in Craig Hovey and Elizabeth Phillips, eds, *The Cambridge Companion to Christian Political Theology* (Cambridge: Cambridge University Press, 2015), p. 24.

3 Phillip Berryman, *Liberation Theology: Essential Facts About the Revolutionary Movement in Latin America and Beyond* (New York: Pantheon Books, 1987), p. 10.

4 De La Torre, 'Liberation theology', p. 25.

5 Luis Martinez Andrade, 'Liberation theology: a critique of modernity', *International Journal of Postcolonial Studies*, 19, 5 (2017): pp. 621–2.

6 Berryman, *Liberation Theology*, p. 10; De La Torre, 'Liberation theology', p. 35; Washington Uranga, 'Farewell to Pastor Miguez Bonino', *Página* 12 (2012).

7 Berryman, *Liberation Theology*, pp. 16–17.

8 De La Torre, 'Liberation theology', p. 27.

9 John C. Cort, *Christian Socialism: An Informal History* (Maryknoll NY: Orbis Books, 2020 [1988]), p. 327

10 Berryman, *Liberation Theology*, pp. 27 and 129.

11 Ibid., p. 27.

12 Rafael Luciania, 'Medellín Fifty Years Later: From Development to Liberation', *Theological Studies*, 79, 3 (2018): p. 589.

13 Ibid., p. 567.

14 Ibid., pp. 88–9.

15 Andrade, 'Liberation theology', p. 625.

16 De La Torre, 'Liberation theology', p. 26.

17 Eric Hobsbawm, *The Age of Extremes, 1914–1991* (London: Abacus, 2010 [1994]), p. 350.

18 Luciania, 'Medellín', p. 569.

19 Andrade, 'Liberation theology', p. 627.

20 Luciania, 'Medellín', p. 569.

21 Ibid., p. 572.

22 Ibid., p. 573.

23 De La Torre, 'Liberation theology', p. 27.

24 Berryman, *Liberation Theology*, p. 23.

25 Luciania, 'Medellín', p. 567.

26 Gutiérrez, *Theology of Liberation*, p. 110.

27 Ibid., p. 584.

28 Ibid., p. 580.

29 Luciania, 'Medellín', p. 587.

30 Chris Bryant, *Possible Dreams: A Personal History of the British Christian Socialists* (London: Hodder and Stoughton, 1996), p. 275.

31 Gutiérrez, *Theology of Liberation*, p. 88.
32 Ibid., p. 89.
33 Ibid., pp. x and 35.
34 Berryman, *Liberation Theology*, p. 13.
35 Gutiérrez, *Theology of Liberation*, pp. 255–6.
36 Ibid., p. 49.
37 Ibid., p. 27.
38 Ibid., p. 108.
39 Ibid., p. 35.
40 Ibid., pp. 149–52.
41 Ibid., p. 176.
42 Ibid., pp. 102 and 110.
43 Ibid., p. 90.
44 Ibid., p. 202.
45 Ibid., pp. 90–1.
46 Ibid., p. 91.
47 Ibid., p. 113.
48 Ibid., p. 116.
49 Christopher Rowland, 'Introduction: the theology of liberation' in Christopher Rowland, ed., *The Cambridge Companion to Liberation Theology* (Cambridge: Cambridge University Press, 2007), p. 5.
50 Gustavo Gutiérrez, 'The task and content of liberation theology', in Christopher Rowland, ed., *The Cambridge Companion to Liberation Theology* (Cambridge: Cambridge University Press, 2007), p. 27; Gutiérrez, *Theology of Liberation*, p. 278.
51 Charles E. Curran, *Catholic Social Teaching 1891–Present: A Historical, Theological and Ethical Analysis* (Washington DC: Georgetown University Press, 2002), p. 183; Gutiérrez, *Theology of Liberation*, pp. 255–6.
52 Berryman, *Liberation Theology*, pp. 132–3.
53 De La Torre, 'Liberation theology', p. 31.
54 Gutiérrez, *Theology of Liberation*, p. 57.
55 Berryman, *Liberation Theology*, p. 50.
56 Gutiérrez, *Theology of Liberation*, pp. 293–4.
57 Berryman, *Liberation Theology*, p. 51.
58 Ibid., p. 53.
59 Gutiérrez, *Theology of Liberation*, p. 228.
60 Luciania, 'Medellín', p. 586.
61 Gutiérrez, *Theology of Liberation*, p. 137.
62 Ibid., pp. 195 and 205.
63 Ibid., p. 291.
64 Berryman, *Liberation Theology*, p. 43.

65 Ibid., p. 55.
66 Rowland, 'Theology of liberation', p. 7.
67 Ibid.
68 Ibid., p. 8.
69 Berryman, *Liberation Theology*, p. 25.
70 Ibid., p. 162.
71 Andrade, 'Liberation theology', p. 626.
72 Gutiérrez, 'Task and content of liberation theology', p. 28.
73 Gutiérrez, *Theology of Liberation*, p. xi.
74 Gutiérrez, 'Task and content of liberation theology', p. 28.
75 Gutiérrez, *Theology of Liberation*, p. 11.
76 Berryman, *Liberation Theology*, p. 64.
77 Luciania, 'Medellín', p. 585.
78 Andrew Dawson, 'The origins and character of the base ecclesial community: a Brazilian perspective', in Christopher Rowland, ed., *The Cambridge Companion to Liberation Theology* (Cambridge: Cambridge University Press, 2007), pp. 142 and 145.
79 Ibid., p. 147.
80 Ibid., p. 151.
81 De La Torre, 'Liberation theology', p. 26.
82 Berryman, *Liberation Theology*, p. 74.
83 Dawson, 'Origins and character of the BEC', p. 153; Berryman, *Liberation Theology*, pp. 97 and 100.
84 Berryman, *Liberation Theology*, pp. 149–50.
85 Ibid., p. 153.
86 Ibid., pp. 102 and 155.
87 Ibid., p. 153.
88 Torre, 'Liberation theology', p. 26.
89 Luciania, 'Medellín', p. 570.
90 Ibid., p. 574.
91 Berryman, *Liberation Theology*, pp. 149–50.
92 Gutiérrez, *Theology of Liberation*, p. 267.
93 Berryman, *Liberation Theology*, pp. 156 and 129.
94 Ibid., p. 156.
95 Gutiérrez, *Theology of Liberation*, pp. 112–13; Berryman, *Liberation Theology*, p. 28.
96 Berryman, *Liberation Theology*, pp. 17–18.
97 Ibid., pp. 114 and 204.
98 Ibid., pp. 100–1.
99 Ibid., pp. 123–4.
100 Travis Knoll, 'Seeking liberation in Brazil', NACLA Report on the Americas, 51, 3 (2019), p. 228; Torre, 'Liberation theology', p. 36.
101 Gutiérrez, *Theology of Liberation*, p. 9.

102 Ibid., pp. 112–13; Berryman, *Liberation Theology*, p. 108.

103 Torre, 'Liberation theology', p. 33.

104 Berryman, *Liberation Theology*, pp. 139 and 143.

105 Gutiérrez, *Theology of Liberation*, pp. 272–3.

106 Ibid., p. 295.

107 Berryman, *Liberation Theology*, p. 33.

108 Torre, 'Liberation theology', p. 26.

109 Luciania, 'Medellín', p. 574.

110 John C. Cort, *Christian Socialism: An Informal History* (Maryknoll NY: Orbis Books, 2020 [1988]), p. 3; Knoll, 'Seeking liberation', p. 227.

111 Anthony A.J. Williams, *Christian Socialism as Political Ideology: The Formation of the British Christian Left, 1877–1945* (London: IB Tauris, 2021), pp. 169–72.

112 Gutiérrez, *Theology of Liberation*, p. 10.

113 Ibid., pp. 262 and 265.

114 Berryman, *Liberation Theology*, p. 33.

115 Gutiérrez, *Theology of Liberation*, pp. 167–8.

116 Ibid., p. 232.

117 Williams, *Christian Socialism*, p. 174.

118 Gutiérrez, 'Task and content of liberation theology', pp. 33–4; Gutiérrez, *Theology of Liberation*, pp. 231 and 238.

119 Berryman, *Liberation Theology*, p. 54.

120 Gutiérrez, 'Task and content of liberation theology', p. 23.

121 Knoll, 'Seeking liberation', p. 227.

7 Liberty to the Captives: Liberation Theology Across the World

1 Jim Wallis, *God's Politics: Why the American Right Gets It Wrong and the Left Doesn't Get It* (Oxford: Lion, 2005), pp. 347–8.

2 Ibid., pp. 348–9.

3 Miguel A. De La Torre, 'Liberation theology', in Craig Hovey and Elizabeth Phillips, eds, *The Cambridge Companion to Christian Political Theology* (Cambridge: Cambridge University Press, 2015), p. 37.

4 Hannah Lewis, 'Deaf liberation theology and social justice', *Religions*, 8, 10 (2017): p. 10.

5 Phillip Berryman, *Liberation Theology: Essential Facts About the Revolutionary Movement in Latin America and Beyond* (New York: Pantheon Books, 1987), p. 163.

6   Bastiaan Wielenga, 'Liberation theology in Asia', in Christopher Rowland, ed., *The Cambridge Companion to Liberation Theology* (Cambridge: Cambridge University Press, 2007), p. 55.

7   Kimberlé Crenshaw, 'Mapping the margins: intersectionality, identity politics, and violence against women of color', *Stanford Law Review*, 43, 6 (1991).

8   Wielenga, 'Liberation theology in Asia', p. 76.

9   Tissa Balasuriya, 'Why planetary theology?', in Deane William Fearme, ed., *Third World Liberation Theologies: A Reader* (Maryknoll NY: Orbis Books, 1986), pp. 326–8.

10 Choan-Seng Song, 'The cross and the lotus', in Deane William Fearme, ed., *Third World Liberation Theologies: A Reader* (Maryknoll NY: Orbis Books, 1986), p. 317.

11 Samuel Rayan, 'The justice of God', in Deane William Fearme, ed., *Third World Liberation Theologies: A Reader* (Maryknoll NY: Orbis Books, 1986), p. 353.

12 Ibid., pp. 348–9.

13 Geevarghese Mar Osthathios, 'The reality of sin and class war', in Deane William Fearme, ed., *Third World Liberation Theologies: A Reader* (Maryknoll NY: Orbis Books, 1986), p. 343.

14 Ibid., pp. 342 and 344.

15 Kim Yong-Bok, 'Messiah and Minjung: Discerning messianic politics over against political messianism', in Deane William Fearme, ed., *Third World Liberation Theologies: A Reader* (Maryknoll NY: Orbis Books, 1986), p. 375.

16 Andrew Eungi Kim, 'Minjung theology in contemporary Korea: liberation theology and a reconsideration of secularization theory', *Religions*, 9, 12 (2018): p. 5.

17 Ibid., p. 7; Yong-Bok, 'Messiah and Minjung', p. 383.

18 Nicole Patierno, 'Palestinian liberation theology: creative resistance to occupation', *Islam and Christian–Muslim Relations*, 26, 4 (2015): p. 447.

19 Ibid., p. 450.

20 Ibid., p. 455.

21 Ibid., p. 456.

22 Ibid., pp. 447 and 458.

23 Ibid., p. 488.

24 Tissa Balasuriya, 'Why planetary theology?', p. 334.

25 Ibid., pp. 334–5.

26 Jonathan Gichaara, 'Issues in African liberation theology', *Black Theology: An International Journal*, 3, 1 (2005): p. 77.

27 Julius K. Nyerere, *Ujamaa: The Basis of African Socialism* (Dar es Salaam: n.p., 1962), pp. 4–5.

28 Ibid., p. 8.
29 Ibid.
30 Gichaara, 'African liberation theology', p. 77.
31 John W. Kinney, 'The theology of John Mbiti: his sources, norms, and method', *International Bulletin of Mission Research*, 3, 2 (1979): p. 65.
32 Gichaara, 'African liberation theology', p. 80.
33 Ibid., p. 79.
34 Ibid., p. 82.
35 Desmond Tutu, 'Black theology/African theology: soul mates or antagonists?', in Deane William Fearme, ed., *Third World Liberation Theologies: A Reader* (Maryknoll NY: Orbis Books, 1986), p. 262.
36 Timothy van Aarde, 'Black theology in South Africa - A theology of human dignity and black identity', *HTS Theological Studies*, 72, 1 (2016): p. 1.
37 Peter Walshe, 'The evolution of liberation theology in South Africa', *Journal of Law and Religion*, 5, 2 (1987): p. 302.
38 Ibid., p. 301.
39 K.J. Pali, 'The leadership role of Emeritus Archbishop Desmond Tutu in the social development of the South African society', *Stellenbosch Theological Journal*, 5, 1 (2019): p. 277.
40 Tinyiko Sam Maluleke, 'May the black God stand please!: Biko's challenge to religion', in Andile Mngxitama, Amanda Alexander and Nigel C. Gibson, eds, *Biko Lives! Contesting the Legacies of Steve Biko* (London: Palgrave Macmillan, 2008), p. 115.
41 Allan Boesak, 'Liberation theology in South Africa', in Deane William Fearme, ed., *Third World Liberation Theologies: A Reader* (Maryknoll NY: Orbis Books, 1986), pp. 265–6.
42 Ibid., p. 267.
43 Ibid., p. 269.
44 Ibid., pp. 267, 269–71.
45 Ibid., p. 269.
46 Aarde, 'Black theology in South Africa', p. 2.
47 Ibid., pp. 3–4, 6–7.
48 Ibid., p. 3; Boesak, 'Liberation theology in South Africa', p. 271.
49 Julian Kunnie, *Models of Black Theology: Issues in Class, Culture and Gender* (Valley Forge PA: Trinity Press, 1994), p. 39.
50 Ibid., p. 35.
51 Pali, 'Leadership of Archbishop Desmond Tutu', pp. 271–2.
52 Ibid., p. 276.
53 Ibid., p. 266.
54 Tutu, 'Black theology/African theology', pp. 262–3.

55 Pali, 'Leadership of Archbishop Desmond Tutu', p. 277.
56 Tutu, 'Black theology/African theology', pp. 259 and 262.
57 Ibid., pp. 257 and 260.
58 Ibid., p. 257.
59 Pali, 'Leadership of Archbishop Desmond Tutu', p. 277.
60 Ibid., p. 276.
61 Ibid., p. 278; Tutu, 'Black theology/African theology', p. 258.
62 Kunnie, *Models of Black Theology*, pp. 35–6.
63 Ibid., pp. 36–7.
64 Pali, 'Leadership of Archbishop Desmond Tutu', p. 270.
65 Ibid.
66 Laurel C. Schneider and Carolyn Roncolato, 'Queer theologies', *Religion Compass*, 6, 1 (2012): p. 8.
67 Ibid.
68 Berryman, *Liberation Theology*, p. 172.
69 Mary Gray, 'Feminist theology: a critical theology of liberation', in Christopher Rowland, ed., *The Cambridge Companion to Liberation Theology* (Cambridge: Cambridge University Press, 2007), p. 108.
70 Ibid., p. 107.
71 Dan McKanan, *Prophetic Encounters: Religion and the American Political Tradition* (Boston MA: Beacon Press, 2011), p. 247.
72 Gary Dorrien, *Soul in Society: The Making and Renewal of Social Christianity* (Minneapolis MN: Augsburg Fortress, 1995), p. ix.
73 Grey, 'Feminist theology', p. 108.
74 Rosemary Radford Ruether, *Sexism and God-Talk: Toward a Feminist Theology* (Boston MA: Beacon Press, 1983), pp. 22–3.
75 Ibid., pp. 23–4.
76 Ibid., pp. 24–7.
77 Ibid., pp. 63 and 32.
78 Ibid., p. 31.
79 Ibid., p. 32. Emphasis in original.
80 Ibid., p. 136.
81 Ibid., pp. 152 and 155.
82 Ibid., p. 155.
83 Henriette Marianne Katoppo, 'Asian theology: an Asian woman's perspective', in Deane William Fearme, ed., *Third World Liberation Theologies: A Reader* (Maryknoll NY: Orbis Books, 1986), p. 365.
84 Ibid., p. 366.
85 Ibid., pp. 359 and 363.
86 Ibid., p. 365; Grey, 'Feminist theology', p. 113.
87 Ibid.

88 Ruether, *Sexism and God-Talk*, p. 66.
89 Katoppo, 'Asian theology', pp. 364–5.
90 Grey, 'Feminist theology', p. 113.
91 Ruether, *Sexism and God-Talk*, p. 66.
92 Ibid., p. 67.
93 Grey, 'Feminist theology', p. 113.
94 Katoppo, 'Asian theology', p. 358.
95 Grey, 'Feminist theology', p. 105.
96 Ibid., p. 111.
97 Ibid.
98 Schneider and Roncolato, 'Queer theologies', pp. 3–4.
99 Gary David Comstock, *Gay Theology Without Apology* (Cleveland OH: Pilgrim Press, 1993), p. 4.
100 Schneider and Roncolato, 'Queer theologies', p. 5.
101 Ibid., p. 6.
102 Ibid., p. 7.
103 Ibid.
104 Ibid., p. 9.
105 Ibid., p. 5.
106 Dorrien, *Soul in Society*, pp. 257 and 261; Ruether, *Sexism and God-Talk*, p. 38.
107 Ruether, *Sexism and God-Talk*, pp. 39–40.
108 Grey, 'Feminist theology', p. 116.
109 Ibid.
110 Ibid.
111 Stephen Mayor, *The Churches and the Labour Movement* (London: Independent Press, 1967), p. 67.

8   Where Next for the Christian Left?

1 Stewart D. Headlam, *Priestcraft and Progress: Being Sermons and Lectures* (London: John Hodges 1878), pp. 19 and 21; Washington Gladden, *Christianity and Socialism* (New York: Eaton & Mains, 1905), p. 23.
2 Dan McKanan, *Prophetic Encounters: Religion and the American Political Tradition* (Boston MA: Beacon Press, 2011), p. 124.
3 Gustavo Gutiérrez, *A Theology of Liberation: History, Politics and Salvation* (Maryknoll NY: Orbis Books, 1973), p. 35.
4 Stephen Mayor, *The Churches and the Labour Movement* (London: Independent Press, 1967), p. 203.
5 Gutiérrez, *Theology of Liberation*, p. 267.

6 R.H. Tawney, *Equality* (London: C. Tinling & Co., Ltd., 1938 [1931]), p. 24.
7 Ibid., p. 122.
8 John C. Cort, *Christian Socialism: An Informal History* (Maryknoll NY: Orbis Books, 2020 [1988]), p. 297.
9 Stewart Burns, *To the Mountaintop: Martin Luther King Jr's Sacred Mission to Save America: 1955–1968* (New York: HarperSanFrancisco, 2004), p. 249.
10 James H. Cone, *A Black Theology of Liberation* (Philadelphia PA: Lippincott, 1970), pp. 120–1.
11 Burns, *Mountaintop*, p. 78.
12 Ellen Wilkinson, 'Slaves of machines', *Burnley News*, 28/11/30.
13 Gutiérrez, *Theology of Liberation*, p. 111.
14 Cort, *Christian Socialism*, p. 211.
15 Gutiérrez, *Theology of Liberation*, p. 27.
16 Martin Luther King, 'I have a dream', reproduced at https: //www.npr.org/2010/01/18/122701268/i-have-a-dream-speech-in-its-entirety.
17 Gutiérrez, *Theology of Liberation*, pp. 167–8.
18 Henry Scott Holland, *Our Neighbours: A Handbook for the C.S.U.* (London: A.R. Mowbray, 1911), p. 152.
19 Gary David Comstock, *Gay Theology Without Apology* (Cleveland OH: Pilgrim Press, 1993), p. 4.
20 Stewart D. Headlam, *The Meaning of the Mass: Five Lectures with Other Sermons and Addresses* (London: S.C. Brown, 1905), p. 73.
21 Gutiérrez, *Theology of Liberation*, p. 116.
22 Stewart D. Headlam, *The Meaning of the Mass: Five Lectures with Other Sermons and Addresses* (London: S.C. Brown, 1905), p. 83.
23 Phillip Berryman, *Liberation Theology: Essential Facts About the Revolutionary Movement in Latin America and Beyond* (New York: Pantheon Books, 1987), p. 55.
24 Carl R. Trueman, *The Rise and Triumph of the Modern Self: Cultural Amnesia, Expressive Individualism, and the Road to Sexual Revolution* (Wheaton IL: Crossway, 2020), p. 51.
25 Paul Embery, *Why the Modern Left Loathes the Working Class* (Cambridge: Polity, 2021), pp. 102 and 97.
26 Trueman, *Rise and Triumph of the Modern Self*, pp. 225 and 268.
27 Ibid., p. 234.
28 Embery, *Modern Left*, p. 22.
29 Briahana Joy Gray, 'How identity became a weapon against the Left', *Current Affairs* (2017), pp. 10–11.
30 Khyati Y. Joshi, *White Christian Privilege: The Illusion of Religious Equality in America* (New York: NYU Press, 2020, pp. 3–4.
31 Joshi, *White Christian Privilege*, p. 12.

Index